M000304321

Linda Vousden

Tonkinese Cats

Tonkinese
Contents

DEDICATION

To the constant memory of my beloved parents
Rosemary and MacGregor Henley:
they would have loved the Tonks.

ACKNOWLEDGEMENTS

My grateful thanks to so many Tonkinese lovers for their interest and assistance; Mr Roger Tabor; Ms Paddy Cutts (Animals Unlimited) and Mr Alan Robinson for their generosity in allowing me to use many of their photographs; Miss Julia May for information on the experimental Siamese colours; Mrs Helen Barnes, Ms Anna Barnes-Henley, Mrs Hazel Forshaw, Mrs Rosemary Harper, Mr Gregor Henley (Germany), Ms Patricia S Mullin (USA), Mr Sean and Mrs Sarah Osborn (USA), Mrs Carol Poole, Mr Earl Raey (New Zealand), Mrs Brenda Rawlinson, Mrs Christine Richards, Mrs Daisy (Cuddles) Slark, Mrs Kathy Wilkinson and Mrs Gesine Wolf (Germany) for assistance with research and editing; Governing Council of the Cat Fancy for permission to print the Tonkinese Standard of Points, Registration Policy and other GCCF documentation; New Forest Nature Quest (Lyndhurst in Hampshire); American Cat Association (ACA), American Cat Fanciers Association (ACFA), Australian Cat Federation Inc, Cat Association of Britain (CA), Cat Fanciers Association (CFA), Cat Fanciers Federation Inc. (CFF), Fédération Internationale Féline (FIFe), National Cat Fanciers Association (NCFA), New Zealand Cat Fancy Inc. (NZCF), The International Cat Association (TICA); to all the kind people who sent me photographs of their lovely cats (I'm sorry I have not been able to include every single one) – and Mr Mike Vousden for everything.

FOREWORD

I wrote of the Tonkinese in the book of my BBC television series *Cats:* This is a new name for an old breed that was reinvented. In anticipation of the new millennia, Linda Vousden's book is a timely recognition of the qualities of this wonderful cat.

When Dr Joseph Thompson produced the first Burmese in America from a brown cat called Wong Mau from South East Asia, the form of the original cat was somewhat overlooked in the delight that greeted the 'new' full Burmese. Similarly, in the early days of the cat fancy it is clear that again such cats were introduced, but that time were overshadowed by the new Siamese.

This brown cat was taken up in the West only when it was 'discovered' genetically.

While doing field research in Thailand for my book and the television series, I was particularly delighted to find these cats living feral and be able to demonstrate that the Tonkinese did have a history. I was able to show the illustrations of the brown cat of the *Cat Book Poems*. It seems that the distinction between the shades of brown was not drawn in South East Asia any more than in the West, and that less attention was given to the brown cat's pointing in a land where many cats have more contrasted pointing. Yet in Thailand today, breeders such as Ed and Malee Rose refer to the Tonkinese type rather than the Burmese as Copper. This may be partly because a distinction has now been drawn between the cats, and the full colour form is already called *Burmese*. However, I think it may also be that Burmese are encountered less often than Tonkinese, which are the normal brown cat of the country, so it is naturally called the Copper.

In the 1993 *Cat Annual* I recalled my first meeting with a historic Tai Tonk: *The Coppers are not commonly encountered as stray and feral cats and I have always been pleased that the first one I met was at the site of Ayutthaya. Its glowing copper body was a splendid contrast to its darker points. Another I met was a true monastery cat, being fed with great attention by a Buddhist monk at Chang Mai, which for many years was part of Burma. I have since found them scattered at different temple sites in Thailand.*

In the strong Tai sun, while the full Burmese has a richness of deep colour, it is the Tonk's body that really glows like burnished copper. Tonkinese can be sociable and affectionate and, when I was met by that first Tai Tonk, it was such a meeting; it approached me, then plumped down, rolling onto its back and exposing its tummy to me and the sun. What a greeting!

A cat of different character was the redoubtable Woot, the stud Copper of Ed and Malee Rose, pre-eminent cat breeders in Thailand. He sired a number of fine Burmese and Coppers. His offspring are a good conformation guide and genetically robust. Unfortunately, fashion whims have led some western breeders of Siamese and Burmese into troubled waters, but lovers of Tonks aspire to keep the integrity of build and so the health of the breed.

Linda cares about the welfare of the breed, and her 'Tonk Tome' sets a benchmark to help establish the breed as firmly as it deserves. Unfortunately, she and other devotees of the Tonk have to battle against a prejudice that, as the Tonkinese arises from a cross between Siamese and Burmese, it must be hybrid, and therefore cannot be a true breed. It is no such thing: it is a breed with an untypical form of genetics, arising from a number of alleles mutating at a single locus, resulting in the Burmese and Siamese genes being incompletely dominant with each other. Breed recognition should not try to force the straight-jacket of what is normal for other breeds onto this different type of genetics. It is a genuine genetic exception, and should be treated as such. The Tonkinese is genetically true, a historic breed of significance, and, as Linda amply demonstrates in this celebration of the Tonk, it is a *proper* cat.

No wonder its fans grow daily in numbers!

Roger Tabor

INTRODUCTION

I owe so much to my parents for instilling in me a respect and love for animals. Our family has always included cats and our first Siamese joined us in 1965 – Sabishi, a daughter of Sabukia Sir Galahad, and Njaom, who was a most loving little cat.

I came to know and love the Tonkinese (Tonks to their friends) via the now classic route; my own Siamese (gentle lilac-tabby Moral and bold cream Grimley) died within a couple of years of each other, both over 17 years of age. I knew that I would never find their like again. In less than 20 years the Siamese type and colour had changed considerably. I had seen articles on the Tonkinese in American cat books but I wasn't convinced that they would have the character of my Siamese. However, my first litter of Tonks (from my special blue Burmese girl, Mistry) had such a profound effect upon me that I became wholeheartedly committed to the breed. From that litter of seven I kept three of the kittens as pets – Caspar, Speckle, and Fable, who is still living up to his name through his wonderful temperament. My Tonkinese family has now grown, as has my involvement with the breed in general – none of which would have been possible without the caring and unending support of my husband Mike.

After 30 years the breed is still a junior. Nevertheless, the nature and beauty of the Tonks is so impressive that their popularity continues to grow among the public and members of the rarefied world of the Cat Fancy, and I believe that the Tonkinese will be numbered among the best of short-haired breeds.

Linda Vousden

Front cover: Tajens Isabella, aged 18 months.
Photo: Animals Unlimited
Title page: Deelando Rachaels Angel (choc).
Photo: Alan Robinson
Back cover: Mymystic Nimrod (choc tabby).
Photo: Animals Unlimited

© 1998 Kingdom Books, PO Box 15, Waterlooville PO7 6BQ, England.
All rights reserved. No part of this publication may be reproduced, stored in a retrieval system, or transmitted in any form or by any means, electronic, mechanical, photocopying, recording or otherwise, without the written permission of the publisher.

Chapter:

The Cat Fancy in Great Britain

The first recorded cat show was at the St Giles Fair in Winchester (1598), but it is generally acknowledged that the 'cat fancy' was born on Thursday 13 July 1871. Harrison Weir, a naturalist, artist, writer and great cat lover, was responsible for the first official cat show, which was held at the Crystal Palace. He wrote, *... I conceived the idea that it would be well to hold 'cat shows', so that the different breeds, colours, markings, etc. might be more carefully attended to, and the domestic cat, sitting in front of the fire, would then possess a beauty and an attractiveness to its owner unobserved and unknown because uncultivated heretofore.*

Harrison Weir's first show consisted of 170 cats in 25 classes, comprising nearly all the cat breeds then known in Britain, including the Manx, Eastern (as the long-haired cats were then called), Chinchilla and Abyssinian. The admission fee was the princely sum of one shilling and there were so many spectators that it was sometimes difficult to see the cats at all. Over 54 prizes were awarded for categories such as best colour, best longhaired cat, heaviest

Some of the old and valuable cups owned by the National Cat Club.

cat and the biggest cat. The judges, Rev J MacDona, Harrison Weir and his brother, John Jenner Weir, marked the cats against Points of Excellence drawn up by Harrison Weir. *The Illustrated London News* gave the show full coverage, saying: *At first the proposal to hold a cat show was received with much ridicule; but nothing succeeds like success. The number of entries and the multitude of visitors are sufficient guarantee that a cat show will in future constitute in the annual attractions of the [Crystal] Palace ... there was a wealth of cat that must have astonished those who are ignorant of the beauty and varieties of the animal.*

As a result of that first show cat shows proliferated at home and abroad. No clubs or official bodies were dealing with the registration of cats so, in 1887, a number of cat fanciers joined to form the National Cat Club with Harrison Weir as its first President. As well as running the Crystal Palace cat shows the club started a register of cats, granted championships and, in 1893, issued the very first feline stud book. In 1899 the National Cat Club founded its journal, *Our Cats*, which was produced weekly for about 14 years. By this time Louis Wain was the President and Chairman of the National Cat Club and a staunch supporter of the Club's principles. His love of cats was expressed in artwork which was to become internationally acclaimed, and he designed the National Cat Club's logo.

By the early 1900s many cat clubs had formed as interest in pedigree cats increased. Nearly all of the clubs were running shows under the rules laid down by the National Cat Club. Then, in 1898, as a result of a dispute with the National Cat Club, Lady Marcus Beresford (a well-known exhibitor who owned about 160 cats and often exhibited as many as 30 at a time) founded The Cat Club, with the same aims as the National Cat Club: to promote the pure breeding of cats, to hold shows and to keep a register of all pedigree cats. By 1903 The Cat Club was struggling with its own problems and asked for amalgamation with the National Cat Club. Louis Wain was very much against amalgamation and informed The Cat Club in no uncertain terms that the National Cat Club was *the* Club; in 1904 The Cat Club ceased to function and the National Cat Club once more became the sole registering body. Unfortunately, disagreements continued within the fancy. In 1908 Louis Wain expressed astonishment when eight clubs broke away from the influence of the National Cat Club and formed the Incorporated Cat Fanciers Association. He said: *...The NCC, despite all its many vicissitudes of fortune, still remains the only club which can hold the cat world together or give it any authority in the eyes of the world.* Two years later the ICFA ceased to exist.

The National Cat Club was most fortunate in having Louis Wain at its helm. Time and again he demonstrated his altruistic view of the Club and the cat fancy. He wrote: *The National Cat Club was formed to advance the interests of the cat, and not the interests of individuals, and to foster and encourage all that pertains to the building up of a really stable and permanent animal.*

Sadly, despite the efforts of people like Louis Wain, disagreements continued within the National Cat Club, so it invited members from 15 other

Chapter 1

clubs to a meeting, at which the Governing Council of the Cat Fancy (GCCF) was formed (11 March 1910). The National Cat Club handed over all rights of registration, transfers and issue of stud books to the GCCF, in return for which it was given the right, in perpetuity, to have four delegates representing it on the Council. The National Cat Club is still the only club which has more than two delegates. The cat fancy's growth was reflected in the number of journals and magazines reporting on cat shows, breeders and all aspects of the fancy. In 1890 the magazine *Fur and Feather* was first published and became, in 1919, the first official organ of the GCCF. In 1901 *Our Cats* magazine started to print a *Who's Who* of exhibitors and exhibits and included comments from noteworthy members of the cat fancy. Mr C Witt, a breeder, judge and reporter said: *The Cat Fancy is quite in its infancy; it has come to stay and once we get over the petty jealousies that exist, and judges and fanciers are credited with better intentions generally than at present, we shall go on and prosper and better prices will be obtained for A1 specimens because of the greater healthier rivalry and competition.* I wonder how he would view the fancy today?

For many years show pens were just wire cages and the cats were bedded on straw with sawdust in their litter trays, all of which was ideal for the transmission of fleas and disease. Although companies like Eucryl produced disinfectants (for instance, Salubrene was advertised as *recognised by Cat Fanciers, non-poisonous and non-corrosive*), no suitable disinfectant was used regularly; judges did not wash their hands and no-one saw any harm in the public stroking the exhibits. Cats and kittens could be sent to shows unaccompanied, often in nailed down boxes or baskets tied with string, and left to the 'tender care' of the various railway companies. It was not uncommon for a cat to arrive too late for a show; nor was it unheard of for a cat to go missing. Hygienic standards at cat shows were learned at great cost; the death rate of cats and kittens attending the early shows was horrendous. No-one was aware of feline enteritis, but many breeders and exhibitors were aware that improvements could be made. Mrs E Cope wrote in *Our Cats : I sincerely trust that before another season the sanitary show pen may become an accomplished fact and that the appalling death-toll which seems to inevitably follow our large shows may vanish beneath the stern hand of the reformer.*

Shows were held on different days of the week, so a cat could be exhibited numerous times within any one month. Breeders who had given up exhibiting still accepted exhibited queens to their studs, which often resulted in whole catteries being wiped out. The GCCF tried to institute a rule that there should be three weeks between shows but many clubs opposed it and threatened to hold shows without GCCF licence if the rule was passed. The continuation of cat shows was under serious threat.

In 1914 only five shows were held and in 1916 the National Cat Club held the last cat show until the end of the Great War. Despite the trials and traumas of that horrendous period, interest in cat shows remained. The first show held after the war was the Sandy Show in 1919. By 1927 the National

Cat Club's Crystal Palace show, organised by Mr Cyril Yeates (later Chairman and then President of the GCCF), had an entry of over 1000 cats, and catalogues were completely sold out by the start of the second day. At that time many cat shows were two-day events but in 1936, the night before the National Cat Club show, Crystal Palace burned to the ground. With great panache the show manager, Mrs Sharman, managed to move the entire show to the Paddington Baths. National Cat Club shows have been one-day events ever since, as are all GCCF-licensed shows now.

With the Second World War the future of cat shows was threatened, and indeed the cat fancy in Great Britain nearly came to an end. Thousands of cats were put to sleep as families were separated, and famous bloodlines were lost as cats were neutered or destroyed. In 1945 the Notts and Derby Cat Club held the first post-War show at the Victoria Baths Hall. There were 662 entries, and an excellent new GCCF ruling meant that each cat had to be accompanied by its exhibitor. Sadly, despite all precautions, many of the entries died of disease after the show but by the early 1950s help against the blight which was to become known as Feline Infectious Enteritis (FIE) was on its way. A vaccine was developed in the United States of America and in Britain Borough-Wellcome also developed a vaccine to be given to six-week-

A decorated pen at the GCCF Supreme Show.

old kittens. Since then several companies have developed and improved upon the vaccines for both the FIE and feline influenza viruses.

No introduction to the cat fancy should omit mention of Mrs Grace Pond, an international judge who has judged cats in Britain, America, Australia, Tasmania, South Africa, Zimbabwe and most European countries. Mrs Pond, authoress of many books on cats, is the president of the GCCF and many other cat clubs representing long- and short-haired breeds. She is also the president of the National Cat Club and first managed the National Cat Club show in 1954 – she was still doing so over 30 years later. It was largely thanks to her efforts that pet classes were introduced to the National show in 1956. Working with Mr Brian Vesey-Fitzgerald she managed to get sponsorship from *The News of the World,* and that year 190 pets were exhibited. It was also thanks to Mrs Pond that the BBC and the ITV have taken a continuing interest in the National Cat Club shows.

In October 1953 the GCCF ran its first show – the Coronation Cat Show. The Council didn't hold another until the 1960 Golden Jubilee Show but, by the 1970s, it had decided to run an annual show of its own. The Supreme Cat Show was founded by Dr W A Groom, and the first one was held in Stafford in December 1976. It is now held at the National Exhibition Centre in Birmingham. Dr Groom visualised the Supreme as being the cat fancy's equivalent of Crufts. He introduced ring-judging so that exhibitors could watch their cats being judged. Exhibitors were also permitted to decorate their cats' pens. The show was to be attended by only the best examples of the breeds – cats had to qualify by attaining meritorious status in other shows before they could be exhibited at the Supreme. Today entries include both pedigree and non-pedigree cats. Awards are granted to the Supreme Best Adult, Kitten and Neuter and the ultimate tribute is to become the Supreme Exhibit of the year. The first GCCF Supreme Show had 543 exhibits; 1996 boasted over 1550 pedigree exhibits plus more than 130 entries in the Household Pet section.

On 20 February 1983 a group of breeders, judges and show organisers met in Oxford and formed the Cat Association of Britain (CA), an alternative governing body to the GCCF. It was registered as a Company Limited by Guarantee so that it would be run solely by its members. It keeps a register of cats (pedigree, half-pedigree and non-pedigree) and holds all-breed championship shows all over Britain. The CA holds its shows on Sunday and so avoids conflicting with the GCCF Saturday-held shows. Like the GCCF it offers Champion, Grand and Supreme Grand Championships, but not just to pedigree cats; registered non-pedigrees may also compete for these titles. In 1986 the CA became the British member of the Fédération Internationale Féline (FIFe).

In 1951 the GCCF recognised just over 26 varieties of cat; today it recognises over 75, including the various colour-ways of the British Short-hair, Orientals, Asians and Long-hairs. As the cat fancy grew, so did the

The National Cat Club Centenary Show, 1996.

number of GCCF-affiliated clubs. In the early 1950s there were 22 clubs, whose membership included over 2100 registered prefixes; today there are more than 120 affiliated clubs, half of which are breed-specific. By 1990 over 30,000 cats were annually registered with the GCCF.

In 1994 the National Cat Club first introduced *The World of Cats* to their annual show. Organized by Miss Pam Weissman it was a resounding success and gave the public the opportunity to get a closer look at many new and established breeds away from the bustle of the exhibits being judged. Possibly the most successful attraction that year, also featured in the BBC's *Cats* programme, was the Tonkinese.

In 1996, when the National Cat Club held its Centenary Championship show, there were over 2000 classes and more than 1500 entries. The Tonkinese were there in competition and on exhibition to help with the celebrations.

Chapter: 2
A Tonkinese History

The earliest records of cats living in domestic association with humans come from Ancient Egypt. There are references to cats in chapter seven of the *Book of Ritual* (11th Dynasty, 3005–2778 BC), and highly ornamented cat coffins have been found inscribed with paragraphs from that chapter. Cats were household companions, also revered as the embodiment of the goddess Pasht, or Bastet. The worship of Pasht was dominant for nearly 2000 years, and Egyptians held their cats in such high regard that to harm them was punishable by death. The Egyptians attempted to ban the export of their cats but, in spite of their efforts, the domesticated cat was carried out of Egypt by travelling merchants to Greece, where it was known as the familiar of the goddess Artemis, to Italy around 300 BC, and into the Far East, where it was to become respected by those of the Buddhist, Moslem and Shinto faiths.

It was in the East that distinct breeds of cat were first recorded, and they are known to have existed in Siam (Thailand) around 400 AD. A belief common in both Burma and Siam was that, when a person of great piety died, his soul transferred itself to the body of a cat, where it would remain until the cat died a natural death; only then could the person's soul move on to Paradise. When a member of the royal house of Siam died it was customary for his favourite cat to be entombed alive with him. The tomb always had a small opening for the cat and, when the cat left the tomb, it was believed to be carrying the soul of the deceased. The cat was then reverently escorted to the temple, where it lived a life of gracious ease. This is undoubtedly one of the reasons why cats thrived especially in the temples, where they were welcome as the guardians of souls. In 1926 a small white cat was an official guest at the coronation of the King of Thailand, as it was believed to be carrying the soul of the late King.

The *Wi Chi-an Maad* cat, as in Ayutthayan manuscripts.

Ayutthaya, the ancient Siamese capital founded in the Chao Phraya valley around 1350 AD, was destroyed by Burmese invaders in 1767, and it was most fortunate that many Ayutthayan manuscripts such as the *Smud Khoi* (concatenated scrolls) and the *Cat Book Poems* were saved from destruction. These manuscripts, now in the Bangkok Museum, are richly illustrated with paintings of many cats, including the blue *Si Sawat* known to us as the Korat, the *Thong Daeng* or Red Gold (Copper) cat with its burnished chocolate coat which we now call the Burmese and the *Wi Chi-an Maad*

(Diamond Cat), a very pale cat with distinctly darker points, which we know as Siamese. There is also a striking looking cat with a brown coat and darker points – clearly the distinctive coat pattern of the Tonkinese.

Note: Phonetic transliteration of Thai words gives rise to variations in English spellings. *Ayutthaya* may also be seen written as *Ayudhaya* and *Wi Chian Maad* as *Vichien Mat.*

The *Thong Daeng* cat, as in Ayutthayan manuscripts.

The history and breeding of Tonkinese, Burmese and Siamese cats have always been so intricately woven that, although the Burmese and Siamese are generally referred to as the Tonkinese's parent breeds, it would be futile to try to establish which was actually the original breed, or even if there was more than one. What is certain is that a good number of the Siamese cats that were brought to the West were not the clearly defined breed which many people have believed them to be for so long.

There is some evidence to suggest that the Tonkinese have been in the West for over 100 years. In the Boston Museum of Fine Arts there is a painting called *Girl with a Cat* by American artist William Morris Hunt (1824–1879), who studied his craft in Europe. The cat in question is brown of body with darker brown points and distinctly blue/green eyes. In the 1890s a cat, which was thought at the time to be a Copper cat, was brought to England by Mr Young of Harrowgate. He described it as *a chocolate variety of the royal Siamese cat... rich chocolate or seal, with darker face, ears and tail; the legs are a*

Siamese-type cats, copied from ancient manuscripts.

Chapter 2

shade darker which intensifies toward the feet. Breeders and exhibitors of pedigree cats have certainly been aware of cats with the tonkinese coat pattern throughout this century. They were originally shown under the name Chocolate Siamese, not to be confused with the chocolate-point Siamese. These cats were later called Golden Siamese, either because the Siamese was thought to have descended from the Asian Golden Cat, otherwise known as the Golden Cat of Malaya (*Felis temmincki*), or perhaps simply for geographic reasons (see **Naming the Tonkinese**).

The Asian Golden Cat can be all black (melanistic) in body colour. It can also be dark brown, golden brown, red or grey, with a darker face and head striped with white. In the southern areas of its habitat range it is only faintly marked with spots on the flanks and belly but in its northern ranges it is more heavily marked with spots and stripes. Its habitat includes deciduous forests, tropical rainforests and occasionally open plains throughout Nepal, Tibet, Assam, Burma, Thailand (Siam), Vietnam (Annam), Cambodia, southern China and from Malaya to Sumatra. Some specimens have been tamed. One such kitten became an affectionate pet before being given to London Zoo.

Frances Simpson referred to both the Chocolate and Royal Siamese in her *Book of the Cat* (1903). She described the Royal as *cream coloured in body with sharply defined seal brown markings on head, ears, legs, feet and tail; eyes a decided blue,* and stated that the show standard for the Chocolate Siamese was the same for the Royal Siamese, with the exception of the body colour. Mrs Forestier-Walker, Mrs Simpson's contemporary, described the Chocolate Siamese as *deep brown in colour showing hardly any markings and having blue eyes.*

There are numerous references to the Chocolate Siamese by early cat fanciers, who consistently described it as having less contrast between point and body colour than the Royal Siamese and eye colour that ranged from varying shades of blue to amber yellow, so we may safely assume that the Chocolate Siamese were predominantly Tonkinese. Although the Royal Siamese was the preferred variety, the Chocolate did have its followers, including a Mrs Sutherland who, until she moved to the South of France, bred them from her Chocolate Siamese stud, Prince of Siam. Unfortunately, those with a preference for the Chocolate over the Royal Siamese were in a minority; the dictates of fashion resulted in the perpetuation of Royal Siamese and the disappearance of Chocolates.

Ch Rogata's Elvyn, a brown Tonkinese.

In his book *Your Cat, Its Care and Treatment* (1927) A de Bary-Saunders describes the Siamese of the day, stating that *The self-chocolate ones with yellow eyes are valuable.* He is surely referring to what we now call a Burmese and, as it is genetically impossible to get a Burmese coat pattern from either a pure Siamese mating or a Siamese/Tonkinese mating, it is clear that both parents of a *self-chocolate Siamese* kitten must have been Tonkinese.

The first genetically-proven Tonkinese was the ancestress of the modern breed of Burmese, Wong Mau. Imported into the United States of America in 1930, she was described as a brown hybrid with darker points on her face, legs, feet and tail. When bred to a seal-point Siamese she produced kittens with a Siamese coat pattern and kittens that resembled her, with darker brown bodies and less contrast between the body and point colour. Her owner, Dr Joseph C Thompson, was a psychiatrist with an interest in breeding cats. He was fond of Wong Mau and interested in establishing the genetic difference between her and his Siamese. In 1932, in conjunction with breeder and geneticist friends, Dr Thompson mated Wong Mau with a Siamese stud called Tai Mau. He then bred her back to one of her sons. The resulting litter had two different coat patterns: a uniformly brown coat and a medium brown coat with darker points. After several test matings Dr Thompson was satisfied that Wong Mau was genetically a Burmese/Siamese hybrid. In his paper he concluded that there were two types of Burmese: the darker phase cats, pure-bred for the Burmese gene, and the lighter phase cats, hybrid for the Siamese gene (Tonkinese). In 1943, a paper published by Dr Thompson, Virginia C Cobb, Clyde E Keeler and Madeleine Dmytryk expanded upon Dr Thompson's findings. A postscript to the paper stated that Lelia Volk of Honolulu believed she had discovered yet another colour variation, darker than the ordinary Siamese. Upon examination by Clyde Keeler it also was found to be intermediate in colour between Burmese and Siamese.

The Tonkinese has played a crucial role in founding the Burmese breed in the United States and Great Britain. The pedigree of many imported Burmese would look very different if those cats were registered today. For example one of the most famous 'Burmese' imports was Mrs Lilian France's Casa Gatos Da Foong (imported in 1949), whose pedigree is shown below. All the cats were brown and the brackets indicate how they would be registered today.

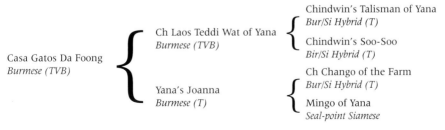

Casa Gatos Da Foong
Burmese (TVB)

Ch Laos Teddi Wat of Yana
Burmese (TVB)

Chindwin's Talisman of Yana
Bur/Si Hybrid (T)

Chindwin's Soo-Soo
Bir/Si Hybrid (T)

Yana's Joanna
Burmese (T)

Ch Chango of the Farm
Bur/Si Hybrid (T)

Mingo of Yana
Seal-point Siamese

Key: T   = Burmese/Siamese (Tonkinese)
       TVB   = Tonkinese variant with Burmese coat pattern

Chapter 2

USA Ch Chango of the Farm, a direct descendant of Wong Mau, is seen in nearly all the Burmese foundation pedigrees. He was born in 1941 and was described as hybrid in appearance, a dark Siamese with aquamarine eyes.

In Great Britain the first Burmese/Siamese cross officially registered as such was Chira Tan Tockseng, imported in 1958 by Mrs R J Grove-White (Ngo and Pya prefixes) to found her Burmese breeding programme, which began one of the early British Burmese bloodlines. The Tonkinese also played an important role in the creation of the cream Burmese in 1964. A tortie Tonkinese (Kudos Farrago) was born from a mating of Southview Havoc (red-point Siamese, sire) with Arboreal Fenella (brown Burmese, dam). Her line resulted in the first cream Burmese, Kudos Gold Guinea:

Kudos Gold Guinea
(1st cream Burmese)

Ch Buskins Blue Sunya
(Blue Burmese)

Ch Blue Bonnetia
(Blue Tortie Burmese)

Pussinboots Blue Moon
(Blue Burmese)

Kudos Farrago
(Brown Tortie Tonkinese)

PARENT BREEDS

Before I go any further I will set the scene with a little information about the cats referred to as the parent breeds of the Tonkinese. The respected geneticist Roy Robinson wrote, *The Tonkinese is one of the newer breeds, comparatively speaking; and a truly elegant cat to boot. The Tonkinese was developed from crosses between two established breeds; made possible by a quirk in feline coat colour genetics. It is not a hybrid, as I heard it described some while ago when specimens were on exhibition for the first time. The word hybrid should be reserved for crosses between different species.* He went on to explain that the Burmese and Siamese both owe their existence to a single gene mutation in the coat-pattern gene.

Reluctance on the part of some members of the cat fancy to accept any 'new' cat was initially a problem. However, neither the Siamese nor the Burmese was wholeheartedly accepted by cat lovers in the West at first.

Siamese

The Siamese must surely be the cat that attaches the most fallacies and fantasies. Immensely popular because of its exotic coloration and unique character, this is a cat with obscure origins. The Hon Russell Gordon, who is said to have made a study of the origins of the Siamese cat, stated that it is derived from a cross between the sacred cats of Burma and the Annamite cats (the Asian Golden Cat). Phyllis Wade, in her book *The Siamese Cat* (1934), theorised that the shape of the Siamese resembled the mummified remains of Egyptian cats so closely that the Egyptian cats probably were transported along with grain in trading ships to the Far East. However, Compton

MacKenzie, in his introduction to that same book, stated his belief that the Siamese was a selected and inbred variant of the Golden Cat of Malaya.

In his *Travels through the Southern Provinces of the Russian Empire in the years 1793–1794*, P S Pallas clearly described (and drew) a Siamese cat he saw near the Caspian Sea, nearly a century before they were seen in Great Britain.

Although it is generally assumed that the Siamese were first brought to England in 1884 there is a disparity of opinions regarding the cat's introduction to the West. Brian Vesey-Fitzgerald wrote in his book *Cats* (1957) that cats remarkably like the Siamese have been portrayed by at least one Dutch and one Flemish master, and the early Victorian Royal Academician, Frederick Smallfield, includes such a cat in one of his paintings.

Mandu, an old-fashioned Siamese.

It is interesting to note the different descriptions of the Siamese exhibits at the Crystal Palace show in 1885. These are believed to have been the progeny of the Siamese cats brought to England in 1884. *The Graphic* wrote that they were *soft fawn-coloured creatures, with jet black legs, an unnatural nightmare kind of cat;* another reporter wrote that they were *singular and elegant in their smooth skins, and ears tipped with black, and blue eyes with red pupils.* Dr St George Mivart, who published the first anatomical study of the cat (1881), described them as being like black-faced pug dogs with remarkable blue eyes and two small bald spots on the forehead.

This fascinating cat became so popular that the Siamese Cat Club was the first club for short-haired cats to have its own specialist show. In 1928 the Siamese Cat Club's fifth show, at Kensington, was attended by Sir Edward Cook, the financial advisor to the King of Siam (Thailand). He noted that in Siam *it seems that the males are much darker than in Britain and the heads, though narrow and pointed, are shorter in the nose. Kinked tails are not un-known but are considered a defect, and cats with kinked tails are never seen in the Royal Palace.*

M Oldfield Howey stated in his book, *The Cat in the Mysteries of Religion and Magic,* that for 200 years Siamese cats were only to be found in the courts of the Royal City of Bangkok, but there is disagreement about whether they were ever exclusively the royal cats of Thailand; indeed the first Siamese Champion (Wankee) was imported from Hong Kong. Without doubt they could, and still can, be found in Thai temples, along with all the other cats, which are cherished as guardians of departed souls. They have the intelligence to realise that the temples are a place to go for comfort and an easy life.

Chapter 2

A modern Siamese with a chocolate Tonkinese kitten.

Ever since their appearance in the West there have been refinements of the breed type (shape) and colour. The seal-point that was known in the 1960s, with its solid body and medium wedge-shaped head, medium-large ears and the lovely glowing cream body colour, is rarely seen today, except in the United States, where it is still bred under the title of 'Apple-head' type Siamese. In 1993 a group of breeders called for re-registration of the 'Apple-head' Siamese to distinguish it from the contemporary Siamese, so in 1994 the 'Opal' cat was officially recognised. In the United Kingdom the numbers of 'old-fashioned Siamese' lovers are steadily increasing; it will be interesting to see how long it takes for them to make their mark on the show bench again.

Burmese

The first recorded 'Burmese' from the East, Wong Mau, was imported from Rangoon (capital of Burma after 1852). She was actually a Tonkinese with the typical characteristics of the breed. Selective breeding with kittens exhibiting just the dark coat pattern and the gold or hazel eyes eventually resulted in a gorgeous cat that breeds true, but it took several decades to convince the cat fancy that the Burmese was not an alternative or defective Siamese. Enough members of the American cat fancy became so convinced that the Burmese were actually Siamese with faulty colouring that the Burmese had to be withdrawn from a major cat show in San Francisco in 1938. Matters came to a head in 1947 when the Cat Fanciers Association Inc (CFA) confirmed that the Burmese was not being bred according to the agreed constitution and withdrew recognition of the breed for six years. Inevitably the Burmese proved itself a true breed, and the appeal of this exotic cat, so full of character, ensured its acceptance.

Lilian and Sydney Frances, well known as breeders and respected authorities on the Siamese (under their prefix Chinki), became interested in the Burmese and contacted Blanche Warren in California. Mrs Warren chose three unrelated cats of the best possible stock to establish the breed in Britain.

The queens, Chindwins Minou Twm and USA Ch Laos Cheli Wat, were mated to different studs and in 1949 were sent to Mrs France with the male Casa Gatos da Foong. Sadly, owing to the change in climate and prolonged duration in quarantine, the kittens did not survive, and later, after only one successful litter, Chindwins Minou Twm also perished. The first time the British public saw the Burmese was at the 1949 Croydon Cat Club show, when Mrs Frances exhibited Casa Gatos da Foong. He was an astounding success, both for his exotic colouring and for his temperament, a characteristic he passed on to his progeny.

The Burmese breed was recognised by the GCCF in 1952, after three pure generations had been produced. At this time there were still very few Burmese breeders but, in 1958, Mrs Grove-White imported the Burmese/Siamese cross Chira Tan Tockseng from the United States. This, along with the cats imported in 1949, became the foundation breeding stock for the British Burmese until 1968, when more American and Canadian Burmese were imported. In January 1955 the Burmese Cat Club (UK) was founded. The club celebrated its 40th anniversary at its show on

Predator Minnie Themoocher, a brown Burmese.

24 June 1995, where it saw its largest exhibit of titled cats – the Grand classes numbered 31 entire adults and 41 neuters.

... and back to the Tonkinese

It is a commonly held belief that the Tonkinese 'originated' in Canada but, while the Canadian Cat Association was certainly the first body to give the breed recognition, and we know that the cat must have originated in the East, the first recorded breeding programme for the Tonkinese was in the United States of America. Milan Greer, a New York pet shop owner and author of *The Fabulous Feline,* became ardently interested in cats when he adopted a nine-year-old Siamese, re-homing his Airedale a month later to make way for her. Greer decided to breed from her and keenly pursued his aim of breeding show-quality cats but, for a period in the 1950s, he was even more interested in another type of cat he had seen, which had a rich mahogany body colour with darker points. He said he was aware that these cats were often destroyed under the assumption that they were defective hybrids who would not breed true. He believed that this hypothesis was wrong and that a strain of very beautiful cats could be developed. He knew that the Burmese had come from *an anonymous brown cat crossed with a Siamese,* from which the Siamese characteristics had been bred out to produce true-breeding Burmese, so he bred his male Burmese, Anyo, to a chocolate-point Siamese belonging to breeders Genevieve Gibson and Helen Arthur. His aim was to breed a cat with the attractive and saleable qualities of both breeds. He cross-bred the offspring, which he called *Golden Siamese,* and claimed to have *bred it five generations pure.* He stated that the Golden immediately proved very popular.

Greer then stopped breeding the Golden, having proved, to his satisfaction, his theory that they were not a defective hybrid. He said that he was leaving it to others to produce enough generations of the breed to qualify for show recognition (seven generations were then required) and returned to his original interest in breeding and showing Burmese. Unfortunately, his experiment on the Golden Siamese came at a time when breeders were far more interested in developing the Burmese lines, which were consistently breeding true to themselves. Possibly this limited interest in the Golden Siamese, coupled with Milan Greer's highly inbred line sold simply as hybrids, was why work on the breed was not continued by other breeders at the time.

Later, in the early 1960s, a Canadian cat fancier from Ontario, Margaret Conroy, crossed a seal-point Siamese with a brown Burmese, hoping to produce a cat with the qualities that she liked best in each of the parent breeds – an intermediate type with a temperament falling between the Burmese and Siamese. Initially her cats too were called Golden Siamese. Several other breeders of the time shared her opinion that the Siamese was becoming too stylised and looked for an intermediate breed with some of the characteristics of the older style Siamese. With their help, Margaret Conroy wrote a standard for her Golden Siamese, and in 1965 she presented it to the Canadian Cat Association (CCA) for approval and the first official recognition of the breed.

American breeders Edith Lux and Mrs Robert Nelson co-operated in a Tonkinese breeding programme and established that they were able to breed the Tonkinese type (head and body shape) consistently and that there were undoubtedly, and consistently, three different coat patterns: the uniform colour of the Burmese, the distinctly pointed coloration of the Siamese, and the intermediate coat pattern exhibited by Wong Mau. Enthusiastic breeders of the cats decided to give the breed another name to re-enforce that it was neither a Burmese nor a Siamese. They agreed on the name proposed by Mrs Lux – *Tonkinese (Tonkanese* in Canada and the United States). This name was chosen because the Gulf of Tonkin in the South China Sea lies on latitude 20°, which runs between Burma and Thailand (Siam). In 1972 the breed was granted recognition by the Independent Cat Federation (ICF) of the United

Imperial Medallist Katalyst Munchinella.

States (the organisation no longer exists) and the Tonkinese's increasing popularity with breeders and pet owners ensured that it was subsequently granted recognition and ultimately championship status by several feline registration bodies (see **Tonkinese Diary** on page 22).

Note: Unfortunately, despite pursuing numerous avenues of investigation, I have been unable to find out more about the early Tonkinese breeders or their cats, so I would very much appreciate any information that readers could send me for future reference.

In 1986 the Tonkinese breed was provisionally accepted by the Cat Association of Britain (CA) as a New Breed, which entitled the Tonkinese to compete for the CA titles of Medallist, Grand, Supreme and Imperial Medallist. When it was elected the British Member of the Fédération Internationale Féline (FIFe) in May 1990, the CA relinquished its authority to recognise new breeds or varieties, but was granted a dispensation by the FIFe to keep the provisional status for Tonkinese; the breed's Medallist awards became CA special national awards. The Tonkinese is presently classified as 'unrecognised' by the FIFe and must await recognition by the FIFe General Assembly before it can be promoted under the CA. For this reason Tonkinese are not seen in competition on the show benches in Europe unless they are registered with a body that is not FIFe affiliated.

Chapter 2

In 1990 a group of breeders who had originally shown their Tonkinese under the CA worked together to found the Tonkinese Breed Club, with the aim of gaining recognition for the breed from the Governing Council of the Cat Fancy (GCCF). On Saturday 11 May 1991 the GCCF, recognising the considerable support for the breed, granted preliminary recognition of the Tonkinese and allocated the unique breed number 74.

In 1996 the GCCF published their breed analysis of the 32,792 cats registered with them during 1995. With 564 kittens registered, the Tonkinese came 9/26 this table, an excellent indicator of its popularity as a new breed when many championship breeds registered far fewer kittens.

TONKINESE DIARY

189? – First recorded Copper-like cat in Britain (owned by Mr Young of Harrowgate)

1936 – First genetically-proven Tonkinese, Wong Mau (owned by Dr J Thompson)

195? – Golden Siamese breeding programme of Milan Greer, USA

1958 – Officially recorded Bur/Si hybrid imported from USA by Mrs Grove-White, UK

196? – Golden Siamese breeding programme of Margaret Conroy, Canada

1965 – First official recognition of the breed, by the Canadian Cat Association (CCA)

1972 – Officially recognised by the USA Independent Cat Federation (ICF), no longer extant

1975 – Officially recognised by the USA Cat Fanciers Federation (CFF)

1978 – Officially recognised by the USA Cat Fanciers Association Inc (CFA)

1979 – Officially recognised by The International Cat Association (TICA)

1979 – Awarded championship status by TICA

1984 – Awarded championship status by the CFF

1984 – Awarded championship status by the CFA

1986 – Granted Provisional (New Breed) status by the Cat Association of Britain (CA)

1989 – Officially recognised by the American Cat Association (ACA)

1989 – Awarded championship status by the ACA

1990 – Officially recognised by the USA National Cat Fanciers Association (NFCA)

1990 – Awarded championship status by the NFCA

1991 – Granted Preliminary recognition by Governing Council of the Cat Fancy (GCCF), UK

1996 – First specialist Tonkinese cat show, held by the Tonkinese Breed Club (UK)

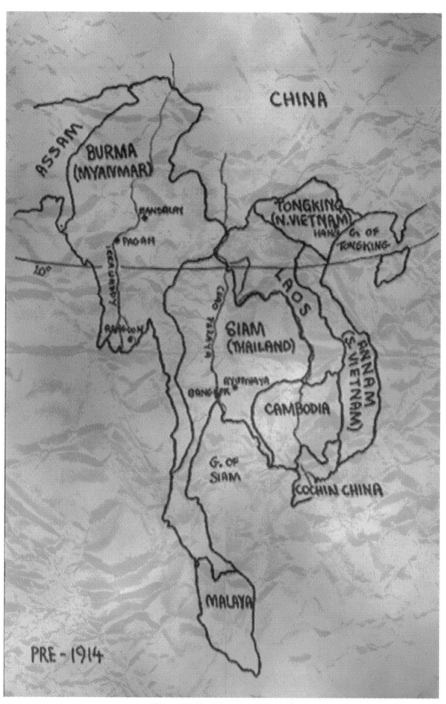

Where the Tonkinese originated.

Chapter 2

NAMING THE TONKINESE

It was inevitable that these cats would be known as either Golden Siamese or Tong-inese. The Thai word for gold is Tong (Thong, Tawng). The Hon Russell Gordon made a study of Siamese cat history and believed that they were derived from a cross between the sacred cat of Burma and the Annamite cats. The northern region of Annam (now Vietnam) was Tongking, which in the mid-1300s was invaded by Kublai Khan's Golden Hordes. Milan Greer called his cats Golden Siamese and later the breed was named Tonkinese after the Gulf of Tonkin (or *Tongking*, according to the age of your atlas), because the Gulf lies on latitude 20° which runs between Burma and Thailand – a fitting piece of symbolism for a Burmese/Siamese cat. The border between Thailand and Burma is the Tanen Tong Dan (The Golden Border).

Finally a piece of serendipity: Muir's *Historical Atlas of the Ancient, Medieval and Modern World* shows Tongking on page 74. The GCCF breed number for the Tonkinese is 74.

Unlike a number of other cat breeds the name of the Tonkinese remains fairly consistent around the cat fancies of the world, although the spelling varies slightly: Tonkanese (Canada, USA), Tonkanesen (Germany), Tonkinees (Netherlands), Tonkinese (United Kingdom, Australia, Italy, New Zealand), Tonkinois (France).

On several occasions, to my surprise, I have been asked to suggest a name for a Tonkinese.

Normally for pedigree cats names are very distinctive, usually having some personal significance for the breeder or owner, or chosen to reflect the cat's personality in some way. A pet name must naturally be acceptable not only to the human family but also to the cat. For example, my brown Burmese queen's pedigree name is Predator Minnie Themoocher (the breeder and I both being Cab Calloway fans) but she didn't want to answer to Minnie; nor did she show the slightest interest in either of the other names I offered her. About two weeks after she came to live with us I noticed her sitting in the gloom under my desk chair. When she blinked her huge luminous eyes she completely disappeared. For this reason, she was named Shadow. I liked the name, my husband Mike liked the name, and most importantly, so did Shadow.

The Thai language is exceptionally intricate and many words have a variety of meanings depending on how they are pronounced and used. Furthermore, Thai script must be phonetically translated into English, so the spelling of translated Thai words varies according the age of the dictionary. Here is a selection of Thai (Siamese) words that you may find useful when naming your Tonkinese.

Adorable	Phitsamai	Lotus	Kohsoom
Beautiful	Chai lai	Love	Rahk
Beloved	Yod rak	Moon	Chanthra
Black	See dam	Moonlight	Saeng som
Black gold	Thong dam	Morning	Chow
Blessing	Som phon	Music	Dohn dtree
Blue	See fah	Naughty	Sohn
Bronze	Thong brawn	Ocean	Samutra
Butterfly	Pee seuuh	Orange	See sohm
Cat	Maa oh	Orchid	Kluai mai
Cat	Warah	Pearl	Ky mook
Cinnamon	Ohp choei	Pleasure	Kwahm yindee
Climbing jasmine	Maliwan	Prince	Chao chai
Cloud	Mehk	Princess	Chao yeeng
Cream	Kreem	Promise	Sahn yah
Dark	Dahm	Red	See daeng
Dawn, Rainbow	Roong	Red gold (copper)	Thong daeng
Day	Wahn	Ruby	Thapthim (Tuptim)
Dearest	Sood sawatt	Sapphire	Nin
Desire	Prasong	Sea	Ta leh
Dove	Nohk kow	Siamese dance	Chui chai
Dream	Kwahm fahn	Silk	Mai
Eyes	Dtah	Snow	Hih ma
Faithful	Pakdee	Special	Phiset
Fame or reputation	Kitti	Star	Dao
Feline	Wila	Starlight	Saeng dao
Floral	Busaba	Storm	Pah yoo
Flower	Malee	Sunlight	Titaya
Fortune	Sawat	Sunshine	Daat
Fortune teller	Maw doo	Sweet lady	Chaem choi
Fountain	Nahm poo	Thank you	Kawp koon
Free	Thai	Tiger	Sua
Gardenia	Phut son	True	Ching
Gem	Mani	Water lily	Bua phuan
Gems	Ratana	Wealth	Sap
Gold	Thong	Whisper	Gra sip
Gold ingots	Thong thaeng	White	See khao
Gold to be added	Thong thaem	White gold	Thong khao
Greeting	Sawatdi	One	Neung
Handsome	Sohpar	Two	Sawng
Honey	Nahm phueng	Three	Sahm
Innocent	Chaisai	Four	See
Ivory	Ngah	Five	Hah
Jasmine	Mali	Six	Hohk
Jasmine	Saraphi	Seven	Chet
Kitten	Look maa oh	Eight	Bpaat
Lady of beauty	Rotchana	Nine	Gow
Lion	Sing dtoh	Ten	Sip

Chapter 2

THE TONKINESE BREED CLUB

With the election of the Cat Association (CA) as the British member of FIFe in May 1990, the opportunities for Tonkinese breed promotion were restricted (see details on page 21). A group of breeders from the CA-affiliated Tonkinese Cat Club therefore decided to found a new Tonkinese club with the aim of achieving recognition for the breed from the GCCF. The Tonkinese Breed Club was established under the sponsorship of the Colour-Pointed, Rex-Coated and Any Other Variety Cat Club. In May 1991 the GCCF, recognising the considerable support for the breed, granted Preliminary recognition to the Tonkinese and allocated the unique breed number 74.

The founding members of the Tonkinese Breed Club were: Mrs B Alston, Mrs H Barnes, Mrs D Bartlett, Dr and Mrs Bishop, Miss D Cary, Miss J Cooper, Miss H Cuthbert, Mr and Mrs Earley, Mrs H Forshaw, Mrs J Elkington, Mrs E Gardener, Mrs J Goodwin, Miss M Hodgkinson, Mrs P Jenkinson, Mr and Mrs Nicols, Mr S Pallister, Dr J Ponsford, Mrs E Pratt-Campbell, Mrs P Spicer and Mrs D Waters. In 1994, the Club applied for affiliation with the GCCF, which was granted on 26 October.

The highlight of the Club's history so far has to be its first show. On 2 November 1996 the Club staged the first-ever specialist Tonkinese show. It was highly successful thanks to the huge support of Tonkinese lovers, the effort of local Club members who ensured plenty of publicity for the show, the many volunteers who helped on the day and, of course, the hard work of its Show Manager (Mrs Doreen Burke) and the Club Committee (Mrs Sylvia

Some of the Tonkinese Breed Club trophies.

Clark, Mrs Rosemary Harper, Ms Sarah Inigo-Jones, Mrs Carol Poole, Mrs Brenda Rawlinson, Mrs Christine Richards, Miss Susan Vogt, Mrs Linda Vousden and Mr Mike Vousden).

Over 70 Tonkinese were entered, a high proportion of which had never been shown before but still demonstrated the relaxed and even temper of the breed. Several Tonkinese variants were exhibited and there was a well-attended Household Pet section. The judges were Mrs Anna Bailey, Mr John Furber, Mrs Joyce Green, Mrs Mary Kalal, Mrs Margaret Kidd, Mrs Beryl Lyon, Miss Priscilla Rowlands and Mr Keith Scruton.

Trophies were donated by Club members and interested businesses, each judge awarded a rosette to the cat or kitten of his or her choice, and many Club members also gave special awards to the Tonkinese of their choice. The prizes were presented by the Honorary Secretary of the GCCF, Mrs Lesley Pring. The Best In Show (BIS) awards went to:

Senior judge Mary Kalal with Mymystic Nemesis.

Best In Show: Clarinath Nightshadow (lilac).

Chapter 2

Reserve Best In Show: Melusine Aquatay (choc), with Melusine Bellaclova (brown tortie) in the foreground.

- *Overall BIS:* Clarinath Nightshadow.
- *Reserve BIS:* Melusine Aquatay.
- *BIS Adult:* Clarinath Nightshadow (74c) male, owned and bred by Mrs Carol Poole.
- *BIS Kitten:* Melusine Aquatay (74b) male, owner Ms M Haas, breeders Mr S and Mrs B Rawlinson.
- *BIS Neuter:* Adhirsh Cato Redbaron (74d) male, owner Miss S A Ward, breeder Mrs P Jenkinson.

A special award for a Tonkinese variant on exhibition went to Melusine Fleur De Lis, brown tortie with Siamese coat-pattern, owner Ms S Bellis-Jones, breeders Mr and Mrs Rawlinson.

Open class results
(* = Best of Colour Group and Nominated Best In Show)

Adult
Brown F	1st: Deelando Gloriana*
Blue M	1st: Samkabar Pliedes*
Blue F	1st: Adhirsh Tamara
Choc F	1st: Romantica Tiramisu*, 2nd: Adhirsh Kandi Kiss

Lilac M	1st: Clarinath Nightshadow*, 2nd: Bonzer Merlin, 3rd: Romantica Oscar
Lilac F	1st: Tonkabella Phoebe Perpetua, 2nd: Ishokats Amber Amethyst
Red M	1st: Romantica Remus*
Cream M	1st: Episcopuss Caesar*
Tortie	1st: Episcopuss Ianthe*, 2nd: Angisan Caramel Passion
Tabby M	1st: Deelando Sonofatiger
Tabby F	1st: Bonzer Duskey Dawn*

Kitten

Brown F/M	1st: Mymystic Nemesis*, 2nd: Fabiola Suliaman
Blue M	1st: Tajens Jumpinjackflash
Blue F	1st: Suantre Sobrina Suzhonese*
Choc M	1st: Melusine Aquatay*, 2nd: Tonkaholics Arabian Knight, 3rd: Tonkaholics Mr Mistofilees
Choc F	1st: Trampuss Tickety Boo, 2nd: Trampuss Troubadour
Lilac M	1st: Suantre Fantasia, 2nd: Mirber Mandarin Ming
Lilac F	1st: Adquash Yum Yum, 2nd: Mirber Contessa Zarta, 3rd: Suantre Kerema Laynese
Cream M	1st: Tonkitu Yoshiki, 2nd: Tonkitu Temujen
Cream F	1st: Adquash Coralie Cleo, 2nd: Episcopuss Maia
Tortie	1st: Melusine Bellaclova*, 2nd: Gymnopedie Araminta, 3rd: Grimspound Majesticlady
Tabby M	1st: Mymystic Mischa, 2nd: Mymystic Nimrod
Tabby F	1st: Mymystic Pagan*, 2nd: Bonzer Chatter Box

Neuter

Brown M	1st: Romantica Marcus Macoy*, 2nd: Mymystic Goldenshadow, 3rd: Carash Glenharm Boy
Brown F	1st: Rohese Calamity Jane
Blue M	1st: Adouzsh Blue Hypnos*, 2nd: Adouzsh Blue Odin, 3rd: Learoyd Serendipity
Blue F	1st: Deelando Bluebell
Choc M	1st: Azulejo Whisky Mac*, 2nd: Tonkabella Lemuel Leon, 3rd: Deelando Rachels Angel
Choc F	1st: Ishokats Fantasque Faline
Lilac M	1st: Learoyd Whiskey
Red M	1st: Adhirsh Cato Redbaron*
Cream M	1st: Adraysh Dawn Chorus*
Cream F	1st: Adhuish Mali Creme
Tortie	1st: Wizadora Petite Fleur*
Tabby M	1st: Bonzer Barnabyboy
Tabby F	1st: Bonzer Moody Blues*

Chapter: 3
The Tonkinese Described

TEMPERAMENT

The Tonkinese – beauty, harmony and balance.

Tonkinese are irrepressible and I doubt that any Tonk lover could better Milan Greer's description of them. In his book *Fabulous Felines* (1961), he describes the cats he bred and called Golden Siamese as the perfect combination of brains and beauty with the better traits of both the Siamese and the Burmese – *a prodigy in fur.*

Tonkinese are intelligent, inquisitive and communicative individuals. If you want a cat that will keep its feet on the ground and merge into your carefully-planned home and well-regulated timetable you should get an ornament, not a Tonkinese. Their outgoing and affectionate nature makes them truly wonderful pets for those who have abundant time and a secure environment for them. They like to keep you company whatever you are doing, a trait which I heard described as a drawback by someone who actually thought he owned his cat. Tonkinese make full use of their surroundings and, if ignored, will demand their fair share of attention with a moderately-toned voice.

Tonkinese have a sense of fun and the occasionally mischievous streak is moderated by their gentle dispositions. They develop strong ties with people rather than places. They enjoy family company and dispense their attentions among the whole family rather than devoting themselves entirely to one person. Please note that, although Tonkinese are undoubtedly happy in the company of people, they do need company of their own kind.

Tonkinese need company of their own kind.

A single-cat household is a very lonely home for any cat, but especially so for a Tonkinese, who will make sure that you know it.

The sensitive and responsive nature of the Tonkinese is so reliable that an American breeder, Joan Bernstein, and her Tonkinese were featured in a *National Geographic* documentary video. Joan uses some of her Tonkinese in a Pets As Therapy *(PAT-cat)* programme. Their temperament is ideally suited to being handled and fussed by people, who gain immense benefits and pleasure from relating with friendly animals. If you want to share your home, and life, with such a cat you must have will-power, patience and a sense of fun.

TYPE

In the make-up of any cat breed the two basic factors are the head and body shape (referred to as the *type*) and the *coat pattern*, which in the Tonkinese is strongly related to the colour of the eyes. In the more detailed descriptions which follow I have included some excerpts from the exhibition standards of other registration authorities as a comparison with the GCCF standard of points. Abbreviations for cat fancy registration bodies referred to in this chapter are as follows:

ACA	American Cat Association
ACFA	American Cat Fanciers Association
CA	Cat Association of Britain
CCA/AFC	Canadian Cat Association/Association Féline Canada
CFA	Cat Fanciers Association Inc (USA)
CFF	Cat Fanciers Federation (USA)
GCCF	Governing Council of the Cat Fancy (UK)
NCFA	National Cat Fanciers Association (USA)
NZCI	New Zealand Cat Fancy Incorporated
TICA	The International Cat Association

Chapter 3

The type of the Tonkinese breed was initially described by breeders with the few cats that were being bred at the time as a basis for the description. In the early stages of the breed in the United Kingdom there was less constancy of type, as breeders' perceptions of the ideal varied according to their preference for the Burmese or Siamese look. Several breeding programmes included back-crossing with the parent breeds, which often meant that a particular line had more emphasis on either Burmese or Siamese type. Within the last few years, many interested breeders have introduced new bloodlines into the gene pool and this, combined with the cessation of back-crossing, has provided enough Tonkinese from different bloodlines for a more accurate assessment of the true (UK) Tonkinese type. What is now acknowledged as the ideal Tonkinese type will be maintained by breeders, who only breed with cats that are generally agreed to be the most desirable and representative examples of the breed.

Ishokats Bijan Valentino (brown) and Ishokats Bianka (choc).

It has been said that the words *medium* and *moderate* are applied too often in the description of the Tonkinese but there is just no getting away from it. That the Tonkinese is not extreme in any aspect of its appearance is a major attraction for many cat lovers.

The Tonkinese is a short-haired cat of moderate foreign type, placed in the *Foreign* group for GCCF registration and exhibition. It is elegant, with a

Wedge too short with distinct nose-break.

Preferred medium wedge with slight nose-break.

Wedge too long with little or no nose-break.

Juvenile female Tonkinese.

Adult female Tonkinese.

Juvenile male Tonkinese.

Adult male Tonkinese.

Chapter 3

lithe and firmly muscular build; the torso is neither cobby (short-bodied) nor elongated but has more of the appearance of a medium length rectangle. The chest is gently rounded in front with the ribs curving slightly outwards, and the flanks are level. The back rises a little from shoulder to rump because the rear legs are slightly longer than the front legs (a typical characteristic of a swift, pouncing predator). The legs are moderately slim but well-muscled and in proportion to the length of the torso, and the feet are neat and oval shaped. The tail is neither thick nor whippy and tapers gently to a rounded tip. It should be long enough to balance the length of the torso.

The Tonkinese head shape is, again, neither elongated with the associated aquiline profile nor short-muzzled with a strong nose-break: it is a well-balanced wedge shape, giving the impression of an equilateral triangle when observed from the front. The top of the head is a lovely rounded shape, ideal for stroking. The ears are oval tipped and fairly large, facing forward and set either side of a generous forehead. The muzzle, neither short nor elongated, tapers gently to a blunt finish without being too rounded or foxy in appearance and the whisker pinch should be evident but not exaggerated. Just below eye level there is a gentle nose-break (sometimes referred to as a 'stop') which, combined with the firm, curved chin, gives the Tonkinese a very attractive profile. The nose is often broader in the male than in the female.

Altogether the appearance of the Tonkinese is that of a stylish and well proportioned cat. It is active, athletic and weighs more than you would expect, judging by appearances. Adult males are proportionately larger than adult females; they are usually more muscular in the neck and shoulders and the head and jowls may be wider and rounder. On average the weight of a mature Tonkinese is around 3.6kg (8lb) for the female and 5.4kg (12lb) for the male.

COAT PATTERN

Many breeds have similar or identical type: for instance, in the Foreign group it is only the colour or coat pattern that separates the Oriental Lilac from the Siamese or Foreign Black. The coat pattern of the Tonkinese makes it a unique breed.

In most breeds with the Himalayan coat pattern you find that, where the temperature drops to about 36°C (96°F) at the extremities of the body (in other words, the *points*: the face mask, ears, feet, legs, tail and the testicles of entire males) the fur is more intensely pigmented. As the legs and feet are fleshier than the other points they don't become quite as cool, so they can be paler in tone than the other points. The coat pattern of the Tonkinese is very subtle, the darker colour of the points gradually blending into a paler shade of that colour over the rest of the body, with even paler underparts. The pattern referred to as the *tonkinese* coat pattern (the lower case 't' distinguishing it from the breed) is found in breeds other than the Tonkinese where the Burmese and Siamese have been used in the breeding programmes: for example the Devon Rex.

The texture of the Tonkinese coat is fine, rich, soft and silky; the fur lies close to the body but may be slightly more full in some cats. These two coat textures used to be referred to as *silk* and *pearl* in the Siamese cats of yesteryear.

COLOUR
Eye colour

The eyes of a Tonkinese are full, set well apart and gently almond in shape – a little more rounded at the bottom than the top and slanting toward the outer edge of the ear. They are beautifully coloured in a range from light green to very light blue shades, but not a clear blue. That is the eye colour of a Tonkinese variant with a Siamese coat pattern. Ideally, the Tonkinese eye colour is a clear blue/green, described as aqua in Canada and America – sparkling

Top: variant with Siamese coat pattern.
Middle: tonkinese coat pattern.
Bottom: variant with Burmese coat pattern.

shades of clear tropical seas. Depending upon the quality of ambient light the emphasis may be on either the blue or the green. The eye colour is so subtle that it is best seen in natural light. Clarity and depth of this beautiful aqua colour is especially prized.

Authority	Eye Colour – Competition Standard
GCCF	Greenish blue or bluish green preferred, with a range from green to light blue allowed, but orange, yellow and deep or vivid blue are not acceptable. Incomplete development of eye colour may be found in kittens.
CCA/AFC	Almond eyes of gemstone quality in shades ranging from aquamarine through the blue-green spectrum.
ACA	Blue-green. Depth, brilliance and clarity preferred.

CFA *Mink coat pattern:* Aqua; a definitive characteristic of the Tonkinese breed, best seen in natural light. Depth, clarity and brilliance of colour preferred.
Solid coat pattern: Green to gold.
Pointed coat pattern: Blue.

CFA Eye colour dependent upon coat-colour. All eye colour should be clear, strong with mid range colours preferred; best seen in natural light.
Mink coat pattern: Aqua; blue-green to green-blue.
Solid coat pattern: Chartreuse; green-gold, yellow-green.
Pointed coat pattern: Blue; light sky blue to deep sapphire blue.

Officially recognised coat patterns and colours

Lilac tabby Tonkinese (left) with brown Tonkinese (right). Photo: Animals Unlimited

In the United Kingdom the GCCF recognises the Tonkinese in the typical tonkinese coat pattern plus the Tonkinese variant coat patterns – solid like the Burmese and pointed like the Siamese – but only cats with the tonkinese coat pattern are eligible to be shown. The GCCF accepts the Tonkinese in the following colours: brown, blue, chocolate, lilac, red, cream, tortie (brown, blue, chocolate and lilac); in the tabby pattern (brown, blue, chocolate, lilac, red, cream) and tortie-tabby (brown, blue, chocolate and lilac). The CA accepts Tonkinese with the tonkinese coat pattern in all of the GCCF-recognised colours but does not accept the tabby pattern.

In New Zealand, the NZCI recognises the Tonkinese in all colours and patterns recognised by the GCCF, but use the term *seal* instead of brown. In Canada and the United States, although there are differences between the various registering bodies, there are generally four recognised Tonkinese colours in three patterns: mink, pointed and solid. The solid pattern is referred to as sepia

A natural mink.

by TICA and the CCA/AFC. The CFA permits the solid and pointed coat-patterned Tonkinese to be shown in its non-championship Any Other Variety (AOV) classes. The ACA only recognises the mink pattern for registration and competition. As TICA has a genetic registration system it recognises all types, colours and coat patterns in cats and the NCFA also recognises all colours and patterns.

It is often thought that the term *mink* is used to reflect the texture of the fur but the term originated because the colour and pattern of the American wild (natural) mink's pelt is the same as the original Tonkinese: dark brown with a medium-dark brown body colour and lighter underparts. The pattern is more distinct during the moulting seasons.

Tonkinese colours: name comparisons
(This table compares only the names of the colours, not the coat patterns)

UK (GCCF)	USA and Canada
Brown	Natural/Seal[1]
Blue	Blue
Chocolate	Champagne
Cinnamon (not recognised)	Cinnamon/Honey[2]
Lilac	Platinum
Fawn (not recognised)	Fawn[3]
Red	not recognised
Cream	not recognised
Brown Tortoiseshell	not recognised
Blue Tortoiseshell	not recognised
Chocolate Tortoiseshell	not recognised
Lilac Tortoiseshell	not recognised

Brown Tabby	not recognised
Blue Tabby	not recognised
Chocolate Tabby	not recognised
Lilac Tabby	not recognised
Red Tabby	not recognised
Cream Tabby	not recognised
Brown Tortie-Tabby	not recognised
Blue Tortie-Tabby	not recognised
Chocolate Tortie-Tabby	not recognised
Lilac Tortie-Tabby	not recognised

Note 1: TICA refers to *Seal* rather than *Natural.*

Note 2: *Cinnamon* is recognised by TICA and NCFA. The ACA, CFF and CCA/AFC recognise it but call it *Honey.* It is acknowledged by the CFA but not accepted for registration or competition. It is not recognised by the ACFA.

Note 3: *Fawn* is recognised by TICA, NCFA and the CCA/AFC. It is acknowledged by the CFA but not accepted for registration or competition.

Tonkinese colour descriptions

The derivation of the following colours is dealt with in chapter 4. Note that these descriptions refer to colour and coat patterns, not to the type (head and body shape).

All breeders will be able to establish which colours occur in their litters; a reasonably straightforward task bearing in mind the colours involved in each particular mating. The Tonkinese breeder must also differentiate between the three possible coat patterns: tonkinese, variant (Burmese

Samkabar kittens: lilac variants (Siamese), brown and brown variant (Burmese).

pattern) and variant (Siamese pattern). By the time the kitten is about 10 weeks old a breeder can be fairly certain of its coat pattern for registration.

Although the eyes are distinctive, bear in mind that it is the tonkinese coat pattern that defines a Tonkinese. Just as a non-variant Tonkinese may have a good or poor tonkinese coat pattern it may have good or poor eye colour. In

Herkatz Milliflora: chocolate variant (Burmese pattern) with good Tonkinese eye colour.

general, however, a tonkinese coat pattern is associated with good eye colour and a variant coat pattern is associated with strong relevant eye colour. By about 10 weeks of age a kitten that still has clear blue eyes is likely to be a variant with the Siamese coat pattern; it is highly improbable that the eye colour will alter. A kitten with obvious yellowish-green eyes probably has a variant (Burmese) coat pattern. A kitten with indistinct eye colour (bluish in the middle changing to dark yellowish-green at the outer edge, or vice versa) has a good chance of developing correct Tonkinese eye colour, but it may take several months. See chapter 8 for more information about the development of coat patterns in kittens.

Cornwood Charlie Barkalot, a mature chocolate.

On the cat's body the hair shaft will be lighter in colour toward the roots, but on the points the colour will be more consistent with the roots. Mature Tonkinese, just like mature Siamese, can become very dark in colour – I well remember a Grand Champion blue Siamese who was so deeply coloured that, if he was a Tonkinese, I've no doubt he would be described as a variant with a Burmese coat pattern. Maturity of coat and the effects of temperature must be allowed for when making assessments of adult Tonkinese. It is desirable for all Tonkinese breeders to show their Tonkinese, or at least visit cat shows. This way they will see enough mature Tonkinese from different bloodlines to get a global view of the development and progress of the breed.

Solid colours

The Tonkinese is not a self-coloured cat but, for the purpose of describing the coat-colours, the term solid is used in the GCCF Standard of Points to refer to colours that are neither tortoiseshell nor tabby patterned. This should not be confused with the American use of the term to describe Tonkinese variants with the Burmese coat pattern.

Mymystic Goldenshadow (brown).
Photo: Animals Unlimited

GCCF competition standard

The body colour should be a lighter shade of the points colour and free from tabby markings.

> **Note:** Ghost tabby markings may be found on the points of Red and Cream adults and should not detract from an otherwise good cat.

Brown (Natural, Seal) The difference between the Burmese brown and the Siamese seal colours accounts for the slight variety of brown in the Tonkinese, which preferably should be a warmer brown on the points than the seal of the Siamese (a rich dark chestnut colour, for instance) with a lighter brown body, more fudge-coloured than chocolate. Very young brown kittens may appear initially to be blue, but are obviously brown by about the age of six or seven weeks. As the cat matures it may become very dark but should still show a difference between its points and the rest of

Trampass Tarragon (brown, Siamese pattern).

the body. The colour on the neck, chest and belly is an even paler shade of the body colour. A variant (Siamese) has an almost white body and tends to resemble a dark chocolate-point Siamese. A variant (Burmese) is a glamorous uniform chestnut or dark coffee brown; very dark in a mature cat.

Samkabar Jasper (mature brown, Burmese pattern).

Authority	Brown - Competition Standard

GCCF   Warm brown with darker brown points. Nose leather, eye rims and paw pads brown (paw pads may be lighter and have a rosy undertone).

ACA   *Mink Body Colour:* Medium-brown shading to lighter hue on underparts. Ruddy highlights acceptable. *Points:* Dark brown. *Nose Leather:* Dark brown. *Paw Pads:* Medium to dark brown with rosy undertones acceptable.

CFA   *Points:* Dark brown. *Nose Leather:* Dark brown (corresponding to the intensity of the point colour). *Paw Pads:* Medium to dark brown (may have rosy undertone).
Mink Body Colour: Medium brown shading almost imperceptibly to lighter hue on underparts. Ruddy highlights acceptable.
Solid (AOV) Body Colour: Sable brown.
Point (AOV) Body Colour: Fawn to cream.

ACFA   *Points:* Rich dark chocolate to sable brown.
Mink Body Colour: Warm light to medium brown, strong contrast to points.
Solid Body Colour: Just lighter than the points.
Pointed Body Colour: Creamy fawn with brown shading. Very marked contrast with points.

Blue A soft slate-grey blue. The body is paler and may have a warm, fawnish, overtone, which can be seen in the blue (dilute) colour of several breeds of

Chapter 3

Mymystic's Addeish Lansdale Fable. Photo: Alan Robinson

Ishokats Dizzy Deirdre (variant, Burmese pattern).

cat. The underparts are a paler shade of the body colour. Very young blue kittens may look an overall 'lavender' colour before their points begin to darken, and it is not unusual for the points to become extremely dark at first and then lighten a little as the kitten grows. A blue kitten's fur may also sparkle with silvery tips. In common with the other dilute colours, a good blue has the appearance of a silvery sheen, especially on the points. A mature blue Tonkinese with the warm overtone tends to retain its points contrast more clearly than a Tonkinese with the silvery-grey blue body. A variant (Siamese) has a very pale, almost white, body, and in kittens the points tend to be closer to the powder blue of the

Siamese than the grey-blue of the Tonkinese or Burmese, but with maturity the colour may darken considerably. A variant (Burmese) is uniform soft grey-blue.

In a blue litter the appearance of a caramel (bronze-blue) kitten indicates the presence of the dilute modifier gene which is not to the advantage of the breed, and the bloodlines should be studied carefully to avoid passing the gene on. See chapter 4 for more information.

Samkabar Nimbus, a typical blue kitten.

Authority   Blue - Competition Standard

GCCF Bluish grey with darker slate-grey points. Nose leather, eye rims and paw pads blue-grey.

ACA *Mink Body Colour:* Soft blue-grey shading to lighter hue on underparts. Fawn overtones permissable but not preferable. *Points:* Slate blue, distinctly darker than the body colour. *Nose Leather:* Blue-grey. *Paw Pads:* Blue-grey with rosy undertone permissable.

CFA *Points:* Slate blue, distinctly darker than the body colour. *Nose Leather:* Blue-grey (corresponding to the intensity of the point colour). *Paw Pads:* Blue-grey (may have rosy undertone). *Mink Body Colour:* Soft blue-grey, with warm overtones, shading almost imperceptibly to lighter hue on underparts. *Solid (AOV) Body Colour:* Slate blue with warm overtones. *Point (AOV) Body Colour:* Off-white with warm grey shading.

ACFA *Points:* Medium to dark slate blue. *Mink Body Colour:* Ash blue to medium blue, often with fawn overtones. Strong contrast to points. *Solid Body Colour:* Just lighter than the points, often with fawn overtones. *Pointed Body Colour:* Silvery blue-white with blue-grey shading, often with fawn tones. Very marked contrast to points.

43

Chapter 3

Chocolate (Champagne)   Probably this colour, more than any other, reminds people of 'old-fashioned Siamese'. Chocolate kittens may be pale milky chocolate to begin with, or almost white in body colour for several

months, before the warm golden chocolate tones begin to develop. In the latter case it is often difficult to distinguish the tonkinese coat pattern from the variant (Siamese) coat pattern. Look first at the paws; the variant has feet closer to the colour of its ears and face, whereas the tonkinese shows paler colour on the feet than the ears and face. Then look at the colouring on the feet and legs. Where the tonkinese has 'ankle socks', the variant (Siamese) is likely to have 'knee

Mymystic chocolate kittens, tonkinese pattern.

socks'. Finally, where the variant (Siamese) probably has a mask covering a fair part of the nose, eyes and muzzle, the tonkinese pattern usually shows just a smudge of colour up the centre of the face along the nose. The chocolate variant (Burmese) is usually easier to discern, as it is coloured more uniformly, but there are some very 'pointed' chocolate Burmese. For this reason, when you are looking at a kitten which has an evenly-coloured chocolate body with slightly darker points, bear in mind that it too could be a variant and be guided by the eye colour.

Chocolate kittens can easily be mistaken for lilac at an early age. At present there seem to be more than one shade of chocolate in the Tonkinese (including torties and tabbies), ranging from a golden/ruddy tone (but not cinnamon) to a quite dark bitter chocolate. The darker shades tend to have more distinct points in maturity. This isn't surprising when

Samkabar Quivical (choc variant, Burmese pattern).

you compare a Burmese chocolate with a Siamese chocolate. In theory we should expect to see the Tonkinese chocolate colour becoming more consistent as we move on through the generations.

Tonkabella Amata Aurora (choc). Photo: Alan Robinson

Authority	Chocolate – Competition Standard

GCCF   Warm chocolate with darker chocolate points. Nose leather, eye rims and paw pads chocolate or pinkish chocolate.

ACA   *Mink Body Colour:* Buff-cream. *Points:* Medium brown. *Nose Leather:* Cinnamon-brown. *Paw Pads:* Cinnamon-pink to cinnamon-brown.

CFA   *Points:* Medium brown. *Nose Leather:* Cinnamon-brown (corresponding to the intensity of the point colour). *Paw Pads:* Cinnamon-pink to cinnamon-brown.
Mink Body Colour: Buff-cream to beige shading almost imperceptibly to lighter hue on underparts. Reddish highlights acceptable.
Solid (AOV) Body Colour: Golden tan to light coffee brown.
Point (AOV) Body Colour: Ivory with buff-tan shading.

ACFA   *Points:* Light to dark chocolate.
Mink Body Colour: Buff/cream to pale tan. Strong contrast to points.

45

Chapter 3

Solid Body Colour: Golden tan just lighter than the points.
Pointed Body Colour: Ecru with buff/tan shading. Very marked contrast with points.

Lilac (Platinum) Lilac kittens are very pale, almost white. Their points develop slowly and usually look as though they are pale golden fawn to start with, which often leads people to think that the kittens might be chocolate. The nose leather and eye rims are good indicators of colour in the lilacs. They are clear pink initially, gradually developing a cool pinkish grey tone, and the paw pads retain just a little more pink. The points will become a distinct lilac

Tonkabella Thaddeus Titus (lilac kitten).

shade, which is preferably a warm pinkish lilac rather than a cool bluish shade. In a mature cat the flanks and 'saddle' over the back will also develop lilac shading and, in a good lilac, the points will show a silvery sheen as in the blue and cream Tonkinese. In a lilac variant (Siamese) the eye colour is your best, and possibly only, guide until the cat is several months old. A variant (Burmese) is a uniform golden fawn colour initially, which will cool to lilac as the kitten matures.

Tonkabella Peregrine Piers (lilac). Photo: Alan Robinson

Lilac variant (Burmese pattern) kitten. Photo: Animals Unlimited

In a lilac litter the appearance of a caramel (a bluish-bronze) kitten indicates the presence of the dilute modifier gene, which is not to the advantage of the breed, and the bloodlines should be studied carefully to avoid passing the gene on. See chapter 4 for more information.

Authority	Lilac – Competition Standard
GCCF	Warm lilac with darker lilac points. Nose leather, eye rims and paw pads pinkish grey.
ACA	*Mink Body Colour:* Pale silvery grey with warm overtones. Not white or cream. *Points:* Pewter-grey, distinctly darker than the body colour. Points may have a lavender cast due to the colour of the skin beneath. *Nose Leather:* Lavender-pink to lavender-grey. *Paw Pads:* Lavender-pink.

CFA   *Points:* Frosty grey, distinctly darker than the body colour. *Nose Leather:* Lavender-pink to lavender-grey. *Paw Pads:* Lavender-pink.
Mink Body Colour: Pale silvery grey with warm overtones shading almost imperceptibly to lighter hue on underparts. Not white or cream.
Solid (AOV) Body Colour: Dove grey.
Point (AOV) Body Colour: Pearly white.

ACFA   *Points:* Pale dove grey to medium pinkish lavender.
Mink Body Colour: Pale silver to light pearl grey, often with fawn overtones. Strong contrast to points.
Solid Body Colour: Warm grey or pearly grey, just lighter than the points.
Pointed Body Colour: Pearly white with silvery-grey shading, often with fawn overtones. Good strong contrast with points.

Cinnamon (Honey)   This colour is not recognised by the GCCF but is included here for information as it is recognised by several other registration bodies. A mature Tonkinese has a golden cream body, preferably with an apricot cast, and the points are light to medium ruddy brown (which is

Romantica Rousseau (red).

lighter in tone than chocolate). The nose leather, lips and paw pads are pinkish tan or caramel pink.

Authority	Cinnamon – Competition Standard

ACA *Mink Body Colour:* Golden-cream preferably with an apricot cast. *Points:* Light to medium ruddy brown. *Nose Leather:* Caramel-pink. *Paw Pads:* Caramel-pink. Medium to dark brown with rosy undertones acceptable.

Fawn This colour is not recognised by the GCCF but is included here for information as it is recognised by TICA, NCFA and the CCA/AFC. The body is pale vanilla with a warm mushroom tone. The points are pinkish buff or taupe. The nose leather, lips and paw pads are pink or pale pinkish tan.

Red A rich red, more orange than foxy, is preferable on the points. The body is distinctly paler with the underparts appearing almost white. A good red colour has an almost translucent clarity. It's interesting to note that the body colour of the red Tonkinese is paler than that of the cream. To get a clear-coated red or cream cat is uncommon, as they are almost always barred in a tabby pattern to a greater or lesser degree. For this reason it is rare to see a red in the true tonkinese coat pattern, and this is usually allowed for in exhibitions standards – see chapter 4 for more information. This colour may be brown or chocolate (or cinnamon) based. A variant (Siamese) kitten is almost

Tonkaholics kitten (red).

completely white, unlike other colours which have a hint of colour even when they are very young. The nose leather, tips of ears and tail gradually take on the red coloration. A variant (Burmese) kitten appears to be red all over, the red becoming richer as the cat matures. Some breeders of red Tonkinese believe that the eye colour of these cats takes longer to develop than in Tonkinese of other colours and have observed that variants with the Burmese coat patterns may have green/blue eyes for up to a year, which then turn yellow/green as the coat-colour matures. For this reason it is difficult to be sure whether the cat has a variant coat pattern or not. See also description of red/cream tabbies.

Chapter 3

Adhirsh Cato Redbaron (red).

Authority	Red – Competition Standard

GCCF Light red with darker points, except for legs, which may present less shading than in the other solid colours. Nose leather, eye rims and paw pads pink. Note: Freckles may appear on the nose leather, eye rims, lips, paw pads and ears and should not be penalised.

Cream It is often difficult to distinguish between the colour of the points and the body colour; while the mask, ears and tail should be distinguishable, it is uncommon for the limbs to be a darker shade of the body colour. The cream colour appears more opaque than the red colour; one judge described it as the difference between poster paint and water-

Rogata's Elrond (mature cream male).

colour, the cream being the former. Some creams become quite 'hot' in colour, giving the appearance of red without its clarity. While acceptable at present, this is not preferable. A good rich cream appears to have a powdering of silver like the blue and lilac Tonkinese. Unfortunately it is rare to see a cream in the true tonkinese coat pattern. The cream colour may be blue or lilac (or fawn) based. See also the description of red/cream tabbies.

In a cream litter the appearance of an apricot kitten (beige-cream, especially noticeable on the ears) indicates the presence of the dilute modifier gene, which is not to the advantage of the breed. Bloodlines should be carefully studied to avoid passing the gene on. See chapter 4 for more information.

Rogata's Grisu (cream kitten),

Authority   Cream – Competition Standard

GCCF   Rich warm cream shading to paler cream with darker cream points, except for legs which may present less shading than in the other solid colours. Nose leather, eye rims and paw pads pink. Note: Freckles may appear on the nose leather, eye rims, lips, paw pads and ears and should not be penalised.

Tortoiseshell You either like or dislike the tortoiseshell colouring, but you are unlikely to be indifferent to it. Those who like it know how fascinating the colour distribution can be. The colour goes all the way through like the letters in a stick of seaside rock; just look at the mottling on top of the paw, turn the paw over and you will see that the paw pads reflect that mottling exactly. Mrs Rosemary Harper, an English breeder well known for her love of tortoiseshells, referred to them as *mosaic cats* – a most appropriate description.

It can be quite difficult to distinguish between tortie tonkinese patterns and tortie variants because of the irregular distribution (mottling) of the base colour and the fact that the body will be mottled all over in both the tonkinese and variant (Burmese) coat patterns. Breeders of tortoiseshells (especially those with experience of browns and blues) have observed that

Chapter 3

people often expect the tonkinese coat-patterned torties to have far more colour restriction on the body than they actually do. It might help you to 'see' the tortoiseshell coat patterns if you think of the solid version of your particular colour and then mentally splash or sprinkle it all over with red or cream.

In the tonkinese coat pattern the points are not solid in colour and may even show more red or cream than the base colour. Nevertheless, the base colour should be darker on the points than on the body and merge gently with the red- or cream-mottled body colour. In kittens the mottling is generally apparent from the start but there are torties who show very little mottling

Tajens Unesco (brown tortie).
Photo: Animals Unlimited

even as mature cats. The amount of base colour on the body of a tonkinese coat-patterned tortie varies considerably. The subtlety of the lilac-tortie coloration makes it particularly difficult to assess the true pattern.

If the mottled base colour on the body is dominated by red or cream this may give the false impression that the cat has a variant (Siamese) coat pattern, but in a variant (Siamese) the base colour over the neck and

Shades of red or cream paint splashed over a 'solid' Tonkinese.

shoulders is not mottled. There is likely to be some mottling on the saddle, flanks and belly, especially in a mature cat. In a variant (Burmese) the base colour is uniform in tone over the body and points but there is a range of tones in the red or cream mottling.

Tonkaholics Speckled Star (brown tortie). Photo: Alan Robinson

In brown and chocolate torties, the red mottling ranges from hot ginger to pale cream, but should generally be a warm colour. In blue and lilac torties, cream mottling ranges from pale cream (almost white) to very hot cream (apparently red). Hot cream is acceptable but not preferable. Blue and lilac base colours may have a warm overtone. It has been observed that in variants (Burmese) the red/cream colour often develops more quickly and is normally darker (hotter) than in the other coat patterns, in keeping with the darker tone of the base colour.

Romantica kitten (lilac tortie).

GCCF competition standard: the base colour should be brown, blue, chocolate or lilac that has been well broken with shades of red or cream. Any large areas of red or cream may show some striping. The distribution of colour on the points is immaterial.

53

Chapter 3

Top to bottom: Blue tortie, blue, and blue tortie variant (Burmese pattern).

Authority	Tortie – Competition Standard

GCCF *Brown Tortie* Warm brown well broken with shades of red. The colours will be darker on the points. Nose leather, eye rims and paw pads brown and/or pink to complement the adjacent coat.

Blue Tortie Bluish grey well broken with shades of cream. The colours will be darker on the points. Nose leather, eye rims and paw pads blue and/or pink to complement the adjacent coat.

Chocolate Tortie Warm chocolate well broken with shades of red. The colours will be darker on the points. Nose leather, eye rims and paw pads chocolate and/or pink to complement the adjacent coat.

Lilac Tortie Warm lilac well broken with shades of cream. The colours will be darker on the points. Nose leather, eye rims and paw pads lilac and/or pink to complement the adjacent coat.

Ishokats Geisha Girl
(brown tortie with clear red mottling).

Tabby patterns Happily the GCCF recognises the tabby (agouti) coat-patterned Tonkinese. It's a most exotic creature, found in all Tonkinese colours. The tortie-tabby has yet to be seen on the show bench and will undoubtedly be one of the most difficult colour/patterns to register accurately.

To have tabby kittens at least one of the parents must be tabby. There is no evidence to support the suggestion that a non-tabby (non-agouti) cat with a tabby parent will produce heavily barred kittens; indeed a number of tabby breeders have observed that some of their clearest coated non-tabby kittens have had tabby ancestors. Conversely, pure non-tabby bloodlines have produced some heavily-barred cats. Breeders of reds and creams are likely to have difficulty in registering their kittens accurately if they include red and cream tabbies in their breeding programmes because of the heavy barring that often occurs in these non-tabby colours. For this reason the GCCF requires that a litter of red and red-tabbies, or cream and cream-tabbies, is registered as an all-tabby litter.

Tabbies are born with extremely pale (apparently white) feet and underparts and, as their body colour develops, it may be heavily ticked along the tail and flanks. The stripes on the mask, and then on the tail and legs, gradually develop. If you are unsure about the colour of your tabby kitten the colour at the tip of the tail is usually a good indicator.

Tip: In a mixed litter of non-tabby and tabby patterns the tabby kittens are quite easy to distinguish from the non-tabby

Tomas, a mature brown ticked tabby.

kittens at an early age – their ears are white fur-lined rather than self-coloured and their masks are extremely pale and may even show some ribbons. However, this is not as easy to see in lilac, red and cream tabbies.

In brown, blue, chocolate and lilac tabbies the coloration of the nose leather is distinctly different from that of their non-tabby counterparts, being pinkish in tone and merely outlined (as if with a coloured pencil) with colour. However it may be solid in colour initially in very young kittens. Tabbies have a pinker tone to their paw pads than their non-tabby counterparts. In accordance with the characteristics of the tonkinese coat pattern there will be paler tabby markings on the rest of the body.

Mymystic Nimrod (choc tabby).
Photo: Animals Unlimited

Don't expect tabby base colours to look the same as their non-tabby counterparts. The influence of the agouti gene appears to tone down the base colours so that the brown, blue and chocolate become a lighter shade of the equivalent non-tabby colour, and the lilac has more pink than blue in it. The base colour in both the tabby and the non-tabby Tonkinese is genetically restricted on the body, but in the tabby the base colour is also restricted on the points, with the exception of the tabby markings. This means that a variant (Siamese) looks exactly like its Siamese counterpart and a variant (Burmese) is uniform in colour over body and points, with strong tabby markings overall.

In the Siamese the tabby pattern is seen principally on the points and, because the point markings are generally the same for each of the four specific tabby patterns, it is irrelevant which pattern is present. However, in the Tonkinese the tabby pattern is also

Mymystic Pasha (blue tabby) at eight weeks.

expressed, in a restricted form, on the body, so it is important to know which specific tabby patterns are carried in the bloodlines. It should be noted that it is possible for more than one tabby pattern to occur in the same litter of kittens (see chapter 4).

In the Tonkinese each of the tabby patterns is expressed similarly on the head, limbs and tail. The head has a well defined 'M' on the forehead, with frown lines running up over the head, clear ribbon tracings running from the outer corner of the eye and the cheek, 'spectacle' markings around the eyes and spotted whisker pads. The ears are a solid colour marked with a paler clear 'thumb print'. The legs have clearly defined broken stripes of various sizes from above the foot to

Mymystic Mischa (lilac tabby).
Photo: Animals Unlimited

the top of the leg; the back of hind legs and under the feet are solidly marked. The length of the tail is marked with rings that are broken on the underside. The tail has a solid-coloured tip. In a restricted form the body markings vary according to the specific tabby pattern:

Mackerel This pattern has at least one unbroken necklace and fine parallel lines down the length of the spine from which fine vertical lines run down the shoulders, flanks and haunches, ending in rows of spots on the belly.

Ticked Apart from the clear tabby markings on the head, legs and tail, the coat is ticked all over.

Spotted This pattern shows necklace tracings and the back, flanks and belly are distinctly marked with round spots laid out in the pattern of the mackerel or classic tabby.

Classic This pattern has broader markings than the mackerel tabby. It has wide necklace tracings and broad parallel lines running down the length of the spine. The shoulders are marked with an 'open-winged butterfly' pattern. The flanks show an unbroken circle with a spot in the centre (sometimes called an oyster mark). The belly is spotted.

Chapter 3

Q: *How can there be a tabby Tonkinese variant with a Burmese coat pattern when there are no tabbies in the Burmese?*

A: I have heard this question asked on a number of occasions and I recall being intrigued by the very same point when I first became involved with the breed. The tabby Tonkinese exists because of the introduction of the agouti gene into its make-up from its Siamese parentage. Once the gene has been introduced it is irrelevant that there are no tabby Burmese because it is the unique behaviour of the tonkinese coat pattern gene that causes the tabby pattern to be expressed in the three coat patterns. The diagrams showing the expression of coat pattern in chapter 4 may demonstrate this more clearly.

GCCF competition standard: the tabby pattern is formed by markings of the solid pattern colour on a background of agouti hairs.

Head Markings: There should be a clearly defined 'M' on the forehead, 'spectacle' markings around the eyes and spotted whisker pads. Ears are solid colour but showing clear 'thumb marks' which are less apparent in dilute colours and mottled in tortie-tabbies.

Leg Markings: Clearly defined varied sized broken stripes. Solid markings on the back of hind legs. The leg markings may be slightly paler in tone than the other points, especially in Red and Cream tabbies.

Tail Markings: The tail is marked with broken rings.

Body Markings: The body markings will depend upon the nature of the tabby but will normally appear as 'ghost' markings against the agouti ground colour. The body markings will lighten down the flanks to the tummy which will be a paler version of the ground colour.

Authority Tabby Pattern – Competition Standard

GCCF *Brown Tabby* Dark brown markings blending into a warm light brown agouti base colour. Nose leather, eye rims and paw pads brown, but may have a rosy undertone.

Blue Tabby Slate blue tabby markings blending into a paler agouti base colour. Nose leather, eye rims and paw pads blue/grey, may have a pinkish undertone.

Chocolate Tabby Darker chocolate tabby markings blending into a paler agouti base colour. Nose leather, eye rims and paw pads chocolate or pinkish chocolate.

Lilac Tabby Darker lilac tabby markings blending into a paler agouti base colour. Nose leather, eye rims and paw pads pinkish grey.

Red Tabby Darker red tabby markings blending into a paler agouti base colour. Nose leather, eye rims and paw pads pink. Note: Freckles may appear on the nose, pads, lips, eyelids and ears and should not be penalised.

Brown Tortie Tabby Dark brown tabby markings broken and overlaid with shades of red. Both elements of tortie and tabby must be present. Nose leather, eye rims and paw pads brown and/or pink to complement adjacent coat.

Cream Tabby Hotter cream tabby markings blending into a paler agouti base colour. Nose leather, eye rims and paw pads pink. Note: Freckles may appear on the nose, pads, lips, eyelids and ears and should not be penalised.

Blue Tortie Tabby Slate grey tabby markings broken and overlaid with shades of cream. Both elements of tortie and tabby must be present. Nose leather, eye rims and paw pads blue and/or pink to complement adjacent coat.

Chocolate Tortie Tabby Chocolate tabby markings broken and overlaid with shades of red. Both elements of tortie and tabby must be present. Nose leather, eye rims and paw pads chocolate and/or pink to complement adjacent coat.

Lilac Tortie Tabby Dark lilac tabby markings broken and overlaid with shades of cream. Both elements of tortie and tabby must be present. Nose leather, eye rims and paw pads lilac and/or pink to complement adjacent coat.

One of the first cream/cream tabby litters, bred by Hazel Forshaw (Ishokats).

Chapter:
Genetics of the Tonkinese

GENETIC BACKGROUND

To understand what you want from a breed you should know something of its make-up and characteristics, a particularly interesting aspect of the Tonkinese.

All the hereditary information required to produce a living being is governed by deoxyribonucleic acid (DNA) molecules, which are arranged in tightly coiled strands called *chromosomes*. Although they vary in shape and size, chromosomes always come in matched pairs. The exceptions are the sex-chromosomes which, disregarding mutations, will be a matched pair in the female (XX), or an unmatched pair in the male (XY). The majority of body cells in the cat contain 18 matched pairs of chromosomes (known as *autosomes*) and one pair of sex-chromosomes.

Genes

These are the units containing the coding instructions that are carried from one generation to the next. They are identically arranged along each of the pair of chromosomes like strings of beads, each one having its own allotted place (locus). Although the genes for a specific trait (such as coat length) are always in identical positions on the paired chromosomes, they may occur in mutant forms called *alleles*.

Alleles

These are not equal: they may be *dominant* (indicated by uppercase letters) or *recessive* (indicated by lowercase letters). Take for example the gene governing coat length. One allele delivers instructions for a short coat to be grown, another for a long coat. The allele for short hair (L) is dominant over the allele for long hair (l), so a cat must inherit two alleles for long hair (ll) to have a long coat. If it inherits one allele for short hair and one for long hair (Ll) it will be short-haired because the allele for short hair is dominant, but will carry the allele for long hair. If the cat inherits two identical alleles (ll), it is described as being *homozygous* for that characteristic; if different alleles (Ll) are inherited it is described as being *heterozygous*.

Genotype

This describes what the cat inherits genetically, which may be homozygous or heterozygous.

Phenotype

This describes what the cat actually looks like: the manner in which the genetic coding is expressed. For example a cat may have the homozygous genotype (LL) or the heterozygous genotype (Ll), but in both cases the cat will be short-haired.

Body colour

In the genetic colour-conformation group, which controls the amount of body colour, the first gene is the albinism gene. It comes in five alleles:

- *The dominant allele (C)* produces full expression of colour. This is sometimes referred to as the *non-albino allele.*
- *The Burmese allele (cb)* is a mutant form, recessive to the full colour allele, co-dominant with the Siamese allele. It produces a slight albinism, reducing black to a very dark brown, and green or green-gold eyes.
- *The Siamese allele (cs)* is a

Lilac Tonkinese/British Black hybrid.

mutant form, recessive to the full colour allele, co-dominant with the Burmese allele. It produces an intermediate albinism, reducing the basic coat colour from black/brown to light beige with dark brown extremities (points) and bright blue eyes.
- *The blue-eyed albino allele (ca)* is a mutant form, recessive to the full colour, Burmese and Siamese alleles. It produces nearly complete albinism with a translucent white coat and very washed-out pale blue eyes.
- *The true albino allele (c)* is mutant form, recessive to all others. It produces complete albinism with a translucent white coat and pink eyes.

As you can see, both the Burmese allele (cb) and the Siamese allele (cs) are recessive to the full colour allele (C), but they are co-dominant with each other. This means that they each have exactly as much dominance or recessivity, so it is possible to have one of each allele producing the combination of Burmese and Siamese coat patterns with turquoise (aquamarine) eyes: in other words the tonkinese coat pattern (cbcs).

The checkerboard table on the next page shows the results of combining the different alleles within the albinism gene. The dominance characteristics are normal except for the combination of Burmese and Siamese alleles. The tonkinese colour-conformation genotype (cbcs) is described as *perpetually*

Chapter 4

heterozygous because it can only result from inheriting the alleles (cb) and (cs). The full combinations are as follows:

	C	cb	cs	ca	c
C	full colour	full colour	full colour	full colour	full colour
cb	full colour	Burmese	tonkinese	Burmese	Burmese
cs	full colour	tonkinese	Siamese	Siamese	Siamese
ca	full colour	Burmese	Siamese	b eye albino	b eye albino
c	full colour	Burmese	Siamese	b eye albino	albino

Coat patterns

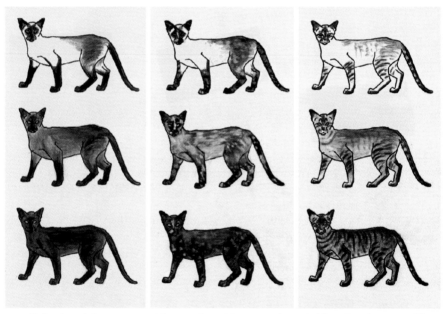

| (Left column) Brown. | (Centre column) Brown tortie. | (Right column) Brown tabby. |
| (Top row) Siamese pattern. | (Centre row) tonkinese pattern. | (Bottom row) Burmese pattern. |

Tonkinese belong to the genetic colour group known as the *Himalayan* group wherein the amount of body colour is controlled by the albinism gene. This gene inhibits the production of pigment when the body temperature is above 36.7°C (98°F). From four weeks of age a cat's usual temperature is 38–38.5°C (100.4–101.3°F) but, at its points (the facial mask, ears, tails, legs and, in entire males, the testicles), the temperature drops to about 35.6°C (96°F), so in these areas the fur is more heavily pigmented than the body. As the legs and feet are well muscled they don't become quite so cool, so tend to be paler in tone than the other points. This can be seen in both Tonkinese and Siamese cats, especially in the lighter colours. (It should be reiterated that Tonkinese, with an uppercase 'T', describes the breed of cat; tonkinese, with a lowercase 't', describes a unique coat pattern best seen on the Tonkinese cat.)

Several breeds, such as the Somali, Balinese and Rex, have a variation of coat conformation (texture and length of coat); the Tonkinese varies in colour conformation (distribution of coat colour), generally known as the *coat pattern*. Like any other breed, the Tonkinese shows slight differences in type (head and body shape). Regardless of whether the type is good, it should be clearly understood that type is not related to coat pattern; the only difference between a Tonkinese and a Tonkinese variant is the coat pattern with its related eye colour.

First-generation Tonkinese kittens, resulting from a Burmese x Siamese mating, all have the tonkinese coat pattern because their genotype (cbcs) provides the breed with its special coloration. Because the Tonkinese is perpetually heterozygous for colour conformation, subsequent generations will have genotypes for the tonkinese coat pattern (cbcs) and for both the Burmese (cbcb) and Siamese (cscs) coat patterns.

Over a number of litters you could expect a consistent percentage of coat patterns from particular matings. The following table shows the expected coat pattern results from matings which include Tonkinese, Burmese and Siamese. For the purposes of this table Tonkinese variants with a Burmese coat pattern are referred to as *solid*, Tonkinese variants with a Siamese coat pattern are referred to as *pointed*.

Parent 1	**Parent 2**	**Coat Patterns of Progeny**
Burmese	Siamese	100% tonkinese
Tonkinese	Tonkinese	50% tonkinese 25% variant (solid) 25% variant (pointed)
Tonkinese	Burmese	50% tonkinese 50% variant (solid)
Tonkinese	Siamese	50% tonkinese 50% variant (pointed)
Tonkinese	Tonkinese variant (solid)	50% tonkinese 50% variant (solid)
Tonkinese	Tonkinese variant (pointed)	50% tonkinese 50% variant (pointed)

Tonkinese variant (pointed)	Tonkinese variant (solid)	100% tonkinese
Tonkinese variant (pointed)	Tonkinese variant (pointed)	100% variant (pointed)
Tonkinese variant (solid)	Tonkinese variant (solid)	100% variant (solid)

These percentages vary from litter to litter. All the kittens will be registered as Tonkinese, assuming that they are bred in accordance with the Tonkinese registration policy. Tonkinese with variant coat patterns are placed on the Reference register and are not eligible to compete in cat shows, but all three coat patterns are recognised and of value within a well thought-out breeding programme. The use of Tonkinese variants of good type from parents with good coat patterns avoids back-crossing with the parent breeds to correct coat pattern. As you can see, the mating of a Tonkinese variant to like Tonkinese variant (solid to solid, for instance) has no value, since the resulting kittens have only the coat pattern of the parents.

It is important to remember that these results only refer to coat pattern and not type, which may be considerably affected by an unbalanced mating. For example, a Tonkinese of good type back-crossed to a Burmese may produce kittens resembling the Burmese type rather than the Tonkinese.

Eye colour

Although there are no specific genes for eye colour, and there is still much to learn about how eye colour is established, it is well demonstrated that the colour of the eyes is intrinsically linked with the colour and

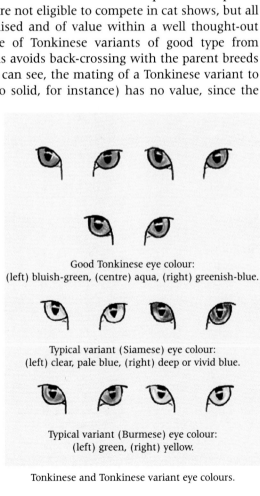

Good Tonkinese eye colour:
(left) bluish-green, (centre) aqua, (right) greenish-blue.

Typical variant (Siamese) eye colour:
(left) clear, pale blue, (right) deep or vivid blue.

Typical variant (Burmese) eye colour:
(left) green, (right) yellow.

Tonkinese and Tonkinese variant eye colours.

pattern of the coat; for example in the Siamese the range of eye colour varies from deep violet-blue in the seal-points to a pale powder-blue in the lilac-points. In the Tonkinese the best eye colour tends to be exhibited by those with good tonkinese coat pattern, varying slightly in intensity according to the coat colour. Tonkinese variants with solid (Burmese) coat patterns tend to have more green/yellow colour in their eyes and Tonkinese variants with pointed (Siamese) coat patterns have a clear blue eye colour. The ideal Tonkinese eye colour is greenish-blue or bluish-green, depending upon your perception of colour.

Geneticist Roy Robinson explained that the variation of eye colour in the Tonkinese is inherited *polygenetically*: in other words, the inherited colour is further influenced by minor genes. This suggests that a desired eye colour may be achieved by selective breeding. However, Mr Robinson also explained that an attempt to influence eye colour by using Tonkinese with variant coat patterns (particularly blue-eyed variants) would have uncertain results and perhaps even be doomed to failure, so selection for eye colour should be confined to tonkinese x tonkinese matings.

Coat colours

Breeders are often asked for a specific colour of kitten. To have some control over the colour of kittens you breed it is useful to have a little basic knowledge of the action of colour genes.

The colours brown, blue, chocolate and lilac are formed by the reduction of colour expression (the manner in which colour is actually displayed on the coat) from black. The partial albinism of the tonkinese coat pattern (cbcs) further reduces the expression of colour to the familiar light-to-medium density body colour with darker points. If a recessive colour allele is inherited from both parents then the alleles will be *active* in the offspring but, if it is inherited from only one of the parents, it will be *carried* in the offspring.

When the sex-linked coat colour gene is not present, correctly-bred Tonkinese are only possible in the colours brown, blue, chocolate and lilac and these colours in the tabby pattern (for registration with the GCCF).

- *Brown* is the dominant colour with the pigmentation distributed evenly along each hair.
- *Blue* is caused by the action of a mutant recessive gene controlling the density of pigmentation – dense colour (D), dilution (d). It dilutes the brown by causing the pigmentation granules along each hair to clump together, allowing light to pass through the spaces between the clumps, which produces a greying effect. Blue is diluted brown.
- *Chocolate* is recessive to brown, the result of a mutation of the brown that causes a reduction in colour from very dark brown to dark brown. Chocolate is modified brown.

Chapter 4

• *Lilac* occurs when the recessive blue and recessive chocolate genes are both active, causing light brown fur with clumped pigmentation granules; the effect is bluish fur with a brownish tinge. Lilac is double-recessive to brown.

Diagram showing the derivation of the basic colours

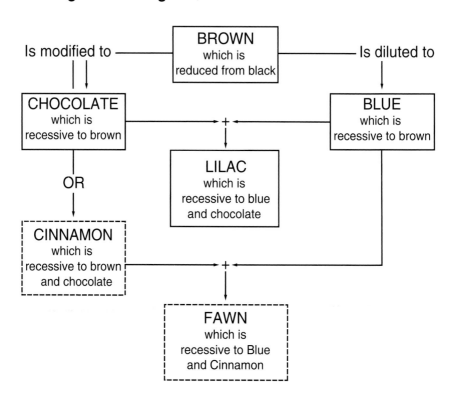

When it is present, the sex-linked coat-colour gene is found on the X chromosome (ordinarily female = XX, male = XY). To put it very simply, the sex-linked gene masks the base colour of the coat by showing it as red or cream. If the base colour is brown or chocolate, the sex-linked colour is red; if the base colour is blue or lilac, the sex-linked colour is cream. If the female is heterozygous for the sex-linked gene, the base colour is mottled with the sex-linked colour, that is, *tortoiseshell*. In normal circumstances (not allowing for mutations) the possible combinations are as shown in the following table. As you can see, to get red or cream females the female sex chromosome must be homozygous for the sex-linked gene.

Sex	Chromosomes	Result
Male	X* Y	Red or Cream males
Female	X* X*	Red or Cream females
Female	X X*	Tortoiseshell females

*Sex-linked gene

Diagram showing how the basic colours
are masked by the effects of the sex-linked gene

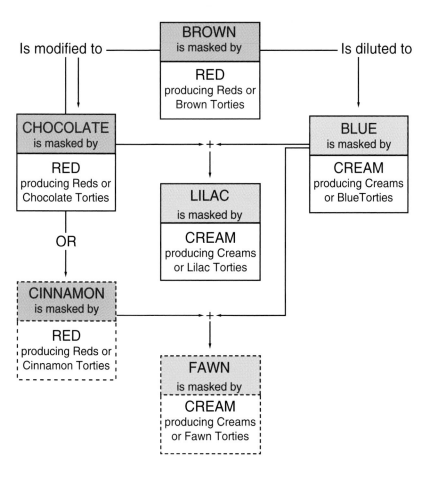

Chapter 4

Tonkinese colour conformation karyotype

The table only refers to the tonkinese coat pattern, but the karyotype (charted record of chromosomes)of Tonkinese variants is the same, with the exception of the albinism gene, which shows the genotype (cbcb) for the Burmese coat pattern and cscs for the Siamese coat pattern.

In the tonkinese colour-conformation karyotype there are four constants:

- In the *coat pattern group*, the *albinism* gene always shows the alleles (cbcs): the combination of the co-dominant Burmese allele (cb) and Siamese allele (cs) that produces the unique tonkinese coat pattern and has the effect of reducing the expression of the colours slightly. For example, black is expressed as very dark brown.
- In the *colour-expression group*, the *colour inhibitor* gene always shows the alleles (ii), allowing full expression of colour throughout the length of the hair.
- In the *colour-expression group*, the *white spotting* gene always shows the non-spotting alleles (ss), allowing full expression of the coat colour without areas of white.
- In the *colour-expression group*, the *dominant white* gene always shows the non-white alleles (ww), allowing full expression of coat colour and pattern.

The variation of alleles in the coat pattern and coat-colour groups produces the difference in the phenotype. In the *coat pattern group*:

- *the agouti gene* that controls ticking may show the alleles (aa) for non-agouti, which is recessive and suppresses ticking and so produces a solid coat pattern, or (A) for agouti, which is dominant and produces ticked hair, in turn producing a tabby coat pattern.
- *the tabby gene*, which controls the manner in which the coat pattern is expressed (solid, striped, blotched, spotted, or ticked), may show the allele (T) for mackerel/striped tabby producing a coat with non-agouti stripes on an agouti background.

Note: For the sake of simplicity, only the mackerel tabby pattern is shown in the karyotype table. The allele for the ticked tabby pattern is (Ta) and the allele for the classic/blotched tabby pattern is (tb). The mackerel tabby allele is co-dominant with the ticked tabby alleles and dominant to the classic tabby. There is no specific allele for a spotted tabby since it is genetically a striped tabby with stripes broken as a result of the influence of polygenes, so the allele for the spotted tabby pattern may be (T) or (tb), the spots following the pattern of either the mackerel or classic tabby.

In the *coat-colour group*:

- *the sex-linked orange-making gene* may show the alleles (oo) for absence of the sex-linked gene, (Oo) for the heterozygous presence of the gene, or (OO) for the homozygous presence of the gene. Males are either orange or non-orange, so a karyotype for a male cat includes only the first of the two alleles (o from oO or O from Oo) to show the sexual distinction.
- *the colour-density gene*, which controls the uniformity of pigment distribution throughout the hair, may show the allele (D) for dense pigmentation or (dd) for diluted pigmentation.
- *the coat-colour gene* comes in three alleles: black (B), dark brown (b) and light brown (bl). In Tonkinese the black allele (B) expresses itself as a very dark brown but, when it interacts with the allele (d) for dilute pigmentation, the colour expressed is blue. The dark brown allele (b) reduces black (in the case of the Tonkinese, very dark brown) to a dark brown that we call chocolate. When the light brown allele (bl) interacts with the allele (D) for dense pigmentation, the colour expressed is cinnamon, but when it interacts with the allele (d) for dilute pigmentation the colour expressed is fawn.

| Colour | Karyotype | | |
	Pattern	Colour	Expression
Brown	cbcsaa--	B-ooD-	iissww
Blue	cbcsaa--	B-oodd	iissww
Chocolate	cbcsaa--	b*ood-	iissww
Lilac	cbcsaa--	b*oodd	iissww
Red	cbcsaaT-	--OOD-	iissww
Cream	cbcsaaT-	--OOdd	iissww
Brown Tortoiseshell	cbcsaaT-	B-OoD-	iissww
Blue Tortoiseshell	cbcsaaT-	B-Oodd	iissww
Chocolate Tortoiseshell	cbcsaaT-	b*OoD-	iissww
Lilac Tortoiseshell	cbcsaaT-	b*Oodd	iissww

Chapter 4

| Colour | Karyotype | | |
	Pattern	Colour	Expression
Brown Tabby	cbcsA-T-	B-ooD-	iissww
Blue Tabby	cbcsA-T-	B-oodd	iissww
Chocolate Tabby	cbcsA-T-	b*ooD-	iissww
Lilac Tabby	cbcsA-T-	b*oodd	iissww
Red Tabby	cbcsA-T-	--OOD-	iissww
Cream Tabby	cbcsA-T-	--OOdd	iissww
Brown Tortie Tabby	cbcsA-T-	B-OoD-	iissww
Blue Tortie Tabby	cbcsA-T-	B-Oodd	iissww
Chocolate Tortie Tabby	cbcsA-T-	b*OoD-	iissww
Lilac Tortie Tabby	cbcsA-T-	b*Oodd	iissww
#Cinnamon	cbcsaa--	blblood-	iissww
#Fawn	cbcsaa--	blbloodd	iissww
#Caramel	cbcsaa--	ooddDm-	iissww
#Apricot	cbcsaa--	OOddDm-	iissww

- means that any allele of the relevant gene may be present.
* means that (b) or (bl) may be present.
# means colour not recognised in the Tonkinese by the GCCF.

Tabbies

Tabby is not a colour: it is a pattern of colour. The agouti gene (A) controls pigmentation by switching it on or off along the length of the hair. This results in bands of colour along the hair, referred to as ticking. All cats are essentially tabby, but the pattern is masked by non-agouti (a), which suppresses the ticking. However, the orange gene (O) defeats the effect of the non-agouti, which is why red and cream cats are usually barred. Don't confuse barring with a tabby pattern; a cat must have a tabby parent to be tabby-patterned but, conversely, you can get a non-tabby pattern from a mating that includes a tabby (heterozygous) parent.

A mixed litter, agouti and non-agouti.

The Breeding Colour Tables are valid for colours in the tabby pattern, but the results are also dependent upon whether a tabby parent is homozygous or heterozygous for the agouti gene. The agouti gene is not sex-linked, so which parent is tabby is irrelevant. Possible combinations are indicated in this table:

Parent 1	Parent 2	Progeny
Non-Agouti	Non-Agouti	100% Non-Agouti
Agouti (Homozygous)	Non-Agouti	100% Agouti (Heterozygous)
Agouti (Homozygous)	Agouti (Homozygous)	100% Agouti (Homozygous)
Agouti (Homozygous)	Agouti (Heterozygous)	50% Agouti (Homozygous) 50% Agouti (Heterozygous)
Agouti (Heterozygous)	Non-Agouti	50% Non-Agouti 50% Agouti (Heterozygous)
Agouti (Heterozygous)	Agouti (Heterozygous)	25% Non-Agouti 25% Agouti (Homozygous) 50% Agouti (Heterozygous)

It must be emphasised that percentages vary from litter to litter. Take for example my first litter of tabby Tonkinese (six) resulting from the mating of a lilac tabby (heterozygous for agouti) with a brown carrying blue and chocolate:

Theoretical Results	Actual Results
50% Male, 50% Female	4 Male, 2 Female
25% Brown, 25% Blue, 25% Choc, 25% Lilac	1 Brown, 1 Blue, 2 Choc, 2 Lilac
50% Non-agouti, 50% Agouti (Heterozygous)	1 Non-agouti, 5 Agouti (Heterozygous)

Cinnamon, fawn and caramel

On 20 October 1993 preliminary recognition was granted by the GCCF to these three colours in the Siamese. These colours are not recognised in the Tonkinese in Great Britain, but there may be some breeders who would like to see them in the breed. It might be argued that, since these colours are in the Siamese lines, they will ultimately end up in the Tonkinese and may be hidden in the genes of some lines already. Therefore, we should seek recognition for all the colours of our parent breeds in readiness for these colours appearing.

The alternative argument is that it is not necessary for the Tonkinese to embrace these colours simply because they may have already infiltrated our gene pool; we should be controlling our colours by careful selective breeding to keep the recognised colours clear, both perceivably and genetically. The

Oriental cinnamon. Photo: Animals Unlimited

Oriental classic fawn tabby. Photo: Animals Unlimited

matter of new colour recognition requires very careful consideration based on a knowledge of the advantages and disadvantages that new colours bring to the breed.

- *Cinnamon* is recessive to both brown and chocolate. As there can only be two genes at any one locus of the chromosome (homo- or heterozygous), brown may carry either chocolate or cinnamon but not both.

  The cinnamon colour is known to have been introduced into the Siamese in 1971 by, among others, a mating of Tranby Red Tutankhamen (a sorrel Abyssinian stud) and Annelida Fair Maid (a seal-point Siamese). Unfortunately, Tranby Red Tutankhamen was found to carry the long-hair gene. The development of the cinnamon was continued by interested breeders but it later included a recessive white gene from Anart's Miiko, a cat imported from the United States, which had the phenotype of the Siamese. The result was that some cats inherited the cinnamon, the long-hair and the recessive white genes. The GCCF became so concerned about the breeding of recessive whites that in 1975 no further progeny from lines known to be carrying the gene were accepted for registration. Later, in 1979, any carriers of the genes were placed on the Supplementary Register and their registration documents were over-stamped with the warning, *This cat is thought to carry the Recessive White gene and is not recommended for breeding.* Breeders are still working to eliminate the necessity for over-stamping with *Recessive White* and *Long-hair* warnings.

- *Fawn* is diluted from cinnamon in the same manner that lilac is diluted from chocolate; the alleles (blbl) for cinnamon interacting with the alleles (dd) for dilute density of colour pigmentation (double recessive).

Chapter 4

•*Caramel* (and also *apricot*, which is not officially recognised in the Siamese) occurs in the presence of either one or two dilute modifier genes (Dm). This is a dominant mutation of the gene for normal pigmentation (dm). The dilute modifier gene only affects the dilute colours, hence its name. It converts blue, lilac and fawn to caramel and cream to apricot.

Siamese breeder Pat Turner was involved in breeding what were known as *unclassified* colours and it was her interest in the effects of the inhibitor gene (gives rise to the silver and smoke varieties in the Siamese and Orientals) that led to her identifying the action of the dilute modifier gene. She mated Scintasilva Sue (a Chinchilla/chocolate-point Siamese hybrid) with Ch Pitapat Zeno (a red-point Siamese, carrying blue). One of the resulting kittens was Scintilla Serene Sunset (a heterozygous Oriental Tortie Shaded Silver, carrying blue, chocolate, Siamese pointing, non-inhibitor and classic tabby). Scintilla Serene Sunset was mated with Ch Darling Red Rufus (red-point Siamese) and produced apricot coloured kittens; later in 1973 she was mated with Taurus Kay Kavalier (lilac-point Siamese) and produced apricot self and smoke kittens. In an effort to establish whether or not Scintilla Serene Sunset carried the long-hair gene from her Chinchilla grandparent she was mated with a long-haired stud Southview Trappist, a

(Left) Oriental fawn classic tabby. (Right) Oriental caramel ticked tortie-tabby.
Photo: Animals Unlimited

descendant of Maureen Silson's recessive white Anart's Miiko. Two kittens from the resulting litter were caramel, which is believed to be associated with the silver colour. In 1976 Scintilla Serene Sunset was mated with a chocolate-point Siamese and produced Scintilla Rosario, a seal-silver-tabby-point Siamese (registered as a 'dove-point') who was later proven to carry the dilute modifier gene.

Since the dilute modifier gene has no visible effect when the dense gene (D) is present (that is, on brown, chocolate, cinnamon or red) it can be passed down many generations and only show its effects when a dilute kitten is produced. The effect of the modifier gene appears to be variable and, as the colour modification may not even be noticeable, a genetic caramel may appear to be blue or lilac. The 'hidden' caramel and the cinnamon may be unknowingly mixed and it would be exceptionally difficult to classify the colour of the resulting kittens (especially lilac, fawn and caramel). The result of this is that you are unlikely to know what colours you are passing on through your breeding line. It would be most inadvisable to cross a bloodline carrying caramel with a bloodline carrying cinnamon. For example, here are the possible colours that may result from the crossing of a brown (carrying blue and cinnamon) with a chocolate (carrying blue and cinnamon, 1 x Dm):

brown(ch)	cinnamon	caramel[blue(ch) 1 x Dm]
brown(cn)	*cinnamon(bl)	caramel[blue(cn) 1 x Dm]
*brown(bl)(ch)	lilac(cn)	chocolate(cn) 1 x Dm
*brown(bl)(cn)	fawn	*chocolate(bl)(cn) 1 x Dm
blue(ch)	brown(ch) 1 x Dm	cinnamon 1 x Dm
blue(cn)	brown(cn) 1 x Dm	*cinnamon(bl) 1 x Dm
chocolate(cn)	*brown(bl)(ch) 1 x Dm	caramel[lilac(cn) 1 x Dm]
*chocolate(bl)(cn)	*brown(bl)(cn) 1 x Dm	caramel[fawn 1 x Dm]

Key: ( ) indicates a colour which is carried.
[ ] indicates the base colour (ie the colour which is modified).
* indicates that there is twice the likelihood of this colour occurring.

In all there are 24 possible coat-colour genotypes. In comparison, brown(bl)(ch) x brown(bl)(ch) can only result in nine possibilities. If you then allow for the effects of double dilute modifier genes you can see how complicated and difficult it may be to recognise and register your kittens correctly. Imagine this when further complicated by the use of tabby (homo- or heterozygous) or the sex-linked colours. Finally you should consider the increased difficulties of sorting out variant coat patterns.

As a breed the Tonkinese is unique, and therefore independent of the Siamese colours. Are the colours cinnamon, fawn, caramel and apricot so desired in the Tonkinese that we are prepared to risk the possible inclusion of the long-hair, recessive white and silver influences? We know that we can breed these colours but, at this relatively early stage of the development of the Tonkinese in the United Kingdom, the question is, 'Should we?'

Chapter: 5
Choosing a Tonkinese

If you are reading this book it's likely that you already have your Tonkinese. If you haven't, I congratulate you on your foresight. It's so important to find out as much as possible about the character and requirements of a prospective pet and there are several questions to ask yourself before bringing home your new Tonkinese.

Is the Tonkinese breed suitable for your lifestyle and your household? Will it fit in with your routines or are you prepared to compromise? Is the cat or kitten in question happy to live with you? It's no use picking a kitten which is patently scared of you or your children when you go to see it. If you're considering a rescue cat, what is its history? Are you ready to get a new cat with its own character and habits or are you trying to replace a recently lost cat?

Don't choose a Tonkinese if:
- You want a beautiful cat to grace your beautifully-decorated home. Tonkinese are not designer accessories.
- You are getting it as a present for someone, unless you are certain that the prospective owner really wants it and is able to care for it for the next 10 or more years. Sadly, too many kittens are discarded when the novelty of kittenhood has worn off.
- You have no other pets and will be away from home for a large portion of the day.
- You want a cat for any reason other than love of the cat in question; otherwise, neither of you will be happy in the long run.

FURTHER POINTS TO CONSIDER
Allergies
The fine coat of the Tonkinese doesn't tend to attract and hold dust quite as much as the coats of many other breeds. I have heard the expression *hypo-allergenic* used regarding them, but there is no evidence to suggest that the Tonkinese are more hypo-allergenic than any other breed of cat. If any member of the family suffers from asthma or an allergic reaction to cats, arrange a visit to a Tonkinese pet owner or breeder to see whether the cats do cause a reaction before choosing and taking home a cat. Having to re-home it later will be upsetting both for your cat and yourselves (see page 87: **What if you cannot keep your Tonkinese?**).

Adaptability to others
Unlike some Foreign breeds, Tonkinese don't usually devote themselves to any one member of the family, but share their attentions equally. I'm sure

they've worked out that they get more attention this way! It might happen that they develop a slight preference for a particular person, and not always the obvious one. All cats vary in their response to adults, children and other pets, but the relaxed and outgoing nature of the Tonkinese is most advantageous in a family cat.

Male or female?

Ultimately this is a question of personal preference. I've always had female cats; they are bright, loving and judiciously independent. Until five years ago I never kept a male cat as a pet. Now I cannot understand why – they are wonderful. I have found that, once males are neutered (between six and nine months is best) they prefer to keep closer to home. Furthermore (and with no disrespect to males!) male cats generally don't appear to be as intelligent as females, so they don't get bored as soon as females. My neutered boys are more cuddly than my girls, but my girls are more welcoming.

Although there is no great advantage in having one sex rather than the other,

(Left) Male: Tonkabella Thaddeus Titus (lilac).
(Right) Female: Tonkabella Questa Quintus (choc).

bear in mind that Tonkinese can be sexually precocious. Females have been known to start calling at the age of four-and-a-half months, although seven to ten months is more usual. Whichever sex you decide upon, you should arrange for your Tonkinese to be neutered at the optimum age unless you are going to breed from it.

How much does a Tonkinese cost?

Although Tonkinese are still comparatively scarce their breeders are well aware that the 'raw materials' for producing Tonkinese are not in short supply. You should expect to pay the same for a Tonkinese as you would for any Foreign breed of cat (Burmese, Siamese, or Oriental). Prices may vary a

Chapter 5

Mymystic Nimrod (choc tabby) and Mymystic Mischa (lilac tabby) Photo: Animals Unlimited.

little from region to region or breeder to breeder. Some breeders charge more for what they consider to be show quality or suitable breeding animals, and a breeder who is using Champion or Grand Champion bloodlines might charge a little more for their Tonkinese.

Rescue organisations are not a means of obtaining a cheap or free pedigree cat. If you are having a Tonkinese from a rescue organisation, remember that such organisations rely entirely on donations to function, and few will permit a cat to leave without having been inoculated or neutered – which is expensive. In all fairness you should offer to make a reasonable donation to the organisation.

The price of the kitten or cat in question is just the first of many payments you will have to make. Over the 15 or more years of that cat's life, there will be continuous payments for food, vet bills, toys, bedding, and so on.

Your new Tonkinese – cat or kitten?

Having made all the right decisions regarding your suitability to live with this wonderful cat you can move on to choosing your Tonkinese.

Most of us pick a kitten rather than an adult cat. Kittens are vulnerable, innocent and appealing. They are unlikely to have developed anti-social habits, they adapt more easily to a new home and we have the pleasure of watching them grow up. It is important to remember that a kitten is a baby cat. This may seem obvious, but it is surprising how many people forget that baby cats differ from adults cats as much as baby humans differ from adult humans. They have an entirely different outlook on life, different needs and different habits, so we shouldn't expect too much from them. They must be allowed to have their kittenhood and all the associated experiences.

A kitten shouldn't be taken from its mother and litter-mates before the proper time. The GCCF recommends that no kitten should go to a new home before the age of 12 weeks, and reputable breeders will not allow the purchase of a kitten before that age. At 12 weeks a kitten is fully weaned, relatively well grown and has had its full course of inoculations. Whatever happens, please don't be tempted to 'rescue' a kitten from a breeder; you will only be encouraging bad breeding practices. It is far better to look for another kitten from a breeder that you are happy with.

The breeder should give you the following with your Tonkinese kitten:

- A properly completed pedigree certificate showing at least four generations.
- A vaccination certificate.
- A transfer-of-ownership/registration certificate.

Some breeders also provide an insurance note to cover the kitten up to 16 weeks of age and they should provide a copy of the conditions of purchase, if there are any. If you have any problems with, or enquiries about, your kitten

Simon (red) and Mymystic's Addeish Blueberry Fortune (blue).

Chapter 5

Caesar (blue).

you should be welcome to contact the breeder who will normally be grateful for any progress reports and will value photographs showing how the kitten is developing.

There are many advantages to choosing an adult rather than a kitten. An adult cat has already survived the vulnerable kitten stage and can cope better with the eager attentions of children, who can unintentionally cause serious injury or even kill a kitten. An adult cat is more experienced and stronger psychologically than a kitten; for example, a hurt kitten might develop a persistent fear of anyone resembling the person who hurt it, but an adult cat would simply put that person in their place with a scratch without developing a permanent enmity or fear. There is great satisfaction in watching a cat who has been made homeless, through no fault of its own, learn to adopt a new life and give you its trust and companionship. Adult cats face a very uncertain future unless they find a good home because, however well-meaning, not all rescue organisations have the time or funding to ensure the quality of home that their cats go to.

I would *not* advise buying a cat or kitten from a pet shop. Good pet shops do not sell kittens or puppies. Please don't feel sorry for a sad-looking kitten in a pet shop. By buying it you would simply encourage dealers to continue their trade. It's impossible to guarantee that you will not be introducing disease into your household and virtually no pedigree breeders would sell their kittens through a pet shop or similar agency. You have no guarantee that the kitten is healthy and properly bred and you are most unlikely to receive a pedigree, registration certificate and inoculation certificate.

If you intend to have a pair of kittens it is preferable to get both kittens from the same litter. It is far easier for a kitten to settle in a new home with a litter-mate for company. Don't be concerned that they will keep to themselves. Tonkinese kittens soon become part of their new family. If you decide to have two kittens from different households, possibly different breeds, try to bring them home within a couple of days of each other and make sure that they are of a similar age. Tonkinese get on happily with other cats (and dogs) but they are an active breed so it is probably best for them to have a companion of a similar nature. A sedate Persian, for instance, just couldn't keep up with a Tonkinese. Where there are other pets, a new kitten usually fares better than an adult cat; if you are introducing an adult, a neutered cat usually fares better than an unneutered one.

Health check

Laryna Lindy Lou (choc tabby).

It's important to choose a healthy animal. For more detail on what you should expect to see in a healthy Tonkinese see chapter 7.

A kitten or cat should be alert and responsive around strangers. It may be curious or cautious but shouldn't be afraid and after accepting your presence in its home it should permit itself to be stroked gently. It should move around comfortably, with good visible muscle tone; the limbs should be strong and the feet and claws clean and firm. The abdomen and groin should be free from swellings and there should be no sign of tenderness. The ribs should be easy to feel, but not obvious under the fur. The anus and genitals should be clean, dry and free from discharge. The coat should be clean and free from fleas and other parasites. The eyes should be clear and bright and free from cloudiness and discharge, and the haws (inner eyelids) shouldn't normally be visible.

Chapter 5

The ears should be clean, held forward and pricked up. The nose should be slightly moist, cool to the touch and clean. The teeth should be clean and unbroken with no excessive tartar build up and the gums should be firm and pink. The breath shouldn't be unpleasant, but may smell a little just after eating.

If you've chosen a kitten, make sure it's fit and healthy, find out when it was wormed and make sure that it has had its inoculations before you take it home with you. Be wary of taking a cat or kitten from a home that is not Feline Leukaemia Virus (FeLV) and Feline Immunodeficiency Virus (FIV) negative. If you are not sure, have the appropriate tests performed before allowing it to mix with your other cats. When you go to see your prospective kitten, have a good look at the mother. Her appearance and temperament are good indications of how the offspring will grow up. A shy, fearful or aggressive queen will probably raise shy, fearful or aggressive kittens. If you've chosen a cat from a rescue shelter, or even from someone who has asked you to give it a home, again be sure that its inoculations are up to date and that it been tested for FeLV and FIV. If it is FeLV or FIV positive, you shouldn't bring it into contact with any other virus-free cats. Find out as much as possible about its medical history, what accidents or illnesses it has had and whether it is entire or neutered.

All of these factors have a bearing on the animal's future with you. A sick or injured cat may appeal to your sympathies and make an excellent and rewarding pet in the long run, but be prepared for extra veterinary bills. If you are determined to rescue an unhealthy animal, consult your veterinary surgeon first. Your vet is the best person to help you make a rational decision – after all, he or she will be the one treating the animal. It's easy to say reject any animal that isn't perfect, but it isn't always easy to do so, because adoption is fundamentally an emotional experience. Those willing and able to care for disabled cats are rare and wonderful people.

Once you have brought your Tonkinese home, arrange an appointment with your vet to give it an introductory check-up.

Transportation

Having gone to a lot of trouble to choose your Tonkinese, spend a little thought on how you will bring it home. A cardboard box is not as good as a proper cat carrier. You might think it's not worth investing in a hygienic, comfortable and safe mode of transport for your cat, but even the annual trips to the vet for inoculation boosters are far easier with the correct equipment. You cannot hope to contain a frightened or ill cat in anything other than a purpose-designed carrier. Sturdy plastic carriers are excellent, as they are lightweight, easily cleaned and quite warm with the appropriate bedding. For cats that struggle to avoid a front-loading carrier the plastic-coated metal baskets are probably best, as they are top-loading. Always line the carrier with a cat blanket, if necessary underlined with clean newspaper for the nervous traveller. Always buy a carrier that is slightly larger than you need; too small a carrier is worse than useless as it can be very distressing for your cat.

Mymystic Nemesis (brown).

Chapter 5

Preparing for the new family member

Before bringing home your new family member make sure that your home is ready to receive and welcome it. In 1962 my parents brought home our first Siamese kitten. She was beautiful and healthy but there was no advice from the breeder regarding her diet or requirements, so we turned to *Foyles handbook of Siamese Cats* (Kathleen R Williams) and Sherley's *Famous Cat Book* for information. When I brought home *my* own Siamese kitten in 1976 the breeder gave me a carefully considered diet sheet – tinned milk, cooked rabbit and fish, raw mince and liver, cat biscuits, wheat cereal and honey all played a substantial part in the diet. Knowledge of feline requirements and the availability of the right products have come a long way since then. There is no point in adding the right pet to your family and then skimping on the accessories. The minimum equipment necessary for your cat is: a warm bed, food and water dishes, a litter box, a suitable carrier and a grooming brush. Have these facilities ready and in place before your Tonkinese arrives home; when it arrives, all it will want to do is explore its new home with the least amount of fuss and bother, especially for the first few hours.

Sleeping arrangements: Cats and kittens need warm, draught-free beds. A manufactured bed or a good-sized, sturdy cardboard box is equally suitable if there is clean, warm bedding (blanket or pet duvet for example) inside. A kitten used to the warmth of its litter-mates at night needs extra warmth initially. It is cruel and unnatural to leave a home-bred cat outside at night.

Toilet arrangements: Even if you decide that your new cat will eventually be going outside to relieve itself, you must still provide a suitable litter tray to start with. A Tonkinese is usually litter trained before it leaves its mother and will be used to a clean litter tray, so it is important to make one easily available. Normally there are no problems but, if your new Tonkinese starts to investigate a corner studiously, carry it to the litter tray immediately, speaking gently to it. After it has used the tray, reward it by praising and petting it. A dirty tray is offensive both to yourself and your Tonkinese, who may decide to make other arrangements if it thinks the tray isn't cleaned often enough. Eventually you may choose not to have a tray in the house. When your cat is used to going outside for part of the day, place the tray in an obvious position near its entrance to the house. This will encourage it to relieve itself outside. You'll usually find the cat takes over its own training at this stage and uses the garden in preference to its outdoor tray. See also chapter 6.

Feeding arrangements: It's important for your Tonkinese to be aware that feeding is a public and social activity. Each pet should have its own food bowl. Place the food and water bowls in a clear, open position, such as a corner of the kitchen which isn't regularly disturbed, so that you can keep an eye on how much your Tonkinese is eating. This is especially important in a multi-cat household, where one cat may be hogging food at the expense of the newcomer. Placing food bowls in a regular place also helps you to see when they require cleaning or topping-up. Food and water bowls are best placed on a washable surface, especially if you have a cat that insists on burying its left-overs or a kitten that hasn't yet learned to put on the brakes before careering into its water bowl! Don't be tempted to chase your new pet with food if it will not eat with the others in the regular area. This merely encourages it to become fussy and irregular in its eating habits. Simply move its bowl further away from the others to give it a little more confidence. A cat allowed to have hiding places in which to eat is also likely to hide any little presents that it brings in for you; at least a cat encouraged to eat in the open will leave presents openly for you.

For details on suitable and unsuitable feeding/drinking bowls, the varieties of food available and the basic dietary requirements of the cat, see chapter 6.

Clean water to drink: A bowl of clean water must always be available. Before putting it down, leave it to stand a while to allow some of the chlorine to evaporate. Chlorine and fluoride are highly scented and quite unpleasant for a cat, who will often drink from a puddle, pond or even toilet bowl in preference to what we see as clean and freshly drawn water. Of course, there are the exceptions who like to drink from a running tap.

A brown tortie with a bowl of clean water.

Toys: These should be as simple and safe as possible. Manufacturers and people care that the toys look like mice, with ears, eyes and tails and whiskers – cats and kittens couldn't care less. Ping-pong balls, cardboard boxes, screwed-up newspaper, cotton reels, hazel nuts, small bags of cat-nip and clean goose feathers are favourites. Thin pieces of string, shoe laces, elastic bands and knitted toys can be eaten and may be dangerous.

Introduction to the new home

Most of the information in this section is written with a new kitten in mind but the principles also apply to the introduction of a more mature cat. This can be a traumatic time, so take everything slowly and gently. It's best to

85

restrict access in the new home to one or two rooms at a time; otherwise you might risk losing your Tonkinese in the first couple of days. Remember that a kitten can hide in the tiniest of gaps. Think of the smallest space you believe a kitten can get into – then halve it.

Introduction to your existing pets: Give your new kitten time to explore the eating, sleeping and litter tray areas before you introduce it to any other animals. Give it the chance to take in the new smells and even to take on some of those smells itself by using the litter tray. Whatever happens, don't force the issue: both new and existing pets feel threatened by each other's strange scent and react. Don't shout at or chastise your existing pet; just move the animals apart as gently as possible and give them both plenty of calming attention. Don't worry about face-to-face growling; this is just their means of beginning diplomatic discussions before establishing hierarchical positions and a treaty. Do not attempt to block their vision of each other; this will just make them more nervous and wary. Eventually the kitten will take on the smells (and rules) of the new home and settle happily with existing pets. Most cats adapt to other species within the family, but the adjustment period may take from one to four weeks or (rarely) even months, so be patient. If introducing your kitten to a dog, have the dog under absolute control. The kitten could hurt the dog, and the dog could easily kill the kitten.

Introduction to children and the rest of the household: For the kitten, its introduction to the human members of the household (especially children) may be just as stressful as its introduction to the animal members. It is natural for children (and adults!) to want to cuddle, play with or pet a new kitten constantly. However, a kitten must be given a good couple of hours to explore its new home, without being fussed or restricted by children, to become confident in its new surroundings and know where there is a safe bolt hole if it needs it. A kitten that is over-fussed to start with may become nervous and frightened, or worse (from your point of view), may scratch a child to protect itself. Remember that the kitten is also a child and needs time to settle in. Meanwhile, the children should be taught that a kitten is not a toy but a living creature with feelings that must be respected. If introduced slowly and gently, kittens and children can become life-long friends.

Going outside: A kitten probably hasn't been outside by the time you collect it from the breeder, and shouldn't go outside for the first couple of weeks after you take it home. This allows it time to adjust to its new and strange home while its immune system builds up after its recent inoculations. When you do let your kitten out, supervise it until you are confident that it won't come to any harm and knows its way home. Remember that Tonkinese are more intelligent and inquisitive than average, and they do like to see the world from the heights!

Alice (brown).

Inoculations, pests and parasites: See chapters 6 and 7.

What if you cannot keep your Tonkinese?
There may be many reasons why a relationship doesn't work out, either from your point of view or the cat's. This is why it is so important to be sure that you are ready for a cat in the first place. Sadly, many a loving cat is re-homed when an unexpected baby comes along or when the owner realises that the cat is more friendly or energetic than they can cope with. Whatever the reason, the most important consideration is finding the right home for it, one that will be caring and permanent.

First contact the breeder. It is unrealistic to expect breeders to be able to take back adult cats but they will usually wish to know that the cat will be moving on and may be able to help, or at least put you in touch with a Tonkinese rescue organization. Try to find a relative or acquaintance willing to provide a loving home. You can advertise in one or more of the cat magazines for a good home for your pet, and many of them don't charge for this service, but be sure to vet the prospective new owners, as the health and happiness of your Tonkinese must be of paramount consideration. As a last resort, contact cat rescues or shelters, which usually advertise in cat magazines. If you find them by other means check them out thoroughly. Not all cat rescues have the time or resources to vet potential homes for the cats in their custody thoroughly and it isn't unheard of for animal research laboratories to obtain cats from such organisations.

Chapter:
Caring for your Tonkinese

A HEALTHY TONKINESE
A healthy Tonkinese is a confident, alert and athletic cat. It should move smoothly, without favouring any particular foot. Its posture should be erect with the head and tail held up and there should be no hesitation in stride or uncertainty in movements. The muscle tone should be well developed and visible. An unusually quiet, listless cat that is hunched in posture is unwell; a drooping tail or head is often a sign of a nervous or ailing cat.

Choosing the right vet
Choose your veterinary surgeon carefully. The continuity of approach and handling your pet receives from your vet will make all the difference to its acceptance of treatment; if you find the right vet to start with, your cat won't have to get used to yet another person prodding and poking it around. Ideally, you want a vet who isn't too far from home, who has open surgeries as well as specific appointments, who is willing to make home visits, who is accessible at weekends, who charges competitive rates with discounts for multi-cat households and who has a particular interest in cats. If you find a vet with all of these features you are extremely fortunate.

Probably the best way to find the right vet is to ask local breeders or cattery owners to recommend one. Don't be afraid to ring around and find out about surgery hours and charges. Unfortunately, we often settle for the nearest vet, not necessarily the right one for our needs. Don't forget that the vet's right hand, a qualified, efficient nurse, makes all the difference to you and the vet in all matters, from arranging your appointments to ensuring that the essential blood test results are available on time for your desperately-calling queen. Ask to see around the surgery and nursing pens (by appointment, of course). Veterinary practices are increasingly aware that breeders and cattery/kennel owners want to be more involved, and many of the larger practices now hold open evenings.

Perhaps you prefer a natural or holistic healer. Homeopathic remedies are known to be extremely effective but should be additional to, not instead of, the services of a vet. A cat with a broken leg or a queen in need of a caesarean must have the immediate attention of a qualified vet, but may well benefit from the post-surgery support of homeopathy.

Inoculations
Your kitten's breeder should have provided you with an inoculation certificate for your kitten. It is essential that your cat receives an annual booster for both feline influenza and feline infectious enteritis. Where possible, avoid contact with sick animals, catteries that will take your cat without an inoculation

Mirber Contessa Zarta (lilac), a typically inquisitive kitten.

certificate and taking your queen to a stud whose owner does not require a recent FeLV test or cannot show you a copy of the stud's recent test.

Insurance

I recommend that you take out insurance for your Tonkinese. This will give you freedom from financial worries should your pet require unexpected veterinary treatment or go missing, incurring the expense of advertisements. It is becoming more common now for breeders to insure their kittens for a short period to cover possible settling-in problems. Inquisitive young cats can get into all sorts of trouble, breeding queens and studs have their own unique problems and elderly cats always need more veterinary attention.

Eyes, ears and nose

Eyes The eyes should be open and clear, with no sign of discharge or cloudiness. A little residue from the tear glands is normal (usually light grey when wet and brownish when dry) and some cats are more prone to this than others. However, persistent, sticky dirt could be a sign of a blocked tear duct, conjunctivitis or an upper respiratory infection. The inner eyelid (haw) is not normally visible. Some cats raise their haws slightly when enjoying a stroke or when concentrating on their food, but the haw should retract quickly and it should be clean and pinkish-brown, according to the colour of the cat. A visible or exposed haw indicates illness and/or parasitic infection. See also chapter 7.

Laryna Lucy Locket (brown).

Ears The ears should be clean and held forward, fully pricked or erect. A cat with a drooping ear or that persistently shakes its head or scratches its ears probably has ear mites. A dark or waxy substance in the ears may also be a sign of ear mites.

Romantica Lorenzo (lilac).

Nose The nose should be slightly moist and cool to the touch. It may occasionally be dry – after the cat has washed its face, for example. It should be clean and free from discharge or encrustation, either of which may be a symptom of an upper respiratory infection, but there may occasionally be a little dirt around or inside the nostrils where the cat cannot reach to clean itself. A persistently hot nose is a sign of illness.

Care programme Unless there is an obvious problem you can leave the eyes and nose to the cat to care for. If you need to wipe away a little dirt from the corner of the eyes or edge of the nose, use a moist cotton wool ball. Wipe the insides of the ears gently with wipes made specifically for cats' ears if necessary, being careful to follow the instructions on the package. A kitten's ears may get rather dusty, so this is a good time to get it used to very gentle cleaning as part of a daily inspection, combined with petting. If your cat has feline companions these are areas that you can usually leave to the cats.

The adult canines alongside the milk teeth.

Mouth and teeth

Mouth The mouth is usually pink and the tongue clean. Some Tonkinese (especially the Torties) have some pigmentation inside the mouth, making health assessment just a little more difficult. Except immediately after eating, the breath should not be unpleasant; bad or sour breath can be a sign of mouth, respiratory or gastric problems or worms. The palate should not be cleft; a cleft palate is a serious congenital defect, which is often fatal.

Teeth In kittens the teeth begin to erupt at about the age of two weeks; by eight weeks a kitten has a full set of 26 deciduous (milk) teeth. From about fourteen weeks it begins to lose its milk teeth and by seven months a full set of 30 adult teeth has erupted. The permanent teeth are larger and have longer roots. In many Foreign breeds of cat the canine teeth are quite long and may protrude below the lips. The teeth, especially the canines and incisors, should be clean and white, with no excessive tartar build-up. They should be firm and unbroken. Missing or broken incisors are of no great consequence as long as there is no pain (pain may indicate an abscess) – cats can manage quite well without them. The gums should be firm and pink. Abnormally pale, bluish, red or dark gums, or gums that bleed when pressed with the pad of your finger or return to colour very slowly, may be signs of gingivitis, periodontal disease, respiratory distress, toxicity problems or other illness.

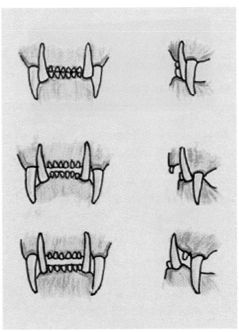

Bite Besides the obvious (painful) definition, this term is used to describe the position of the cat's upper and lower teeth when the jaw is closed. The incisors should meet, the four canines neatly slotting through one another. Deformities include undershot and overshot jaws, which give an imperfect bite and may cause eating problems. This is scarce in Tonkinese; their good depth and width of muzzle deters crowded teeth.

The bite:
(top) correct; (centre) overshot;
(bottom) undershot.

Teeth	Time of Eruption	Number
Incisors	Deciduous: 2–3 weeks	Upper jaw: 6, Lower jaw: 6
	Permanent: 4 months	Upper jaw: 6, Lower jaw: 6

Chapter 6

Canines	Deciduous: 4–6 weeks	Upper jaw: 2, Lower jaw: 2
	Permanent: 5–6 months	Upper jaw: 2, Lower jaw: 2
Pre-molars	Deciduous: Not present in kittens	
	Permanent: 5–6 months	Upper jaw: 6, Lower jaw: 4
Molars	Deciduous: 4–6 weeks	Upper jaw: 6, Lower jaw: 4
	Permanent: 7 months	Upper jaw: 2, Lower jaw: 2

Care programme When you collect your kitten it may be teething. Some kittens don't notice this period; others react in a variety of ways. They may have slightly upset stomachs, lose their appetites or paw at their mouths. If the kitten is distressed about its mouth, ask your vet to check that its teeth are coming through properly. Teething kittens will want to chew on various firm objects. I find a small cardboard box is useful for kittens, to sleep in, play in or simply chew on. It's unlikely that you'll see any of the baby teeth your kitten loses. They are normally swallowed harmlessly. Examine your Tonkinese's mouth and teeth regularly from an early age, using clean, soap-free fingers. This will make life much easier in the future, especially if you intend to show your cat.

Provided that its diet is well balanced, a cat's teeth will look after themselves up to a point, but check them regularly. Give your cat biscuits and pieces of cooked meat large enough to be chewed rather than swallowed whole. The shearing and crunching action helps to clean the teeth and gums. There are many proprietary brands of animal toothpastes and gels now available – and yes, each cat should have its own feline toothbrush, or you risk passing on any infection from one cat to another. Elderly cats in particular suffer from the

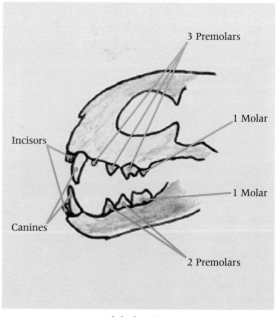

Adult dentition.

effects of poor dental condition and, in extreme cases, a build-up of plaque can result in foul breath, loss of appetite, pain and severe kidney problems.

Limbs and hindquarters

Legs and tail These should be firm and strong, with no signs of scabs, lumps or tenderness; the abdomen and groin also should be free from lumps and swellings. You should be able to feel the ribs easily, but they should not be obvious under the fur. Lumps in the groin or navel area may indicate hernias.

Anus The anus should be relatively clean, dry and free from discharge. It should be pink or pale brown, according to the colour of the cat: usually a red, swollen, or draining anus indicates diarrhoea and/or a parasitic infestation.

Genitals These should be clean and free from discharge. In males, a draining or swollen penis indicates a problem, possibly urolithiasis (FUS). In females, a discharge may indicate a gynaecological disorder.

Care programme An elderly cat may need your help in washing itself as it becomes less supple. Its anal region especially will need to be cleaned. Gently wash the area with cotton-wool moistened with luke-warm water, and then dry it gently. A heavily pregnant queen will also benefit from such attention.

Feet and claws

Feet and claws should be clean and strong, with no encrustation and no soft or spongy pads. Polydactylism (extra toes) is not uncommon in cats generally (although I have not heard of it in Tonkinese) and doesn't usually cause the cat any problems, but such a cat should not be bred from. Cats normally have five toes on each front foot and four on each rear foot.

Care programme Cats don't scratch to sharpen their claws: they scratch to prevent their claws from becoming too long and to remove the outer sheath of newly-developing claws, just as we clip our nails. Examine their feet and claws weekly, checking the pads for cuts or abrasions and the claws

Cats like to keep their nails in trim!

for breaks, splits, infection or abnormal growth. Elderly cats are less able to strop their claws, which can grow round into the pad itself. They may also suffer from cracked pads, which is painful. Cats scratch on carpets and furniture if there is no alternative: outside they use tree trunks, and indoors you can provide one of the many scratch posts available from pet shops.

Your cat will keep its claws clean and healthy with regular use, but you may wish to clip them regularly if you have a 'house cat'. To examine the claws, gently but firmly hold the paw in your hand. Then, with thumb and forefinger above and below the toes, squeeze lightly to extend the claws. When you examine each claw you will see the sensitive quick (the pale pinkish area within the claw), which is well supplied with blood and nerves, so be very sure that you clip just the tip of the claws (see diagram on opposite page). Use clippers specially designed for cats' claws, as nail clippers and scissors splinter the claw. Your cat must become used to having its claws clipped, particularly if you have a queen, elderly or show cat.

Beau (brown), Samson (choc) and Ellie (brown tabby) in the cat tower.

Unless advised by a vet, because of injury, you should never have your cat de-clawed. This is cruelly painful for the cat and deprives it of its natural defence.

Coat

The Tonkinese coat should be clean, glossy and close-lying, even on the more full-coated cats. It should be free from fleas and other parasites. In elderly cats the coat often becomes greasy looking and clumps together (*staring*); in a younger cat this is a sign of sickness.

Care programme Tonkinese don't require grooming; they just need to be stroked. Actually, this isn't too far from the truth. They have such close fine fur that usually all they need is a thorough daily stroking (and which Tonkinese owner wouldn't be pleased to do this?) combined with a weekly brushing with a rubber-toothed brush or grooming mitt to remove loose hairs. When grooming your cat remember not to put pressure on the spine and, although most cats love to be stroked under the chin and along the jawline, you should avoid the throat itself. It's not necessary to bath a kitten and rarely necessary to bath a cat.

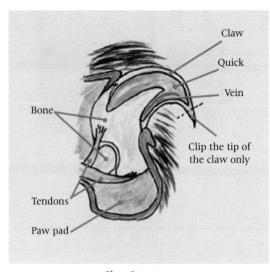

Claw

Quick

Vein

Bone

Clip the tip of
the claw only

Tendons

Paw pad

Claw Structure.

Grooming is both relaxing and good for your cat and therapeutic for yourself, so get into the habit of grooming your Tonkinese regularly, although it may not appear to need it when it's young. Brush your cat more often in the moulting seasons (spring and central heating time) to keep the coat free of loosened hairs. The fur of elderly cats becomes 'clumped' as a result of a decrease in the production of sebaceous oils, so they need even more regular gentle grooming. This is when you'll find that the grooming habit has been worthwhile – brushing an elderly cat that isn't used to it can be rather difficult! Besides removing loose fur, regular grooming allows you to keep an eye on any changes in the condition/weight of your cat and be aware of the earliest signs of any abnormalities or parasites.

Fleas and worms

(see chapter 7 for further details)

Fleas are a natural hazard for cats that go outside, and are as unpleasant for the cat as for you. A regular programme of de-fleaing and worming is recommended. De-fleaing should include treating the areas the cat lives, sleeps and plays in (your home and garden pen)

Treedancer Lilac Korene (lilac). Photo: Alan Robinson

and all bedding. A kitten should leave its breeder's home free of any infestation or parasites; find out from the breeder when your kitten is next due to be wormed. If your Tonkinese goes outside and develops a habit of catching mice and birds, use a 'total wormer' recommended by your vet. Do not over-worm your cat or kitten.

Chapter 6

Caring for older cats

A healthy Tonkinese can expect a long life. It may live well into its late teens, which equates to a human age of 70–80. In old age your Tonkinese (and indeed any other cat) needs your support and consideration most of all. Generally, the older cat will be slower, less in control, more susceptible to the cold and less able to tolerate richer foods. You can help by making sure that your cat is kept warm and comfortable, that the daily routines are regular and that food and facilities are not too far away (for example an aged cat may have problems climbing stairs to the litter

Kipper (choc), still fit at 13 years old.

tray). Increased grooming periods and, if necessary, a change of diet can also ease the life of a less able cat. The care of an older cat covers a great range of topics and considerations, both physical and psychological, which are outside the scope of this book. I recommend that you read *The Ultrafit Older Cat*, which I found to be one of the most comprehensive and readable books on this subject (see **Bibliography**).

DIET

If your Tonkinese is fed on a complete diet (in other words, one that covers all its nutritional requirements) it does not need to be given dietary supplements. The addition of a vitamin/mineral supplement may even be harmful. If cats are predominantly fed on 'moist' food (tinned food, fish, meat) they also get a high percentage of their required fluid intake, but clean water should always be available. If the cat's diet contains more semi-moist foods or dry 'complete food' biscuits, it is even more critical that water is constantly available.

Food bowls

Each cat should have its own food bowl. The softer plastic bowls and dishes, such as

Cats like fresh, clean water.

those made of polyethylene or polypropylene, are usually the cheapest, but they slowly release chemicals that cats can smell and to which they may also develop an allergic reaction, visible as a rash or irritation under the chin. Hard plastics such as Melamine are slightly more expensive but far more suitable, as they are hard-wearing, easily cleaned and safe to eat from. The only suitable metal bowls are stainless steel; other metals can react with food and water. Glazed ceramic bowls or glass bowls are also highly suitable. Remember that very light-weight bowls are easily upturned.

Milk

Milk should not be substituted for water, because it is a food, not a drink. Apart from humans, who drink milk for the taste of it, it's unnatural for mammals to continue to drink milk after they have been weaned. If your cat has developed a taste for it, you should not offer milk straight from the fridge, as the chill may upset the cat's digestive system. If possible, encourage it to drink milk specially formulated for cats in preference to cows' milk.

How often should a cat be fed?

It's a common mistake for people to give an adult cat a large meal at either end of the day. Cats have very small stomachs; they don't gorge themselves, like dogs, to hold reserves of food, but eat only what they want at the time. If you find your cat leaves a lot of its tinned food, reduce the portions and leave biscuits out during the day in case it becomes hungry between meal times. This also helps keep its teeth in good order. Such a feeding programme is particularly suitable in a multi-cat household, where cats often prefer to free-feed from the biscuit bowl rather than having to eat together. Don't be surprised if your cat prefers to live on biscuits rather than moist foods – just make sure that the biscuits you provide are one of the complete varieties, which are now quite easily available from pet shops.

Cat foods

The number of cats you have, the availability of brands, the state of health of your cats and their age all affect your choice of cat food. The cost of the food should not be a prime consideration. Never feed your cat a diet of dog food or human food, as both lack nutrients that are essential to a cat.

There are three basic types of cat food:

- *Complete* foods contain all of the nutrients necessary for the feline diet. A cat need not eat anything else at all, but water must be readily available.
- *Balanced* foods contain a well balanced mixture of minerals, carbohydrates and so on. Use these as an addition to, rather than instead of, other foods.

97

• *Treats* may be labelled *gourmet, premium,* or *supreme*. These are designed to tempt the cat rather than provide a proper diet. This group also includes dried or cooked fish, chicken, liver, cat sweets, special biscuits and so on.

Commercial cat foods are very convenient and come in three types:

• *Tinned foods* generally have the most flavour. Good tinned food contains a well-balanced mixture of protein, fats, carbohydrates, and minerals. Exceptions to this are the *premium* or *gourmet* foods, which are often formulated for taste rather than nutrition. Ensure that the food you use as a staple is labelled *total* or *complete* nutrition, which is defined by law (the label *balanced* is not). A disadvantage of tinned food is that it can only be left in the bowl for a short period before it becomes stale, especially in hot weather.
• *Semi-moist foods* have the advantages of minimal odour, a long shelf life and a one-day bowl life. Semi-moist foods generally contain a great deal of preservatives, so be sure to read the labels carefully.
• *Dry foods* have two distinct advantages over other types: they have a very long shelf and bowl life and, if the components are too large to be swallowed whole, they will help to clean the cat's teeth as they are chewed. Most commercial dry foods are complete, nutritional diets.

Your Tonkinese may also enjoy the occasional meal of lightly-grilled, chopped chicken, poached white fish (carefully flaked and cooled) or other prepared foods. The following table indicates some of the foods which are often given to cats regularly in addition to, or instead of, a normal feline diet. These foods are treats and care should be taken not to unbalance the diet by giving them too often.

(Left) Tonkabella Diggory Dai (choc).
(Right) Tonkabella Daffy Dorothea (brown).

Eggs   Source of protein, vitamins D and B12, choline, sulphur and iron. Cooked egg is a good source of protein for a cat but raw egg white contains an enzyme which destroys biotin; biotin deficiency causes dry flaky skin and hair.

Fish   Source of protein, iodine, selenium and magnesium. Raw fish contains an enzyme (thiaminase) that destroys vitamin B1; B1 deficiency leads to brain damage. Cooking the fish destroys the harmful enzyme but excess fish in the diet can result in an extremely painful disease called steatitis (Yellow Fat Disease) due to a build up of unsaturated fatty acids.

Kidney   Source of protein, vitamin B1 and cobalt; very high in phosphorous, very low in calcium. Cats fed excessively on kidney develop nutritional secondary hyperparathyroidism.

Liver   Source of protein, vitamin B1, niacin, choline and cobalt, high in vitamin A and phosphorous, low in calcium. In pregnant queens, vitamin A can be depleted by up to 50%, so the occasional addition of liver to her diet can be beneficial. Cats fed excessively on liver develop hypervitaminosis A, which leads to excess bone growth (usually of the spine and forelimb elbows).

Meat   Source of protein, very high in phosphorous, very low in calcium, iron, magnesium, copper, sodium and iodine. Ratio of calcium to phosphorous in a cat's diet should be approximately 1.5:1 but in meat the ratio of calcium to phosphorous is 1:20. Young cats fed excessively on meat develop nutritional secondary hyperparathyroidism. Pregnant queens fed excessively on meat suffer iodine deficiency, which leads to birthing difficulties and kitten deformities. Meat should not exceed 20–25% of a cat's total diet.

Feeding kittens

It's very important that kittens are fed as their breeders recommend for three to four weeks at least. Kittens need dietary continuity to avoid upset stomachs and provide a sense of security. When you first bring it home, the kitten is probably still on four small meals a day (which should be reduced to three meals a day by the age of six months), as well as freely-available biscuits. Use good brands of kitten food, which are especially formulated for your kitten's digestive system and nutritional requirements. There are now several on the market. However, you may find that the kitten has already started to eat adult food mixed with kitten food.

TOILET ARRANGEMENTS

Any commercial litter tray is suitable, but you may find one of the covered trays preferable for several reasons: the appearance of it, the increased control of odour or simply because you have a cat that digs a deep well to squat in.

Mymystic Snowshadow and Mymystic Opalshadow (both choc).

However, a new kitten may have difficulty getting into and out of a covered tray, so find out what it's used to and provide something similar initially; it will be reassuring for the kitten to have a familiar tray. The tray should be large enough to accommodate the cat comfortably. If you use a covered tray, make sure it's high enough for the largest of your cats to scratch around in. Site the tray in a quiet part of the house, as some cats prefer privacy while using trays; while squatting they are in a very vulnerable position. Cleanliness is essential, but don't go overboard; strong bleach shouldn't be used, as the odour may altogether discourage your cat from using its tray. There are several suitable disinfectants (such as Formula H or Pet Virkon). Don't assume that an antiseptic or disinfectant suitable for infant humans is suitable for cats. A clean tray will encourage your cat to use it rather than go elsewhere.

Most commercial cat litters are suitable, or in dire emergency you could use shredded newspaper for a short period. With small kittens you have to take into account the effect of the litter on their tender paws: wood pellets may be a little hard to start with and, with young or small kittens, I strongly recommend that you avoid the use of clumping litters. While they may be soft underfoot, the clumping properties have been known to cause injuries in young kittens who have flicked litter into their eyes or eaten it.

'Hurry up, it's my turn!'

SAFETY IN THE HOME ENVIRONMENT

Reading this section is enough to make any caring cat owner paranoid about the safety of their cats, but your cat has probably come in contact with at least one of the 'dangers' every day and come to no harm. It is included simply as a guide to some of the easily avoided problems in your home and garden; it would be impossible to write a fully comprehensive chapter on feline safety. It's also impossible to provide a totally safe environment for your cat and still let it live the life of a cat. So if you just note these 10 simple points you'll have the basics for making yours a safe home for your cats.

Kittens need extra vigilance and care in the garden, especially if there is a pond.

- A Tonkinese is a cat. Cats are naturally curious. Tonkinese (especially kittens) can get into, fall down or get stuck in the smallest of gaps.
- Tonkinese are upwardly mobile. Don't expect them to remain on the ground when there are tables, shelves and higher planes to reach. Kitchen counters offer a bewildering array of dangers.
- Cats don't have fingers, so everything must be tried out with the mouth.
- Cats can't spit out (except for tablets!) so anything that starts in the mouth must continue in that direction – even if it's a shoelace, elastic band or a thread with a needle on the end.
- Kittens don't understand that they cannot necessarily get out of the bath, toilet bowl or pond.
- Cats have a restricted sense of temperature. They love to sit next to hot radiators and, since they are so inquisitive (especially kittens), they are at risk from hot cooker plates and grills. They may be happily half-way over the grill, gas-fire, barbecue or hob before they realise that their feet are burning.
- Cats don't understand the concept of sunburn, which they can get through glass as well as lying outside.
- Cats don't know that a plant, creature, garden chemical, or bleach is unpleasant to taste and may be poisonous unless they try it first – see the lists of chemicals and plants to avoid on pages 103 and 104.

Check kitchen appliances before you switch on.

•Cats don't always judge the speed of travelling vehicles accurately, especially when they are used to the road being quiet.

•Cats don't know that there are people outside with whom they shouldn't be friendly.

First aid box

Here is a short list of proprietary items for the Pet First Aid Box. All of these products are easily available from a good pet supplies store.

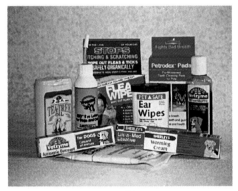

First aid kit.

•Philip's Vetzyme Antiseptic Ointment

•Philip's Vetzyme Antiseptic Lotion

•Sherley's Worming Cream (a mild general wormer, easy to use)

•Sherley's Lik-A-Med (a mild laxative, easy to use but should not be used as a habit)

•Pet Safe Ear Wipes

•Tea Tree Wipes and/or Lotion

•Flea wipes (produced by United Pet Supplies, available by mail order from Purrsonal Touch)

POISONOUS SUBSTANCES

Drugs

Cats lack certain enzymes found in humans and consequently are unable to cope with substances that are not necessarily toxic to humans. Several medicines prescribed for humans were originally, and successfully, used to treat animals, but most human medicines are specifically designed for humans and must not be used for your cat, unless under the strict supervision and recommendation of your vet.

Aspirin Do not give a cat aspirin or any medicine containing aspirin. In cats it's toxic to both the liver and bone marrow. However, your veterinary surgeon may prescribe aspirin for certain conditions, in which case it must be used strictly as prescribed.

Paracetamol Should never be given to a cat, nor should any medicine containing paracetamol. In cats, paracetamol affects the function of haemoglobin and results in death due to oxygen starvation of the body tissues.

Chemicals

Keep chemical products securely out of reach and take great care when disposing of containers. Only use products that are specifically labelled as being suitable for use with animals – there are now plenty to choose from. The following is a list of some common chemicals which should be avoided or only be used with extreme caution in a household with cats.

- All pest control products – label cautions are not always as clear as they should be.
- Alphachloralose – used in rodent and bird poisons.
- Bleach – use with extreme care and wash off thoroughly.
- Calciferol – used in rodent poisons.
- Caustic soda – soda crystals used for laundry or cleaning drains.
- Chlorhexidine – used in disinfectants and antiseptics.
- Chlorphenoxyacids – used in herbicides.
- Ethylene glycol – used in antifreeze.
- Hexachlorophane – used in disinfectants and medicated soaps/solutions.
- Metaldehyde – used in slug bait.
- Methalene blue – used as an antidote for some poisons in humans, it is highly toxic to cats.
- Organochlorines (Chlorinated Hydrocarbons) – used in insecticides.
- Organophosphates – used in insecticides. These may also be found in some flea treatments, in which case they are safe to use provided that the instructions are followed carefully.
- Paraquat – used in herbicides.
- Phenolic compounds – used in disinfectants, such as TCP, Dettol and Jeyes Fluid. Generally any substance which becomes milky or cloudy when diluted should be avoided.
- Sodium Chlorate – used in herbicides.
- Strychnine – used in rodent poisons and mole baits.
- Turpentine – highly toxic and rapidly absorbed through the skin.
- Warfarin – used in rodent poisons.

Romantica Lilith Venezia (lilac) in the snow.

Chapter 6

Antiseptics

Many antiseptics that we use are highly toxic in cats. If you need to bathe a wound but don't have any proprietary animal antiseptic (such as Philip's Vetzyme Antiseptic Lotion), a saline solution is acceptable, especially if it's an area that the cat will lick. Mix one teaspoon of salt into one cup of boiled, and cooled, water. Cats cannot detoxify phenols.

Plants

If your cat doesn't have outside access make sure that it has a pot of grass. Cats get essential folic acid from grass, which isn't always present in sufficient quantities in the modern feline diet. Most pet shops sell tubs of grass seed for cats, or you could grow your own. It's best to use broad-leaved grasses. Without access to grass, cats try to eat house plants. Tradescantia, the spider plant, is very popular. However, several house plants are poisonous, and the following are best avoided:

Addeish Katey Clare among the garden plants.

- • All Bulbs
- • Azaleas
- • *Ricinus communis* (Castor Oil Plant)
- • *Dieffenbachia* (Dumb Cane)
- • *Hedera* (Ivy)
- • *Hyacinthus* (Hyacinth)
- • *Viscum album* (Mistletoe)
- • *Euphorbia pulcherrima* (Poinsettia)
- • *Ficus* varieties (Rubber Plant, Weeping Fig)
- • *Philodendron scandens* (Sweetheart Vine)
- • *Solanum* (Potato Flower, Ornamental Nightshade)

Cats, like most animals, have an innate awareness of which plants are harmful to them, but this occasionally fails them; especially kittens, who are happy to try anything once. While you can't protect your cat from all poisonous plants, you can take steps to avoid including known poisonous plants in your own garden and you have complete control over the plants and flowers in your home and your cat's pen. It's unusual for a cat to bother with anything more than grasses or cat-mints in the garden but, in overgrown areas or underneath trees or shrubs that drop seeds, it's easier for a cat to pick up a seed, berry or leaf inadvertantly. The plants which are particularly dangerous in this instance are Laburnum, Solanum varieties (Nightshades), Yews, Cytisus varieties (Broom), Lily of the Valley, Foxgloves and Aconite (Monkshood). Although it's highly unlikely that a cat will bother with them it's worth knowing that all plant bulbs are poisonous.

A secure pen in the garden often includes an area of grass, which should be kept short to prevent the grasses setting seeds. Many grass seeds are barbed to help them disperse and set in unaccommodating terrain, and they can do a great deal of damage to a cat that accidentally inhales or eats them. It can be extremely difficult to remove a grass seed that has worked its way into a cat's ear, eye or nasal passage, and very painful for the cat. Don't forget that many dried flower arrangements include ornamental grass seed heads. You might see the herb rue recommended as a safe deterrent against cats tramping across your garden, and this is for a very good reason – the sap of the herb can cause extensive and painful blistering. A few years ago *Gardening Which?* magazine carried an article about the dangers of rue, including some horrific photographs showing blistering on arms and legs on which the affected area measured up to 20cm in diameter. Obviously, some people are more sensitive to plant sap than others, but the risks to yourself and the poor cats make me believe that rue is not an acceptable deterrent against a vagrant cat. Other plants that can be irritants are Euphorbia (Spurge) and plants with hairy leaves.

One plant that is perfectly acceptable in the garden is Nepeta, also known as cat mint or cat nip, because of the cat's habit of nipping out the top leaves.

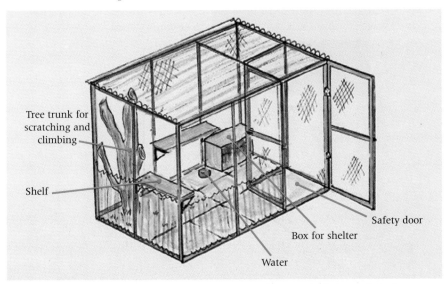

Tree trunk for scratching and climbing

Shelf

Safety door

Box for shelter

Water

Garden pen: part grassed, part paved and covered to provide shelter and shade.

Chapter 6

The three varieties, *mussinii*, *fassinii* and *cataria*, are all easily grown and produce flowers attractive to bees, so be careful where you plant it. *Mussinii* and *cataria* are usually preferred by cats, who are either indifferent to catnip or, more usually, become euphoric.

GARDEN PENS

Mymystic cats in their garden pen.

We have all seen outside pens at a cattery or at the home of a cat breeder (especially if they have a stud) but now more and more pet owners are aware of the advantages of an outside run for their cats. It might be argued that cats are naturally free-ranging animals that should not be confined to the garden. However, the combination of the outgoing, friendly nature of the Tonkinese and the dangers of thoughtless and irresponsible people and increasing levels

Mymystic's Addeish Caspar Lilacflush suns himself.

of traffic enhance the value of a secured area in your garden (see plan on page 105).

Read the section on running a stud in chapter 8 for more information on outside pens. Basically, the pen should be roofed, with an area of constant shade, contain shelves at various levels for exercise and for the cat to lie on and contain a fixed tree branch for scratching. The more cats sharing the pen the larger it needs to be. We have quite a large garden and have put up a pen about 4.5m x 7.6m (15ft x 25ft), with a long tunnel running to the cat-flap in our back door. The pen is usually occupied by at least five cats at a time and is more than comfortable for them. The size of pen is determined by the amount of space you have available. Remember that the purpose of the pen is to give your cats exercise as well as fresh air. According to the layout of your house and garden it could be accessed directly from a window or perhaps, like ours, a tunnel running from a cat-flap. It will need a door (ideally a double safety door) for you to get inside and maintain it. Don't forget that there should always be fresh water in the pen.

A cat who has access to fresh air and room to stretch and have a mad dash from level to level, and who can chew on fresh grass, wear down its claws naturally, bask in the sun and watch the birds, is unlikely to fret about not being able to roam the neighbourhood. And think of the peace of mind you will get from knowing that your Tonkinese is safe and sound.

HOLIDAYS AND CATTERIES

A good cattery is not just a business – it must also be a vocation.

When I left a career in computing, clutching my generous redundancy money in my paws, I seriously considered setting up a cattery. I spent over a year looking into the logistics of it and had long telephone calls with the indomitable Sophie Hamilton-Moore, who was the Boarding Cattery Officer of the Feline Advisory Bureau (FAB)(see **Useful Addresses**). I studied the FAB's excellent book on setting-up a cattery (which includes everything from building the houses to the paperwork required) and visited many local catteries and the local authorities. The financing was catered for and I was all prepared to enrol on the FAB's training course. Then, when everything seemed set to go, I abandoned the idea – not because of the finance, nor because I felt I couldn't cope with the hard work involved, but simply because I had too many other interests to spend 24 hours a day, 7 days a week running a cattery. I wasn't ready to devote all my time to what was necessary for the welfare of people's pets. If you are interested in setting-up a cattery I strongly recommend that you keep closely in touch with the FAB.

When you go on holiday you'll want, and are required by law, to ensure that your pets are properly cared for while you are away. The friendly neighbour who pops in twice a day to feed your pets (and if they are indeed a good neighbour they will also clean out litter trays, or there will be considerable problems when you return) may be fine for a weekend away from home but, for a longer period, you need to know that your cats are supervised. An experienced cattery proprietor knows the signs of a pining or ailing cat and will not hesitate to consult a vet, knowing that any fees will be covered. More importantly, he or she has an understanding of cats and their needs. A good cattery caters for the distressed cat that won't eat its usual diet, spends time with a cat with a specific grooming requirement and ensures that any medication your cat needs is given properly. For my money a good cattery wins hands down over the well-meaning but busy neighbour or the home-sitter.

Before you choose a cattery, it might help to know a little of what constitutes a good cattery, because there is undoubtedly a higher percentage of indifferent and poor catteries. In 1989, *Which?* magazine did a survey of catteries around the country and found that less than half were adequate, despite being licensed by the local authority. A wide discrepancy was found in the standards used by the inspectors, common problems being lack of hygiene, lack of space and poor exercising facilities. Sadly I suspect that their findings would be no different today.

To find the right cattery for your cats, start looking many months before you plan to use it; the better catteries have regular customers, who book six months or more in advance. Ask your vet, friends, relatives and various breeders for recommendations and send for a list of FAB-approved catteries (see **Useful Addresses**). These catteries have to meet a higher standard than those approved by the local authorities. Dismiss any place that won't allow you to make an inspection visit (by appointment, of course), but bear in mind that in the best catteries there will be areas that you are not permitted to enter, such as isolation and inhabited pens.

The British Veterinary Association recommends that the housing units are at least 2m (6ft) high with a floor area of at least 0.8sq m (9sq ft). There should be lighting and infra-red heating for each unit, access to daylight and good ventilation. The pens should be separated or divided with solid sneeze barriers to prevent cross-infection. There must be an isolation pen for ill cats. The outside runs should be roofed, have at least one shelf off the ground for the cat to lie on, and have a scratching post. It is essential that there is a safety gate to prevent the escape of frightened cats. The flooring inside and outside the house should be undamaged and hoseable. Sophie Hamilton-Moore said: *Simplicity and cleanliness are more important than luxury.* Check with the cattery what it wants you to take with your cat (bedding and toys for instance) and don't forget to take your inoculation certificate for the proprietor to see.

Romantica Sheba Noelle (choc), Romantica Lilith Venezia (lilac) and Adouzsh Hypnos (blue).

There should be a separate reception/office area and you should expect your cats to be inspected on arrival; the proprietor has the right to refuse your cat. When I first contacted the cattery that we use I was put through an inquisition before I was permitted to ask anything about the cattery. When the proprietors were satisfied that our cats were wholesome and loved we were welcomed with open arms, and our cats have spent many a wonderful holiday with them, coming away fit, healthy and happy with their own little Easter presents or Christmas stockings! Some catteries have 'family' pens, large enough to cater for several cats from the same home. Very few catteries will take in an unneutered male over the age of eight months.

Learoyd Heidi (lilac).

When you take your cat along, give yourself plenty of time before you have to leave to catch your train or plane. A good cattery will keep a small biography of each cat (date of birth, likes and dislikes, habits, temperament, grooming requirements, medication, inoculation records, disabilities, veterinary contact, emergency contact), so there will be some form filling each time you check your cat in. When you come home from your holidays your first priority may be to refill your empty home with cats, but catteries are not open 24 hours of the day, so arrange a specific pick-up time.

Here are some points to remember when checking out your cat's prospective holiday home:

- Is the cattery licensed?
- Will they let you look around before you take your cat there?
- Do they insist that your cats are inoculated and inspect the certificate before accepting your cat?
- Will your cat's diet and any special medical or grooming needs be catered for?
- Are the pens adequately heated, lit and ventilated, and are they spacious enough?
- Are the facilities clean?
- Are the houses and pens secure?
- Will your cat be treated as an individual?
- Is the cattery manned full time?

I'll leave the last words to Sophie Hamilton-Moore, who said: *You can judge a cattery by the way they behave towards their charges. Do they treat them as individuals or just as furry fivers?*

109

Chapter: 7
Health and the Tonkinese

A comprehensive chapter on feline health is outside the scope of this book but I would be remiss if I didn't include a brief description of some of the ailments and diseases that are common today. I recommend that you supplement your home library with a book on cat health care.

WHEN TO TAKE YOUR TONKINESE TO THE VET

Obviously you will be making an annual trip to the veterinary surgeon for your booster vaccinations. It is a good idea to ask for a little extra time and have your vet give your Tonkinese a check-up at the same time. This should cover a physical examination and a check on vital signs. I have listed below other occasions when you should call your vet:

Call vet the same day for:
- Abortion, any difficulties giving birth, distressed queen, retention of afterbirth.
- Breathing difficulties, choking, persistent coughing.
- Burns.
- Collapse, loss of balance, lameness, fits, unconsciousness.
- Depressed appetite with other symptoms, rapid weight change.
- Drinking, greatly increased.
- Eye/ear problems, head shaking, ear flicking, unusual discharge.
- Injury, with pain/wound, heavy/persistent bleeding.
- Insect bite to head/throat with swelling.
- Pain.
- Particularly abnormal behaviour.
- Persistent attempts/straining on the litter tray, blood in the stools or urine.
- Persistent sneezing.
- Persistent vomiting and/or diarrhoea – fluid, putrid or bloody.
- Poisoning.
- Signs of shock.
- Swelling – hot, painful or with discharge.
- Temperature change, obvious, persistent.
- Uncontrollable scratching or biting at skin.

Call vet after 24 hours for:
- Bad breath or other foul odour besides soiled fur.
- Diarrhoea – no sign of blood or distress.
- Itching – moderate with no excessive scratching.
- Lameness – able to bear weight, not affecting other functions.

• Depressed appetite – no other symptoms.
• Vomiting – two to three times, no other symptoms (not necessary to call vet if vomiting just after eating grass).

If your cat has been stung on the paw by a wasp or bee, ensure the sting is removed and reduce swelling with cold water. A sting on the face or throat may require veterinary attention.

This is only a guide. For your cat's sake, don't hesitate to take it to the vet if you are concerned about its health for any reason.

Emergency transportation

If the cat is injured, especially if broken bones are suspected, call your vet immediately for advice on immobilisation before transporting it. If you don't have a proper cat carrier available you could use a cardboard box, provided that it has plenty of air-holes. If this isn't possible then wrap the cat securely in several layers of material such as towelling until it is completely immobilised. It will be frightened, and will probably panic, making it defensively aggressive. Talk constantly to the cat in a soft tone to relax it as much as possible. The chances of panic in this case are increased by the cat's inability to move its legs. Do not allow a child to hold a restrained cat. Children lack the strength and nerve to hold struggling cats.

BUILDING UP IMMUNITY

A veterinary surgeon can tell a great deal about the health of a cat from blood tests and will refer to *antibodies* and *antigens*.

When the body is entered by a foreign substance (that is, a substance that is not a normal constituent of the body) it reacts to the threat of damage by producing antibodies. An antibody is a chemical compound, a protein, with the ability to render a specific foreign substance harmless. A foreign substance that causes the production of antibodies is known as an antigen (most of which are proteins). Common examples of antigens are bacteria and viruses. Another example of an antigen is the serum injected for the treatment or prevention of infectious diseases – for example, the cat flu vaccine stimulates the body to produce its own defence against the disease. The antibody produced to deal with an antigen is unique to that antigen and will not react with any other antigen. The blood of any individual contains tens of thousands of individual antibodies directed against different antigens. These form a distinct group of proteins in the blood serum called the *immuno-globulins*. Most antibodies are acquired by contact with antigens, but kittens passively acquire some antibodies from their mothers. These persist for a few weeks after birth to provide an early protection against infection. In rare cases, antibodies may be formed against the body's own cells rather than against foreign substances. This is known as an *auto-immune* disease.

Vaccination

When the body encounters a particular antigen for the first time it normally takes about a week to produce detectable amounts of antibody, and two weeks for the maximum level of antibody to be reached. Once the antigen has been eliminated successfully the levels of antibody fall again, but a 'memory' of the antigen is retained in the plasma cells. This means that, if that antigen is encountered again, the necessary antibody level can be produced much more quickly than before. When the antibody is produced by the animal itself, as a result of contracting the disease or having been vaccinated, the immunity is referred to as *active*. If the animal receives antibodies from another source, such as from the mother's first milk (colostrum), this form of immunity is referred to as passive. Passive immunity is not as prolonged as active immunity. For full details of the vaccination of kittens, see chapter 9.

A vaccine contains antigen and is used to stimulate the body's production of antibodies. There are two main types of vaccine:

- *Killed* (dead or inactivated): The antigenic material is obtained from dead micro-organisms. The antigen is eliminated quickly and often the first dose merely sensitises the immune system.
- *Live*: the antigen is in the form of living organisms that have been weakened (attenuated) so that they will stimulate the production of antibodies but not cause the disease. The live micro-organisms actually multiply in the host for a short time until the antibody levels are high enough to destroy them.

Annual boosters are necessary to maintain the required levels of antibody which, in the absence of the antigen, gradually diminish. Vaccinations should not be given if there is any indication of a disease being present; if there is, the antibody-producing cells will be fully occupied in fighting the existing disease.

AILMENTS AND DISEASES
Abortion
See chapter 9.

Acne, Feline
The skin becomes irritated, producing excess sebaceous oils, which combine with dirt and block the skin pores, just as in humans. The cause may be hormonal or due to irritations such as flea dirt or bites, allergic reaction to plastic food bowls or an accumulation of dirt from food itself. It is more usually seen as a rash, pimples, pustules or small abscesses on the chin and around the lower lip. Flea control and regularly cleaning of a cat prone to acne help to control the problem. Veterinary treatment is required in persistent and extreme cases.

Allergies in cats
See also Asthma (page 115). Symptoms may be coughing, sneezing, conjunctivitis, diarrhoea, wheezing and bald patches. Many cats are allergic to lactose and should only be given water to drink. Other causes of allergic reactions are aerosols, certain types of litter (especially dusty litter), household cleaning products, cigarettes, plastics, cosmetics. In short a cat is just as prone to allergic reactions as we are. See section on **Zoonoses** (page 126) for information on allergic reactions to cats.

Chapter 7

Amputation

Whatever the reason for amputation, cats can manage very well with just three legs. Their rapid recovery and adjustment is largely because of the fact that, unlike ourselves, cats are not emotionally affected by the concept of amputation. Euthanasia is not the first option to be considered.

Anaemia

This is a deficiency in the amount of haemoglobin, the red oxygen-carrying cells in the blood. Possible causes include loss of blood, the body's failure to produce new blood cells in the bone marrow, excessive breakdown of blood cells within the bloodstream, kidney disease (especially in elderly cats), and FeLV-related infections or tumours. Anaemia may also be caused by a parasite called *Haemobartonella felis*, which is thought to be transmitted by 'biting' insects such as fleas. The parasite fixes itself to the red blood cells, causing antibodies to be produced to destroy them. Slight cases of anaemia may go unnoticed, especially in cats with dark skin pigmentation, which is why the mouth should be checked regularly. Anaemic cats usually have pale gums and eyelids and tend to be lethargic. Anaemia is treatable, but it is not a disease in itself and is usually the sign of an underlying problem.

Aortic thrombosis

This is the formation of a blood clot in the aorta, the main artery supplying the hind limbs with blood. When the blood supply is suddenly blocked, the cat suffers muscle spasm in the hind legs, which become completely paralysed. It is extremely painful for the cat. This is a particular affliction of elderly cats and can be associated with an underlying heart problem. Although the situation is not always hopeless, euthanasia is often recommended.

Arthritis

This causes painful swelling and stiffness of the joints. It is a fairly uncommon condition in cats because they are relatively small animals and it is unusual for them to be overweight. Elderly cats are more likely to suffer arthritis than younger cats because their joints have been used more. Arthritis cannot be cured but the discomfort can be alleviated and controlled with anti-inflammatory drugs. This must be strictly under the supervision of your vet, as several anti-inflammatory drugs are highly toxic in cats.

Ascites

This is the accumulation of fluid, mostly water, in the abdominal cavity, causing the abdomen to swell uncomfortably. It is not a disease in itself, and may be relieved by drawing the fluid off, but it is a symptom of several diseases, including heart failure, organ disorders and FIP (see page 120).

Asthma
Cats suffer from diseases corresponding to human asthma, bronchitis and emphysema. Although the causes are not fully understood, it is suspected that often they are caused by allergies. The most common symptom is coughing with varying degrees of wheezing and dyspnoea (difficulty in breathing). These symptoms should not be ignored, as they often indicate a more serious problem that may be treatable if diagnosed early enough.

Blindness
Any sign of problems with the eyes should be treated immediately. Various diseases can affect the eyes and cause blindness, apart from actual accidents. Cataracts are more common in elderly cats and, although it is possible to remove them surgically, it is unusual to do so on an elderly cat. Cats cope very well with blindness in one eye but, because they rely much more on their sight than on their sense of smell, many cats are unable to cope well with complete blindness, although older and less active cats are more able to do so.

Burns
While someone is alerting your vet and making transport arrangements you should immerse the affected area in cold water for several minutes. Keep the cat as calm as possible, and do not apply any ointments, as they will only have to be cleaned off before the vet can begin treatment. The area of burn may be wrapped in a wet towel during transportation to the vet.

Cat flu (feline influenza)
This is a highly infectious disease of the respiratory tract with an incubation period of 2–10 days. Although there are several contributing agents it is mainly caused by two viruses, **Feline Calicivirus (FCV)** and **Feline Viral Rhinotracheitis (FVR)**, the latter being the most common and severe of feline respiratory diseases. Initial symptoms of FVR are loss of appetite, lassitude and sneezing, followed by fever, possibly coughing and discharge from the eyes and nose. Because of the cat's low resistance, secondary infections such as conjunctivitis and bronchopneumonia are common. Young cats are affected more severely and, of those treated for FVR, approximately 25% die. FCV may result in severe respiratory infection or just a mild clinical infection such as mouth ulcers. Cats with flu must be isolated and kept in a draught-free, warm, dry environment, but with plenty of fresh air. Depression can impede recovery significantly, so it is important to keep the cat clean, dry and comfortable. Some cats that recover suffer permanent after-effects such as a persistent cough, noisy breathing, sniffles or weepy eyes, which may be aggravated by stress or cold, damp weather. Many cats make a full recovery but remain carriers of the viruses, shedding them in times of stress such as when giving birth or when confined (for example, in a cattery or when being

shown). This makes them a risk to other cats and they should not be bred from. Immunisation against these viruses is essential for kittens, and is usually administered at nine and twelve weeks. Annual boosters are necessary.

Cat Scratch Fever

See section on **Zoonoses** (page 126).

Chlamydiosis, Feline

Chlamydia psittaci is one of the contributing bacterial agents of cat flu, but it can initiate nasal disease on its own. Although its role in rhinitis is comparatively minor compared with other agents of cat flu, it can result in severe, prolonged conjunctivitis. It is usually treated with antibiotics. Vaccines are now available against it.

Cleft palate

See chapter 9.

Constipation

Unless your cat normally uses a litter tray you may not be aware of a problem other than general listlessness. Constipation is a particular problem in less active and elderly cats. A proprietary brand of feline laxative, such as Sherley's Lik-A-Med, may be given according to package instructions. As an emergency measure, one teaspoon of medicinal liquid paraffin may be given daily for a maximum of three days. If the problem isn't resolved in that time, consult your vet. Prolonged use of liquid paraffin can result in vitamin deficiency, as it physically inhibits the absorption of vitamins in the digestive system.

Coughing

See also **Kennel Cough** (page 121).
Although the cause may not be serious, coughing should always be taken seriously and referred to your vet as soon as possible. Causes may be:

- Fur ball, grass, dry food caught in the back of the throat.
- Foreign body stuck in the throat, in which case the cat may paw at its mouth or drool and breathing may be difficult. Seek veterinary attention immediately.
- Allergies.
- Worms.
- Tonsillitis or other throat infection.
- Heart disease, growths in the mouth or respiratory system.

Cystitis

Inflammation of the lining of the bladder causes pain in the lower abdomen and when urinating. There is a desire to urinate more frequently and the cat may be feverish and lethargic. Cystitis is usually caused by bacteria. The cat may be seen straining on its litter tray, wetting on furniture or the carpet, and it may cry out. Urgent veterinary attention is essential. Antibiotics are usually prescribed, as well as urine acidifiers, and changes in diet are usually advised to prevent recurrence of the problem. The cat should be encouraged to:

- Drink more. The addition of salt (an eighth of a teaspoon daily) does not harm the cat but makes it more thirsty.
- Avoid dry foods so that water is taken in via the food, Add a little water or fresh chicken stock if necessary.
- Empty its bladder regularly. Put your cat on its litter tray (kept scrupulously clean) at least four times a day.

Dander and dermatitis

When hair is shed by a cat it often causes a slight chipping of the dead skin around the hair follicle. These little flakes of skin are *dander*. A cat, like a human, may suffer from dermatitis or another skin condition that causes it to shed skin flakes, not related to the shedding of hair. Consult your vet if there is a persistent presence of dander.

Dehydration

This is not an illness but a serious symptom of many illnesses, and must be addressed immediately. Veterinary attention is necessary. Skin is normally elastic: after a pinch test it immediately resumes its normal position: a dehydrated cat's skin becomes non-elastic, its coat is often rough and the cat is lethargic and rapidly loses weight. In very hot weather cats, especially kittens, may go off their food and need to be encouraged to take fluids. An electrolyte solution can aid re-hydration. It contains the balance of mineral salts and vitamins essential for normal body functions. Commercial mixtures are available from your vet, but you can make up a solution as follows. The mixture may be stored in the fridge for up to 24 hours and may be given as the sole feed for up to 24 hours only.

Electrolyte Solution: 1 pint (500ml) boiled and cooled water.
$2^{1}/_2$ teaspoons (12g) glucose powder (not sugar).
$^{1}/_4$ teaspoon salt.
Pinch of sodium bicarbonate.

Escherichia coli (generally referred to as *E coli*)

This bacterium occurs normally in the intestines of most animals, but certain strains may be harmful and cause infection. Kittens with *E coli* infection often die despite the most careful treatment. They suffer from constant pale and offensive diarrhoea, soon becoming dehydrated. Urgent treatment is needed.

Eye problems

It is normal for the residue from the tear glands, which keep the eyes moist, to gather in the corner of the eye and dry out. In humans we refer to this as *sleep in the corner of the eye*. In cats it is usually light grey when wet and brownish when dry. Any other discharge or accumulation of dirt is not normal. Any signs of abnormality of the eyes such as swelling, redness, discharge, or injury should be treated urgently by your vet. Don't be tempted to wash the eyes out yourself: damage to the eyeball is permanent. Swollen eyelids in a newborn kitten is an emergency; it indicates infection (see Ophthalmia neonatum in chapter 9) and can result in blindness. In some cats, such as Burmese and some Tonkinese queens, the colour of the iris changes slightly during certain stages of the oestrus cycle or during pregnancy and lactation. With these exceptions, any changes of the iris colour or cloudiness should be brought to the attention of your vet immediately as it may indicate serious illness. See also chapters 6 and 9.

Feline Calicivirus (FCV)

See **Cat flu** (page 115).

Feline Infectious Enteritis (FIE)

Also known as **Feline Panleucopenia (FPL)**.

This virus affects the bone marrow and gut lining of young cats and the spleen, liver and lymph nodes of older cats. It is spread by both direct and indirect contact and can survive away from a host for a considerable time. It is highly contagious, with an incubation period of two to nine days. The effects of the virus can be so sudden that it has been known for young cats to die before the owner notices any symptoms. More typically the cat becomes acutely depressed, refuses food and water, vomits and rapidly dehydrates. When you are nursing a cat with the virus it is vital to sterilise or destroy by incineration everything used, including clothing and footwear. A 0.5% solution of formalin has been found to inactivate the virus within 24 hours. The cat must be isolated during the illness and it is usual for a cattery to be quarantined for about six months after an outbreak to ensure that the virus is not passed on. In view of the virulency of the virus and the high mortality rate of affected cats it is essential that kittens are fully inoculated against FIE, and annual boosters are necessary to maintain antibody levels.

Feline Leukaemia Virus (FeLV)

Isolated in 1964, this virus was found to thrive in the lymphoid tissue and bone marrow of the cat – the areas that produce blood corpuscles. It only affects cats. It causes malignancy of the white blood cells and is associated with several fatal illnesses (including leukaemia and lymphoma) and forms of anaemia. It is more usually found in cats over three years of age. Kittens under eight weeks that come into contact with FeLV die very quickly. The virus is transmitted by direct contact, cat to cat, via saliva, urine, faeces, milk or nasal secretion, and in the uterus to unborn kittens. Once the cat is infected there are three possible results:

- 40% of cases make a complete recovery, eliminate the virus and develop an immunity.
- 30% of cases make an apparent recovery but the virus lies dormant in the bone marrow and may reactivate at a later date.
- 30% of cases show continued infection with the virus circulating in the bloodstream (viremic). Of these 80% die within three years. These persistently viremic cats show signs such as high temperature, lethargy, anorexia, enlarged lymph nodes. They can be further divided into neoplastic, exhibiting leukaemia and lymphosarcoma, and non-neoplastic, exhibiting infertility, non-regenerative anaemia, mouth ulcers and chronic infections – in other words, a cat that is persistently unwell, apparently recovers, then a few months later becomes ill again due to immunosuppression from the virus.

Cats in the last two groups may develop an immunity to FeLV-related diseases but not to the virus itself. They constantly excrete (shed) viruses and associated diseases and their kittens do not develop such an immunity. The incubation period of associated diseases ranges from a few weeks to several years, according to the type of disease. It was this variation that caused such difficulty in isolating FeLV itself. Since cats can produce protective immune responses, the presence of antibodies indicates exposure to the virus but not necessarily current infection. For this reason, tests for FeLV look for antigen. Cats vaccinated with the leukaemia vaccine do not give a positive reading when tested for FeLV. The kittens of a vaccinated queen have good immunity to the diseases, which will be maintained if they too are vaccinated. It is best to get all cats tested before considering vaccinating, as it is pointless to vaccinate cats that already carry the virus. Vaccinations are initially a course of two, followed by annual boosters. Kittens born to vaccinated queens do not need testing before vaccination provided that the vaccination is carried out before they are three months old, when the immunity they have retained from the queen has worn off.

Note Many breeders prefer not to have their kittens vaccinated against FeLV, cat flu and enteritis at the same time. This is because the potent combination of vaccines can make the kitten very unwell for a period.

Chapter 7

Feline Immunodeficiency Virus (FIV)

FIV causes the feline equivalent of human AIDS. It appears to be transmitted mainly by biting (a natural hazard during mating), so breeders are advised to have their cats tested for FIV at the same time as blood tests are made for FeLV. The tests for FIV look for antibodies, and a positive antibody titre (level of antibodies in the blood) indicates current infection. Cats may be infected long before symptoms start to appear, even several years. Infection is seen as an initial period of mild disease characterised by lethargy, anorexia and swollen lymph nodes, lasting for several weeks to months. This may be followed by a period of several months of apparent health, but eventually the immune system begins to fail and the disease becomes terminal.

Feline Infectious Peritonitis (FIP)

This viral disease is invariably fatal, and there is no accurate test other than biopsy or post mortem, no reliable vaccine and no cure. It is still uncertain how the disease is contracted. FIP attacks the liver, kidneys and other organs and causes leakage of fluid into the abdomen (see **Ascites**). Tests for FIP look for a positive coronavirus (group of specific viruses) antibody presence, but FIP is only one of the feline coronaviruses that cause a range of diseases from slight diarrhoea to full blown FIP, so an antibody-positive test result may or may not indicate the presence of FIP. Cats with a high antibody-positive level may recover without ever contracting FIP; however, according to Langford Veterinary College, there have been cats with negative coronavirus antibody levels that have died of FIP. Generally, less than 10% of antibody-positive cats contract FIP, but coronavirus antibody-positive cats should not be bred from.

Feline Panleucopenia (FPL)

See **Feline Infectious Enteritis (FIE)** (page 118).

Feline Viral Rhinotracheitis (FVR)

See **Cat Flu** (page 115).

Feline Urolithiasis Syndrome (FUS)

Also known as **Feline Lower Urinary Tract Disease (FLUTD)**. Cats can suffer from 'stones' in both the bladder and kidney, which may be small specks of crystal or, in extreme cases, the size of a plum-stone, but are normally present as fine gravel-like material. This urinary gravel irritates the bladder walls, causing cystitis and, in male cats particularly, can block the urethra. Early signs are the cat spending a lot of time in the litter tray trying to urinate, straining and possibly crying in pain, tail twitching and excessive washing under the tail. These early signs are very similar to those of constipation. If in any doubt, treat them as signs of FUS. Do not hesitate to consult your vet; a blockage must be treated immediately, or it can be fatal. Treatment may involve a combination of diet change, drugs and surgery.

Flat Chested Kittens (FCK)

See chapter 9.

Kennel Cough (Bordetellosis)

Bordetella bronchiseptica is the bacterium that causes kennel cough in both cats and dogs. In cats, the symptoms are coughing and sneezing, and there may also be discharge from the nose and eyes for a few days. The condition is easily treated with antibiotics. Since the bacterium inhabits the surface of the mucous membranes, rather than entering the bloodstream, the treatment is usually administered intra-nasally (in other words, as nose drops). It is called *kennel cough* because it is more commonly seen where there is a concentration of animals in confined quarters, such as kennels or catteries. The cats that are affected often have a history of exposure to dogs with the infection, but cats have also been known to contract the infection at the larger and busier cat shows.

Kidney diseases

About 25% of cats over the age of nine years have some form of chronic kidney disease. It may take months or even years for an owner to be aware of the symptoms. It may be caused by a great variety of problems, ranging from infection to congenital abnormality and heart disease. The disease progresses so slowly that often the cat is able to compensate for some time. Then the signs appear rapidly, so that we are given the impression that it has 'happened overnight'. Signs include excessive drinking and/or urinating, weight loss, lethargy, depressed appetite, poor coat condition, occasional vomiting, bad breath and anaemia. It is important that a cat with kidney problems does not become dehydrated. Veterinary advice and treatment is essential; if it is diagnosed early enough, correct treatment can retard or even halt progressive chronic nephritis. Unfortunately, the problem is often diagnosed late into the progress of the disease and treatment can then only alleviate the cat's discomfort for a period. Euthanasia is recommended in severe cases.

Ophthalmia neonatum

See **Eye problems** in chapter 9.

Pyometra

This is a hormonal condition of the uterus. Structural changes, often due to ovarian cysts, lead to a thickening of the wall of the uterus and the development of microscopic cysts. This results in inflammation and eventually the production of a purulent fluid filling the uterus. Symptoms include enlargement of the abdomen, discharge from the vulva, lethargy, loss of appetite and condition and vomiting. If caught soon enough it may be treated with drugs but often it isn't noticed in time and the only treatment is the removal of the uterus and ovaries. Pyometra may be fatal if not treated in time, but it is no longer a case for automatic euthanasia.

Skin cancer

White and very pale cats are particularly at risk from the effects of ultra-violet radiation. If not diagnosed in time, it may be fatal. The cat's ears and nose are most vulnerable. You can protect your cat by keeping it indoors during the period of most intensive radiation (in the United Kingdom between 10.00 am and 4.00 pm), even if the sky is overcast; if this isn't possible, you can apply a total sun block (one suitable for children) twice daily along the inside and outside edge of the ears. This is also useful for cats who insist on sitting all day in a sunny window, as they can get sunburn through the window.

PARASITES

Fortunately, few of the parasites affecting our cats are of any danger to us, but they should never be taken lightly. Many potential health risks are involved, which can be quite debilitating and cause considerable loss of condition and quality of life in a severely affected cat. It may not be possible to prevent occasional infestation, but there is no reason to allow cats to suffer when protection against parasites is usually simple and relatively inexpensive.

Fleas

Fleas are widespread and very active, especially in warm weather. Prior to the advent of central heating, the flea population decreased considerably in the

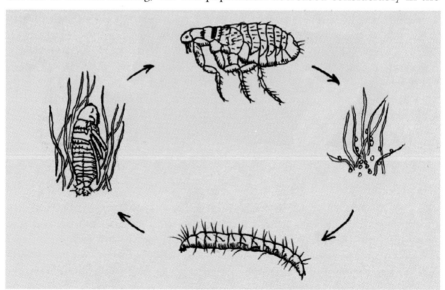

The life cycle of the flea: egg, larva, pupa, adult.

colder months, but now the flea is a full-time pest. The cat and human flea are different species, but people may still be bothered by the occasional flea bite, although the risks are slight. Fleas are blackish brown, shiny and about 1.5mm (a sixteenth of an inch) long. They live on the blood of animals, and it is the biting that causes the cat irritation and discomfort. Some cats may also have allergic reactions to fleas bites. The usual places to see flea dirt are at the base of the tail, at the base of the ears and under the chin, or you may see the flea itself. There are a many proprietary treatments to eradicate and control fleas. If in doubt consult your vet. Fleas carry worm eggs.

Lice

Lice are small and slow moving, and they may be seen in the coat looking like scurf. Lice eggs are tiny, clear and bead-like, usually cemented to individual hairs, and they should be combed out and burned. Re-infestation is a problem, so follow veterinary advice carefully.

Mites

Ear mites are seen as a dark waxy substance in the ear, which often has an unpleasant odour. Ear mites are relatively easy to control but spread easily to other animals in the household. The symptoms of ear mites may also be produced by other parasites or other forms of otitis (ear inflammation).

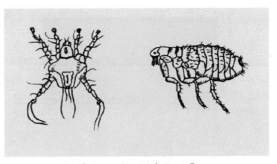

(Left) ear mite, (right) cat flea.

Ticks

These are blue/grey and look like warts. They attach themselves firmly to the cat's skin by biting, so they must not be pulled off; otherwise the head may remain and cause infection. They suck the cat's blood and cause debilitation. Surgical spirit applied to the point of attachment usually makes the tick relax its jaws so that it can be removed with tweezers. The cat's skin should then be cleaned with a veterinary antiseptic and dried.

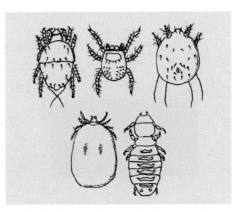

Top (left to right): fur mite, harvest mite, head mange mite.
Bottom (left to right): sheep tick, louse.

123

Chapter 7

Worms

The major internal parasites in this country are not blood suckers, but feed on microscopic particles of food inside the gut. A large number of such parasites in the stomach or bowels of a cat can interfere with the digestion seriously enough to cause poor condition in adults and threaten the life of kittens. A cat in poor condition is likely to contract other illnesses simply because it has less energy and reserves than a healthy cat. While the risk of worms passing from cat to person shouldn't be minimised, it should be kept in perspective, and habitual hygiene and common sense overcomes most potential problems. Pregnant women and young children are more at risk than other people.

> **Note:** Since the symptoms of worm infestation are similar to symptoms of a virus infection, it is most inadvisable to worm a sick cat without checking with a vet first.

Roundworms These can be several centimetres in length and look like thin garden worms. They may be coiled in a mass. Usually, few worms are found in the adult cat, but a cat that hunts and eats prey such as rabbits and birds may harbour them in considerable quantities unless treated regularly. Roundworms are passed easily from cat to cat through the thousands of microscopic eggs passed in the faeces. Once swallowed, these eggs hatch in the stomach and the hatched larvae travel in the bloodstream to muscle tissue

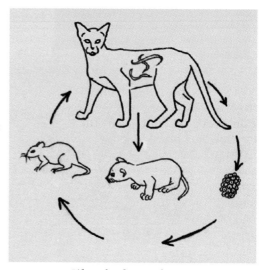

Life cycle of a roundworm.

or, in the pregnant cat, through the liver and lungs, where they are coughed up and swallowed, to grow to maturity in the stomach. In the larval stage, roundworms tend to become encysted in the muscle, where they generally cause no trouble in the male cat. In a pregnant queen the larvae can become activated by the effect of the cat's hormones and develop into mature worms, resulting in pre- and post-natal infestation of the kittens. A queen should be treated for roundworms before giving birth (preferably about six weeks into pregnancy) and again when the kittens are about six weeks of age. Young kittens may be severely retarded in growth and display abdominal distension and loss of appetite because of worm infestation. They may also suffer from the presence of the larval form of the worm, which migrates through the liver and lungs. The treatment for roundworms is no longer starvation: many tablets, liquids and creams are available to suit all ages. As the roundworm has a persistent life cycle, it may be in the cat at different stages at any one time, so a single dose is not enough. You will need to repeat the treatment again, according to the severity of the infestation.

Tapeworms These require intermediate hosts to complete their life cycle – possibly mice or rabbits, but usually fleas. The mature segments passed by the cat contain thousands of microscopic eggs, which stick to the cats fur and are swallowed by fleas, or may be hatched into soil and eaten by rodents. The tapeworm larva hatch in the new host and form worms. When that host is eaten by a cat, the cycle is completed. Thus it is important to eliminate not only the worm from the cat but also the intermediate host.

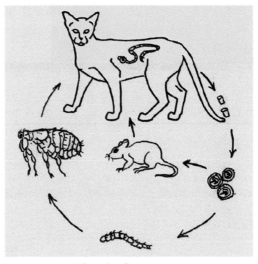
Life cycle of a tapeworm.

A tapeworm is a string of independent segments capable of existing alone, terminating in a sharp hook, the *scolex* (referred to as the *head*), which attaches itself to the lining of the intestine. The worm may be up to a metre long and is yellowish-white in appearance. The worm is more commonly found in adult cats than kittens, possibly because the adult is more skilled at grooming itself well enough to catch fleas. A cat may harbour more than one tapeworm at a time. The presence of a tapeworm may only be recognised when the mature segments start to appear via the rectum or with the faeces, or occasionally if the cat vomits a whole worm. When shed, the segments are alive and capable of movement and look rather like grains of rice. A tapeworm may be difficult to treat; if the whole worm, including the scolex, isn't eliminated the worm will regrow. Use a specific treatment and be sure to control fleas to prevent reinfection.

Lungworms These look like small roundworms and live in the pulmonary artery of the lung, causing respiratory symptoms and pneumonia. The cat can be infected by eating birds or rodents that are carrying the lungworm larvae. It is uncommon and not readily diagnosed by an owner: symptoms include persistent coughing, lethargy, depressed appetite and weight loss. This can be successfully treated by a vet.

Hookworms These are true blood-sucking worms and, if present in large quantities, can lead to debility and anaemia. They are more common in warmer climates and rarely causes problems in this country. They are only about a centimetre long and not easily recognised. Consult your vet if you suspect their presence.

Ringworm This is not a worm but a parasitic fungus. See the section about **Zoonoses** below.

ZOONOSES

From the Greek words *zoo* (meaning living, animal) and *nosis* (meaning disease), *zoonoses* are any diseases that can be transmitted to humans by animals. Fortunately, with the exception of rabies, no cat diseases present a significant risk to the healthy human.

Allergies

Strictly speaking, allergies are not zoonoses, but they are worthy of mention here. Allergies are caused by allergens, which are nearly always proteins. Common allergens are pollen, spores, hair, dander, oils, and saliva. Hay fevers are usually pollen-based, while a rash or other dermatitis (skin problem) is often oil-based. Those who suffer from allergic reactions usually do so

Friends: Romantica Sheba Noelle (choc), Adouzsh Hypnos (blue) and Romantica Rousseau (red).

because they lack either the enzyme necessary to break down the offending protein or the mechanism necessary to produce the required enzyme. For those who are highly allergic to anything, cats included, the first step should be to consult a specialist in the treatment of allergies.

Most people who are allergic to cats are sensitive to cat saliva, dander or fur. Cat fur comprises four types of hair: vibrissae (whiskers); guard hairs (the longest and oiliest hairs, which give the coat its sheen and water repellency); awn hairs (almost as long as guard hairs, giving the coat its density); and the layer of short, fine down hairs which act as the cat's temperature regulator. In a typical coat there are eight to ten times as many down hairs as there are awn hairs, and six to eight times as many awn hairs as there are guard hairs. Nearly all hairs shed by a cat are awn and guard hairs, which often cause a slight chipping of the dead skin (dander) around the hair follicle.

There is no such thing as a hypo-allergenic cat; even the so-called hairless Sphynx can provoke an allergic reaction by shedding dander. However, there are some steps that you can take to minimise the problem of your allergy:

- Groom your cat daily to prevent accumulation of loose fur.
- Wear a dust mask while emptying litter trays.
- Keep carpets, curtains, bedding (yours and your cat's) and surfaces as dust and hair-free as possible.
- The use of an ioniser or air purifier may help.

If you are usually allergic to cats you must consider to what degree you are prepared to put up with your allergy. It would be cruel to 'give it a try and see what happens' and then end up re-homing your Tonkinese through no fault of its own.

Cat bites and scratches

Please take cat bites and scratches seriously; the medical profession certainly does. Up to 50% of cat bites result in infection and, unless they are treated immediately, this increases to 100% after 12 hours. Naturally there is a greater risk of infection in those whose immune systems are diminished, such as infants, the elderly and those suffering any form of illness. The most common infection is *Pasteurella multocida*, which may be detected in the synovial (joint) and cerebrospinal (spinal column) fluids, but not always in the blood. Cat bites are primarily treated with Penicillin, or Tetracyclines and Chloramphenicol if you are allergic to Penicillin.

Keep up to date with your tetanus booster. A booster every ten years is normal but, for people who participate in any hobby or profession involving the regular handling of cats, a booster every three years is recommended. Keep all conditions as hygienic as possible. Some people are more sensitive to cat scratches than others. Have the wound treated immediately. Besides the obvious risks of local infection there is a comparatively rare disease known as 'cat scratch fever'. A cat bite or scratch can result in minor symptoms including headache, a mild fever, swelling of the lymph glands under the arm and a rash around the area of the scratch. These may be so mild that the recipient does not realise he or she is suffering from the disease but, more seriously, the disease may result in a very painful swelling or even hospitalisation. In extreme cases, cat scratch fever has been fatal.

Clean any scratch thoroughly with soap and water, apply a mild antiseptic and cover it with a light, breathable bandage to keep the dirt out. Check the scratch again in six to eight hours; it should show signs of healing by then. In the unlikely event there is inflammation or swelling, or if pain still persists, foreign matter may have entered the wound, so seek medical attention for possible infection. Always seek medical attention for deep scratches and any cat bite.

Rabies (Hydrophobia)

Rabies is a notifiable disease: the police must be informed immediately of any cases of rabies. Cats are far less liable to contract rabies than dogs, but the bite of any rabid animal can be fatal to humans. The disease is transmitted through saliva. The effects of rabies are swift and dramatic. Within a couple of days the animal becomes violent, savage, self-destructive and then paralysed, and death follows within days. Signs are foaming at the mouth and a vacant, wild staring. The rabid animal also has a morbid fear of water. Any infected animal must be destroyed. Anyone bitten by an animal suspected of having rabies must seek urgent medical treatment.

Ringworm (Feline Dermatophytosis)

Although the name suggests that this is a worm, it is actually a fungal parasite that feeds on the protein *keratin*, which is found in large quantities in skin, hair and nail tissue. The fungal parasite commonly found in cats and dogs is *Microsporum canis*. It may be transmitted to a human from a cat or vice versa. Some cats show no initial symptoms but pass the parasite on to other cats, and some only have a small thinning patch of fur, but severe cases exhibit larger bald patches (not always circular), crusted and infected. The lesions are commonly found on the head, face, tail and forepaws, but any part of the body may be infected. If you suspect ringworm in your cat, see a veterinary surgeon immediately. Treatment will be prescribed and may also be prescribed for your other cats as a preventive measure. Be sure to inform your vet if you have an expectant queen, because some treatments for ringworm (for example, Griseofulvin) cause deformity in unborn kittens.

Ringworm is not fatal and is easily treated, but it is highly infectious and it takes a long time to eradicate it from the household. The spores can remain in the environment for over six months, particularly in wood and paper. For this reason, the GCCF has set up a trust to look into this depressing infection. Cats known to have ringworm must be completely isolated from other cats, cat owners and anything to do with the cat fancy. Eradication is helped by careful hygienic precautions. The use of disposable bedding is necessary, and anti-fungal disinfectants or bleach should be used wherever possible. Regular vacuuming of carpets and soft furnishings may also help.

Toxoplasmosis

If a woman catches this disease during pregnancy there is a substantial risk that her child will become infected; this has given rise to the annual media scare about the risk of keeping or handling cats. I am grateful to the Toxoplasmosis Trust (see **Useful Addresses**) for providing information on this subject.

Toxoplasmosis is an infection caused by the parasite *Toxoplasma gondii*, a single-cell organism invisible to the naked eye. It is found in meat, cat faeces and the soil in which cats defecate. It can affect almost all mammals, most of which are infected at some time in their life. Once infected, the host never entirely rids itself of the parasite, which usually remains dormant for the natural life of that host. Toxoplasmosis is not dangerous in normal healthy adults or children; it is only dangerous if their immune systems are undeveloped or depressed. Toxoplasmosis is very difficult to diagnose in adults, because symptoms range from none at all to mild flu-like symptoms, or occasionally a prolonged and debilitating glandular fever type of illness. Once a person has had the disease they are protected for life unless they suffer from an impairment to their immune system. If a woman catches the disease during pregnancy it is likely to cross the placenta to the foetus and, if infected during early pregnancy, the baby may be miscarried or stillborn; if infected later in pregnancy the baby may suffer severe abnormalities or disabilities.

Toxoplasmosis is caught by eating anything infected with the parasite. The principal source of infection in humans is believed to be uncooked or partially-cooked meat. The significance of the cat is that it is the only known host in which the reproductive cycle of the parasite takes place. The domestic cat catches the disease by eating birds, mice or other raw meat. It sheds the infectious organism in its faeces for 14 days after becoming infected, after which time a healthy cat will not normally be a source of infection again. However, sick cats may re-shed infected faeces. The faeces only become infectious 24 hours or more after leaving the cat's body. In the earth, cats' faeces may remain infective for up to 18 months. There is no risk of catching toxoplasmosis from cat's urine or saliva, or from handling or stroking cats, and you are most unlikely to catch it from a cat bite or scratch.

Precautions: Always wash your hands before handling food or eating; always wash fruit and vegetables before eating them; cook meat thoroughly. When gardening wear gloves and avoid hand-to-mouth contact. Clean litter trays daily (minimum), using gloves and a scoop, and scrub the tray out weekly

Chapter 7

(minimum); clean up any accidental soiling thoroughly and promptly. Be especially careful if you are pregnant; if possible get someone else to clean out litter trays and pens. **Remember:** you have to swallow the organism to catch the infection.

BEHAVIOURAL PROBLEMS

We are becoming increasingly aware and more understanding of feline psychology. Not before time – pity the poor cats who were thrown out into the cold night as a matter of course, or the kittens who had their noses rubbed in urine when they strayed from the litter trays! As intelligent creatures, cats have as vast a range of psychological behaviour patterns as we do, often complicated (for us that is) by their apparent lack of social conscience. The subject of behavioural problems is beyond the scope of this book but there are several good books on the subject, including *Claws and Purrs*

Brown Tonkinese kitten.

and *Do Cats Need Shrinks?*, both by Peter Neville. However, I would like to touch briefly on the subject of the *aggressive cat*.

It is important to remember that kittens are feline children, so are not responsible for their actions. They often bite or scratch without even being aware that they are doing so, thus inflicting pain or injury. As these wounds are unconsciously inflicted, injury can easily occur to an eye or face. Cats have an instinctive knowledge of the value of eyes and will not attack them unless they feel utterly threatened, but they may well scratch the face close to the eye as a strong warning. Adult cats can normally place their bites or scratches precisely; the exceptions are the unintentional injuries inflicted by a cat in panic. For example, don't be caught holding a cat or kitten in your arms when a friendly dog jumps up at you!

A Tonkinese is mentally and physically active and needs stimulation to prevent it from becoming bored. Bored cats can be destructive, but cats are never ill-tempered, destructive or dirty without good reason – they don't misbehave deliberately. You should never punish a cat; instead, look for the cause of the aberrant behaviour and put it right. Cats don't have a social conscience as we understand it and, since they are not aware of the concepts of right and wrong, you are simply inflicting a form of torture if you punish them.

EUTHANASIA AND BEREAVEMENT

Eastern cultures have many traditions concerning death, but Western cultures are uneasy with the concept. From an early age it seems to be a closed subject, so we don't discuss our feelings about it. Consequently, we are often confused and frightened by our reactions. The depth of grief we feel and the manner in which we express it is highly subjective, but there is usually a common pattern. There is the initial shock of the event itself, however long we may have had to prepare for it; coming to terms with finality; understanding the pain of loss and anger at the obscenity of meaningless activities continuing around us, oblivious to the importance of our loss; guilty acceptance that life must go forward, regardless of its missing element. In grief we experience most, or all, of these emotions. When a beloved cat dies we are faced with the insensitivity of people who never understand how deeply we feel such a loss: 'Why are you so upset? It was only an animal!' This reaction often makes us suppress our feelings and grief behaviour; the pain is difficult enough to bear without having to cope with ignorant ridicule. For many people the loss of a pet is as painful as the loss of a child, but it isn't 'socially acceptable' to grieve in the same way. Nevertheless, we need to grieve, and it may take a long time to come to terms with our feelings.

Making the decision

A terminally-ill pet depends upon us to relieve its pain promptly in the kindest possible manner, but making the decision in favour of euthanasia is traumatic. Logically, we know we have made a humane decision; simultaneously and illogically, we suspect that the decision to have our cat put to sleep was precipitant. Guilt is so difficult to come to terms with. At some time you probably will have to make the decision to have a cat put to sleep painlessly, so bear in mind that the feelings of guilt and precipitancy are quite normal. An increasing number of centres offer grief counselling, and the Society for Companion Animal Studies produces useful booklets about animal bereavement (see **Useful Addresses**). It may help you to make the right decision if you ask yourself these questions:

- Is my cat getting any pleasure out of life? Does it still enjoys its food and react with pleasure to my attentions, or is it persistently suffering from digestive and toilet problems and difficulty in moving around its home? Does it exhibit pain and/or fear when I touch it and complete withdrawal from any stimulus?
- What will happen if my cat doesn't receive adequate treatment?
- Am I equating my cat's difficulties with my own? A cat doesn't suffer

Chapter 7

the emotional stress that we would over the loss of a limb, sight or hearing.

- Have I fully discussed prognosis and treatment options with my vet?
- If I'm not entirely happy with my vet's advice, have I sought a second opinion?
- Will the benefits my cat gets from treatment outweigh the pain it will have to endure during the treatment?
- Even if my cat makes a temporary recovery or reprieve from pain, has its quality of life really improved?
- Have I explored every valid medical option, including alternative treatment such as homeopathy and acupuncture?
- Am I doing everything possible to make my cat comfortable and to relieve its pain and depression?
- Am I capable of giving my cat the care, attention and nursing needed?
- Am I keeping my cat alive because I feel guilty about having it put to sleep?
- Have I fully discussed/explained the need for euthanasia with the rest of the members of the family? (Don't add to your difficulties by making yourself the villain.)

Caspar (right, lilac) with Fable.

Barely two weeks after I had written the above, Mike and I had to make the very painful decision to have our wonderful Caspar put to sleep. He was only four-and-a-half years old, but a lymphoid tumour of the lungs had been diagnosed and there was no prospect of recovery. While still feeling the raw pain of the loss of our gentle giant, I can assure you that, because we considered all these questions before we made our decision, we have been given a clarity of mind and a small measure of comfort in the midst of our grief.

What is involved in euthanasia?

A subject we don't like to discuss is the process of euthanasia and what happens afterwards. Although you may prefer your vet to come out to your home, it is often better to have your cat put to sleep at the surgery where the vet has the help of a nurse and the ideal facilities to carry out the task. Naturally, you are going to be upset so, for your own sake, make an appointment outside the usual surgery hours; your vet will understand. If you are particularly distressed, your vet may prefer you not to be present, as your distress may upset your cat. However, many people wish to be with their cats at this time and are often surprised and relieved at how painless and quick the procedure is.

Euthanasia is nearly always carried out by the injection of an overdose of barbiturate – a drug used in much lower doses as an anaesthetic. The injection may be given intravenously in the front leg or, in the case of elderly cats that have become thin, directly into an organ such as the kidney. The only discomfort is the slight pricking of the needle. Within seconds, the cat becomes unconscious, the heart stops functioning and the cat dies peacefully. Don't worry if you notice some slight muscle twitching, bowel evacuation or apparent sighs of breath: these are reflex actions of the body and do not mean that the cat is still alive.

The resting place

Whether your cat is put to sleep or dies naturally you'll need to decide upon a final resting place. It's unlikely that you'll feel up to discussing details with your vet or pet cemetery service at the time of your bereavement, so it's far better to consider these matters beforehand. Veterinary surgeries are obliged to dispose of animals that are put to sleep at surgeries in a lawfully prescribed manner, which could mean deep burial in a landfill site or incineration. However, many surgeries can arrange for pets to be cremated, or they may permit you to take your cat's body or ashes home with you for burial in your garden. To ensure that the body is not disturbed, make the grave about a metre deep. It is often a comfort to mark the grave with a special stone or plant. Burying your pet with its favourite blanket or toys is also a comfort, as this involves some ceremony and helps you to say your farewells. You might feel that a pet cemetery is a more suitable and permanent alternative to home burial. Your vet should be able to advise you and may be able to arrange for the cemetery staff to collect your cat's body from the surgery. The pet cemetery staff should be able to help with the burial, the choosing of a casket and headstone. Make sure that you know what is involved in their services: what their fees are, whether there is an annual maintenance fee, and whether the cemetery is on consecrated ground – if it is not, the land may be sold later for

A final place resting place.

development. It may seem callous to consider such mundane questions at this time, but it will prevent possible further distress later on.

Chapter 7

Feline bereavement

Do cats grieve, or do we simply assign our own emotions to our pets when we are in a state of bereavement? We readily accept 'pining' (languishing, and

Cats make their own relationships: Adhirsh Cato Redbaron (red) with Learoyd Serendipity (blue).

growing weak with pain and grief) in a dog, but not so readily in a cat. Perhaps this is because lethargy in a dog is more obvious and, whereas a dog whines, which we can equate with our own crying, a cat normally suffers in silence.

Cats do grieve. They are reasoning creatures who develop specific social relationships.

An example of a person assigning her own emotions is the woman who had two cats, one of which was run over and killed outside the home. The woman was 'devastated' (*sic*) and the dead cat's brother lost its appetite and sat throughout the day on the pavement near the site of the accident. The woman couldn't bear to see the cat upset and, after one week, she took him to the vet and arranged for him to be put to sleep. She claimed that the cat couldn't come to terms with the loss of his brother, but her decision was more likely based on the fact that the cat was a constant reminder of her loss.

When we lose a beloved cat we choose one of three alternatives:

- We immediately get another cat, either to fill the painful gap in our lives or as a 'replacement' cat. The latter is always a mistake, since each cat makes its own place in our hearts and is irreplaceable.

• We decide we can't ever go through such pain again and don't have another cat.
• We give ourselves time for mourning and reorganisation of our lives before taking in another cat.

Although there are times when grief is not a factor (indeed, in certain cases the survivor may positively bloom, often when it has been subdued or dominated by the deceased), if the household has a grieving cat the effects of our decision are even more significant for the cat than for ourselves. We may expect a newcomer to be the peer of our cat, but they will always establish their own relationships.

Sometimes we have to accept that extra love and attention isn't enough and steps may have to be taken, however painful, for good of the grieving cat. Such a case is that of Claude, whose feline partner, Jaom, developed a fatal pancreatic illness and had to be put to sleep. The family was very upset, but Claude became distraught; he refused all food and began to chew his front paws. Despite veterinary treatment, Claude continued to mutilate himself, and the vet had to put him on a drip when he became dehydrated. Nothing could be found to interest him and the family began to think it would be kinder to have him put to sleep. As a last resort, they contacted a couple whose own cat had recently died and told them about Claude. It was then decided to see if Claude would respond to a complete change of environment. He was taken to the couple's home and gently placed in a basket beside the lounge fire. Whether it was the complete absence of Jaom's scent, the strange appearance of the room or the new voices of the couple, Claude started to take an interest in his surroundings for the first time since Jaom died.

Claude didn't look back. He had the devoted attention of the couple, and lived contentedly for several years afterwards. Although the family had to cope with the loss of both Claude and Jaom, there was considerable comfort in knowing that Claude was alive and well.

How can we help a grieving cat?
In cases of pet bereavement we have the advantage of knowing in advance that behavioural changes may be expected and should keep a close watch for signs.

How can we help our cats come to terms with their loss when we don't really understand what they are feeling? We usually know when a person wants comforting or to be left alone and generally people deal with the death either by ignoring and forgetting the matter (in which instance grief plays little or no part) or by understanding and coming to terms with it. It's difficult to help a grieving animal and, while time may heal all, the immediate future may be critical to a cat's physical and psychological well-being. Since we are unable to communicate with our pets in depth we cannot apply the usual abstract consolations such as discussing their bereavement,

Chapter 7

reviewing happy memories and building a future. We must be practical and, although the symptoms of grief may be psychologically and/or practically dealt with, it has to be remembered that grief is an emotion and the cause cannot be remedied.

First we must accept that the cat is not developing anti-social habits; vigilance, tolerance and patience is required from us. After a period of time (which cannot be specified) the cat will probably come to terms with the absence in its life but, during its mourning period, we need to be more tolerant than usual: cats, like people, should be allowed to express their grief to overcome it. We are more able to accept the death of a person or pet if we actually see the deceased, and the same applies to our pets. If at all possible, allow your cat to see and smell the body of the deceased to help it understand that its friend has died rather than disappeared. Animals accept death more readily, because they are not encumbered with such concepts as faith and perpetuity. Make sure that the surviving cat isn't placed under any further stress at this time. For instance, don't introduce new animals to the house too soon, even if it's what you need, and don't chastise the cat for anti-social behaviour. If there is a companion animal or human in the house during the day, complete confinement to the house may be advisable for a while, provided that the cat doesn't react too strongly to it, as it gives the cat a prolonged period of companionship. If the cat believes that it too might be 'taken away' it may become defensively aggressive; reassure it by spending extra time in the same room, without making overt attempts to confine it, such as by picking it up, by following it around, or by looking at it continually. Offer small, tempting meals several times a day to a cat that has gone off its food, but consult your vet if it refuses to eat for more than a couple of days, especially if it isn't taking in fluids.

Self-mutilation must be handled very carefully. Such an extreme reaction to the loss of a companion cannot usually be dealt with simply by diverting the cat's attention, and the use of an elizabethan collar might induce more stress-related behaviour. Spend extra time with the cat, if it permits you to, calming and reassuring it by talking, stroking and perhaps grooming it. Let it sleep in your room in case it needs to be reassured during the night. Injuries must be treated by a vet but very small skin abrasions can be dealt with at home, using a veterinary antiseptic, to avoid the added stress of transporting the cat to the vet. In extreme cases, where the cat will not tolerate company and the self-mutilation is persistent, it might be advisable, after discussion with your vet, to have the cat mildly sedated for a couple of days to help it over the initial stages of its grief. The careful use of anti-depressant and/or anti-anxiety drugs has proved beneficial in such cases, particularly when the self-mutilation is triggered by grief and has not been habitual behaviour, and mild sedation can also improve the appetite.

Over-attachment must be dealt with sensitively. It is understandable that a cat who has lost a companion might fear the loss of others in the household and be reluctant to be left alone, but this could become a permanent habit. Constant companionship with your cat may be consoling for you both but it shouldn't be permitted to continue for long. The cat should be distanced from you very gradually until it realises that, even when it cannot see or hear you, it has not been abandoned. In an extreme case a kitten pen would be very useful as it is large enough to contain a litter tray and cat bed quite comfortably. The cat may be kept in the pen in the room with you, reassured by your presence, without having to be in constant physical contact. Let it out of the pen several times a day for food and a cuddle so that it knows it's not being permanently confined, and take the pen into your room at night. After a while the pen may be

Ishokat's Beki Saffron with Biba Belle.

placed in a different room within earshot, so that the cat knows you're there even if it cannot see you, and is still let out frequently for your attention. If possible, encourage it to return to the pen by itself and, once it has done so a couple of times, you can leave the pen door open. It is essential to make these steps gradually and firmly so that the cat is encouraged to return to a normal affectionate relationship with you, knowing that it will not be abandoned.

Although our verbal communication with our cats is limited, empathetic relationships with cats do exist. Cats are sensitive to changes in our emotions, which is why vets sometimes prefer to put a cat to sleep without the presence of anxious and distressed owners. As well as having to cope with the loss of a companion a cat also has to cope with the changes in our behaviour. In the earliest stages of grief we are often unusually subdued:

Give sorrow words: the grief that does not speak whispers the o'er-fraught heart, and bids it break. MACBETH (IV:iii)

Making provision

One final point in this chapter – you should consider what will happen to your cats should you die before them. Make provision in your will for your cats and their care. The Cats Protection League and RSPCA (see **Useful Addresses**) both produce cards to carry so that your cats may be cared for in the event of accidents or emergencies. If possible, make arrangements with a person that you trust to find homes for your cats, making sure that you have their agreement before you write it into a will and allowing them the flexibility to make the most suitable arrangements. Make sure that instructions to contact this person are easily and immediately available.

Chapter: 8
The mating game

BUSINESS OR PLEASURE?

Breeding Tonkinese should not be considered a business but a self-supporting hobby, in which the welfare of the cats and the breed as a whole must be the primary concern. There are three categories of breeder:

- *Pet owners* who have one or two litters from their queen because *it would be nice to have kittens*; perhaps the aim is to recover the cost of the pet or to keep one of the kittens as company for their pet.
- *Professional breeders.* By definition a 'professional' is one able to make a living from an activity or interest in which enthusiasts and amateurs engage; when related to breeding animals it is usually referred to as *farming* unless the animal in question is rare and/or commands a very high price or the breeder also runs a cattery as a business.
- *Well-informed enthusiasts*, from the breeder with just one queen to those with larger feline households. In this category there are even rare enthusiasts who are able to make some profit from their hobby.

Cuddly Romantica kittens. Think very carefully before you decide to breed a litter.

If you are thinking of having just one litter from your pet, please consider that you will be putting her through the strains of calling, pregnancy, birth and a late spaying just for the 'fun' of having kittens. It is also worth noting that a breeder's first litter is by far the most expensive. For example, even before your queen is mated, the cost of her blood test and the stud fee represent most of the price of one kitten. If you are concerned that your pet needs company, why not get a pair of kittens from the same litter to begin with? It's wonderful for them to grow up together, and leaves the worries, hard work and expense to the breeder, who already has the knowledge, experience and facilities for breeding cats. It is a complete fallacy that a female cat needs to have kittens.

If you are seriously thinking of breeding Tonkinese then, although breeding shouldn't be treated as a business, it doesn't mean that proven business practices shouldn't be employed.

Establish your objectives

Why are you breeding? Do you have a breed programme planned for the future that considers temperament, colours, patterns, type and bloodlines – working either on your own or in conjunction with another breeder? How far are you prepared to travel to take your queen to a suitable stud and, more importantly, how far is your queen happy to travel? For how long and how often do you intend to breed from a particular queen? Can you cope with several queens and their litters? Do you have the time, space, resources, energy and family support? Are you intending to breed often enough to invest in a prefix? Do you have a suitable vet, one who is happy to cater for the extra needs of a breeder? Can you afford the expenses? Can you offer all your cats a lifestyle that suits their needs? Are you prepared to be responsible for the lives you bring into this world?

Produce a product that people want

Do some market research. What did you look for when you first bought your Tonkinese? There is plenty of competition from other breeders, so consider carefully what you want to offer: good temperament is essential. Which colours are you planning to breed? Will you get what you desire from a particular mating? Take advice from the stud owner on colours, but remember that in the end you alone are responsible for the stud you choose and the resulting colours and type. When you have kittens to offer they must be healthy, fit and well balanced temperamentally. If you want to get the best from your cats they must be given the best in nutrition, environment and loving companionship.

Charge a price that people will pay

Financially your objective is to break even or, hopefully, to make a small profit to put back into the next litter. The first litter is normally the most expensive because of the initial outlay on equipment such as heating pads, bedding, maternity pen and extra food bowls. When setting a price for your kittens, consider your overheads: vet's fees (for inoculations, blood tests and unforseen treatments), stud fees, extra heating, advertising, foods and materials during the queen's pregnancy and the 12 or more weeks of rearing kittens, and so on. All of this has to be balanced against a price that people will pay for your kittens: a price that is generally standard among breeders of Tonkinese.

Find the correct market

Where should you advertise? Where did you look for your Tonkinese? Ask experienced breeders where and where not to advertise. To attract suitable customers you'll need to sell yourself, as reflected in the way your cats behave and the way in which they are seen to be treated. Your advertisements will always be in competition in breeders' directories: a surname beginning with

Chapter 8

'A' has an obvious advantage over one beginning with 'W'. Elsewhere you can make your advertisement distinctive. Think about your logo, typeface and the photographs you use. Keep a record of your advertisements: where, for how long, the costs and the response. This helps to build up a valuable picture of cost-effective advertising. Keep a note of people who refer prospective owners to you and return the compliment when you can. We don't always have kittens, and a network of friendly breeders is by far the most effective way to sell them. If you want the best homes for your kittens it's important to vet your prospective owners. They should certainly vet you regarding the condition of your cats and the way they are raised.

These points are just the start. With all worthwhile activities the most important maxim is, 'If in doubt ask, and if you don't understand, ask someone else!' Ask questions of more experienced breeders and read up on your subject – there are many good reference books. Keep in mind that, if you ask specific questions about feline behaviour, you'll get a variety of answers because each person's answer is based upon experience of their individual cats. Once your hobby is actually managed by you, and not just in the hands of time and luck, you will find it to be a genuine pleasure.

YOUR HEALTH

(See also the section about **ZOONOSES** in chapter 7)
This aspect of breeding cats is often forgotten or taken for granted. A calm disposition is always advantageous (kittens, queens and potential new owners can all be trials) and you'll need plenty of time to spend with developing kittens. You need a strong back unless you have raised facilities and a housemaid, as you will be bending up and down like a yo-yo, especially when the kittens are being weaned and using their litters trays. You'll need to keep up to date with your tetanus boosters, and you'll need plenty of time and energy to spend with developing kittens – I know I've mentioned it already, but this is so important it bears repeating.

APPLYING FOR A PREFIX

A prefix is a breeder's identifier. If you intend to have just one or two litters there is no benefit in owning a prefix but, if you are going to continue breeding, a prefix is worthwhile. The reason for this will become very clear when you start to look for studs for your queens. Particular bloodlines may be more desirable in terms of compatibility of type, coat pattern and colour quality. More to the point, you'll want to study the bloodlines to ensure that you are not mating your cat with one too closely related to your own or known to exhibit or carry faults. A particular advantage of owning a prefix is that, as the quality of your cats becomes known among breeders and exhibitors, you'll find that people may specifically seek your kittens.

You should purchase your prefix from the authority with which you

SAMPLE ONLY

THE GOVERNING COUNCIL OF THE CAT FANCY
APPLICATION FOR PREFIX REGISTRATION

Office use only:
Application No: .... Batch File: .... Further selection: ....

APPLICANT (1)	APPLICANT (2) *(if joint prefix application)*
Surname	Surname ....
Christian name(s)	Christian name(s) ....
....	....
Mr./Mrs./Miss	Mr./Mrs./Miss ....

Full address ....

....

Telephone No: ....   Post Code ....

I/We acknowledge that in any matter relating to the breeding, exhibiting or treatment of cats or to any Cat Show I/we consent to be bound by and to submit to the Constitution and Rules of the Cat Fancy as the same may be amended from time to time.

PREFIX to be registered (please give names in order of preference)

(1)

Signature: ....
(Applicant 1)   (please sign — do not print)

(2)

Signature: ....
(Applicant 2)   (please sign — do not print)

(3)

Date of Birth if under 18: ....

Name of Parent/Guardian: ....
(block capitals, please)

(4)

Signed by Parent/Guardian: ....

(P.T.O. for additional choices)

To be completed by affiliated Cat Club Secretary: (IMPORTANT: Applicant(s) please note that YOUR Club Secretary must sign this section)

It is hereby certified that *Mr./Mrs./Miss ....

*Mr./Mrs./Miss ....   *delete where not applicable

is a member/are members of the ....

Signed: .... (Club Secretary)   Date: ....

IMPORTANT   Please read notes enclosed with this form

Please return this application form when completed, together with fee of £50.00 for single or joint application, to:

GCCF, 4-6 Penel Orlieu, Bridgwater, Somerset TA6 3PG

Office use only:
Date received by GCCF

This form is available from the GCCF for breeders wanting to buy their own prefixes.

intend to register your kittens. In the 1970s a prefix with the GCCF cost £5; today it costs £50 but, once approved, it's yours for life and remains unique to you. To apply for a GCCF prefix, complete the relevant form (obtainable

141

from the GCCF) and have it signed by the Secretary of an affiliated cat club, of which you must be a member. If your queen is pregnant you must have confirmation from the GCCF that they have received your application before she gives birth if you want to use your prefix for that particular litter. Even then, you are not allowed to use your prefix until it has been approved, which may take up to three months.

What happens if you don't have a prefix? In October 1982 the GCCF began to apply an administration prefix to kittens registered without a breeder's prefix. Each year the GCCF prefix changes and the prefix itself indicates whether the cat is long-haired (LO), short-haired (SH), Burmese (BU) or Siamese (AM). It also indicates the year in which the cat or kitten was registered by using abbreviations from a mixture of numerics. For example, the first year in which the GCCF applied their administration prefix was year ONE, so in 1982/1983 the GCCF prefix was ADONE. Therefore a Burmese kitten registered in that period without a breeder's prefix would have the GCCF prefix ADONEBU and a Siamese would have ADONEAM. The first GCCF prefix used for a Tonkinese, before official breed recognition, was ADREESH (ADministration prefix, year thREE, SHort hair category). So far the GCCF prefixes have been: ADONE (October 1982 to December 1983); ADUE (1984); ADREE (1985); ADQWE (1986); ADIVE (1987); ADIXI (1988); ADKRI (1989); ADHUI (1990); ADRAY (1991); ADDEI (1992); ADINN (1993); ADOUZ (1994); ADHIR (1995); ADQUA (1996); ADWEL (1997).

WORKING WITH THE TONKINESE BREED

When creating a breed of cat you must eventually stop using the parent breeds in your breeding programme. Before this happens it is necessary to have an agreed breed type. The obvious danger is that enthusiastic breeders may race to 'fix' what they believe to be the ideal type by substantial inbreeding. The example of Milan Greer (see chapter 2), who bred five generations of Golden Siamese (Tonkinese) from cats who were closely-

Burmese queen Chamboza Maiway with her first-generation Tonkinese kittens.

related, demonstrates that it is possible to lose the integrity of the breed for the sake of a particular line. Milan Greer believed he had bred five generations true but, possibly because it was inbred, his line was not producing the range of coat patterns that we now know must exist within a well-balanced Tonkinese breeding programme.

A good Tonkinese breeding programme has two objectives: to produce Tonkinese as described in the Standard of Points and to produce subsequent generations that improve as a result of careful and selective breeding. To perpetuate the Tonkinese as a breed (rather than cross-bred Burmese x Siamese offspring with the tonkinese coat pattern) we need to breed Tonkinese with Tonkinese, and to do this there must be sufficient studs from healthy and unrelated lines to establish firm breed foundations. It would be most unwise to sacrifice a healthy gene pool for the sake of rapid promotion in show status.

This breeding programme is being followed by all conscientious Tonkinese breeders, using only Tonkinese and Tonkinese variants of vigorous health, good type, good coat-colour, good eye colour and excellent temperament.

1   *First mating:* Burmese x Siamese, producing first-generation Tonkinese. This should remain in practice until the Tonkinese gene pool is considered substantial enough, at which time such matings will become undesirable for the progression of the breed. This is indicated in the Tonkinese registration policy.

G C, R W Connacht's Caramel Quinn of Lenape DM (choc) with kittens.

Chapter 8

2 *Second mating:* 1st generation Tonkinese x 1st generation Tonkinese producing 2nd generation Tonkinese variants (Burmese coat pattern), Tonkinese with the tonkinese coat pattern and Tonkinese variants (Siamese coat pattern), in a ratio of 25:50:25 respectively.

3 *Subsequent matings may be:*
  a Tonkinese x Tonkinese, producing subsequent generations of Tonkinese and Tonkinese variants (in the ratio given in 2 above).
  b Tonkinese x Tonkinese variant (Burmese coat pattern), producing Tonkinese and Tonkinese variants (Burmese coat pattern) in a ratio of 50:50.
  c Tonkinese x Tonkinese variant (Siamese coat pattern), producing Tonkinese and Tonkinese variants (Siamese coat pattern) in a ratio of 50:50.
  d Tonkinese variant (Burmese coat pattern) x Tonkinese variant (Siamese coat pattern) producing all Tonkinese with the tonkinese coat pattern.

Ideally you would mate first generation Tonkinese with first generation Tonkinese, second with second, and so on. However, this is not critical as long as the ancestries of the queen and stud are equally balanced Burmese/Siamese. Where you have an imbalance of Burmese/Siamese, you may be able to redress the balance by appropriate selection of the breeding pair. On the page opposite I have given an example of a second-generation Tonkinese kitten. There are several points worth noting about this pedigree:

•The kitten's dam (2) is well-balanced Burmese x Siamese, resulting in first generation Tonkinese.
•The kitten's sire (1) is, at first sight, unbalanced, with a predominance of Siamese.
•The first generation Tonkinese dam (10) is the result of Burmese x Siamese, and may be of good type. Her progeny, dam (4), is likely to be more Burmese in type because she is from a back-cross, Tonkinese x Burmese. Dam (4) is still first generation.
•The back-cross mating of dam (4) x Siamese sire (3) may correct any imbalance of the dam's Burmese type in the resulting progeny, sire (1), who is still first generation. Ideally it would have been better to mate dam (4) with a Tonkinese that is more Siamese in type, as this would have resulted in second generation Tonkinese with more balanced type.
•The next logical step in this breeding programme would be to mate the second generation Tonkinese kitten with a good Tonkinese of balanced breeding, ideally second generation.

Tonkinese Kitten (2nd Generation)

Parents	Grandparents	Great-grandparents	Great-great-grandparents
Sire (1) TONKINESE (1st Generation)	Sire (3) SIAMESE	Sire (7) SIAMESE	Sire – SIAMESE (15)
			Dam – SIAMESE (16)
		Dam (8) SIAMESE	Sire – SIAMESE (17)
			Dam – SIAMESE (18)
	Dam (4) TONKINESE (1st Generation)	Sire (9) BURMESE	Sire – BURMESE (19)
			Dam – BURMESE (20)
		Dam (10) TONKINESE (1st Generation)	Sire – BURMESE (21)
			Dam – BURMESE (22)
Dam (2) TONKINESE (1st Generation)	Sire (5) SIAMESE	Sire (11) SIAMESE	Sire – SIAMESE (23)
			Dam – SIAMESE (24)
		Dam (12) SIAMESE	Sire – SIAMESE (25)
			Dam – SIAMESE (26)
	Dam (6) BURMESE	Sire (13) BURMESE	Sire – BURMESE (27)
			Sire – BURMESE (28)
		Dam (14) BURMESE	Sire – BURMESE (29)
			Sire – BURMESE (30)

Chapter 8

What generation is my Tonkinese?

On several occasions I have been asked, 'How can I tell what generation my Tonkinese is?' Once we have pedigrees showing only Tonkinese breed numbers the question of generation will be irrelevant but, until then, there is a very simple formula you can use:

$$(\text{The } \textbf{Lower} \text{ Generation of the Parents} + 1)$$
$$=$$
$$(\text{The Generation of Their Kittens})$$

Confused? This table gives some examples and, for the sake of argument, I've called the Burmese and Siamese both generation 0.

Parents (Generation)	Formula	Offspring
Burmese (0) x Siamese (0)	0 + 1 = 1	Tonkinese, 1st generation
Burmese (0) x Tonkinese (1)	0 + 1 = 1	Tonkinese, 1st generation
Siamese (0) x Tonkinese (3)	0 + 1 = 1	Tonkinese, 1st generation
Tonkinese (1) x Tonkinese (2)	1 + 1 = 2	Tonkinese, 2nd generation
Tonkinese (2) x Tonkinese (4)	2 + 1 = 3	Tonkinese, 3rd generation

Choosing your queen

Choosing a queen, whether you breed your own or not, is probably the most important decision you will make, so do consider the questions posed in the **Business or pleasure?** section. Before you breed from your queen, make sure that:

• She is registered on the active register under your name (by ownership transfer if necessary).
• She is in excellent health and of suitable age, weight and temperament.
• Her vaccinations are up to date. If her boosters will be due during pregnancy or while she is nursing it is advisable to have them done at least one month before mating. Booster vaccinations can be highly dangerous to kittens developing in the womb.
• You will be with her when the kittens are born.

Choosing the right stud

Why does the stud appear to be more important than the queen? Within any breed there are far more queens than studs, so the studs available need to be of the best possible quality. When they prove to be so they are highly sought after. A stud is more in the public domain than a queen and his results, good or bad, are traceable and consistently more visible. Most breed clubs produce a stud book. Other places to find details of studs are cat shows, advertisements in cat magazines and by word of mouth.

Can you take a GCCF-registered queen to a CA-registered stud? The simple answer is, 'Yes', but you will have to register the kittens on the GCCF Reference register, which means that neither the kittens nor their progeny are eligible to be shown under the GCCF for three generations.

What are you looking for in a stud? The main considerations are good health, a clean bloodline known to be free of genetic abnormalities (including unrecognised colours), preferably a line which is unrelated to yours or at least

Adkrish Sittana (brown).

with the minimum of common ancestors, a stud who will give you the colours you want to breed and a stud who complements your queen. In other words, look for the best possible stud: one who is acknowledged to have good type, colour, coat pattern, strong eye colour and good temperament. Look for a balance of background breeding; if your queen's pedigree is weighted on the Burmese side then you might want to even it up with a stud whose pedigree shows more Siamese influence. Look for a stud that may help to counteract any weaknesses in your queen; for example if she has a shallow nose-break look for a near-perfect stud who has a good nose-break.

It is quite common for a breeder to inspect the stud and queen's accommodation first when the calling queen is taken along for mating. However, if the conditions are not really acceptable, the queen's owner may be too embarrassed to take her straight home again. I've had a number of desperate telephone calls from people looking for a stud because their queen is in the middle of calling. The result is that they either have to take their queen to the first available stud or to wait until she calls again, neither of which is a satisfactory option. Forward planning gives you time to see what studs are available, perhaps see them or their progeny at shows, and find out about their good and bad points from their owners or from breeders who have used them. You will certainly want to discuss the stud fee, see the stud's pedigree and take a look at the stud and queen's quarters before you take your queen along. If you are unhappy with anything, simply start looking elsewhere, because you have given yourself the time to do so, and you'll have time to find a second choice if your chosen stud isn't available when your queen starts to call.

Chapter 8

Tajens Irredescent Opal (lilac). Photo: Animals Unlimited

Do not assume that your queen will be accepted by the stud owner. Many studs are *limited*, which means the owner requires certain conditions to be met. These vary and are entirely up to the stud owner. For instance, a queen may not be acceptable if she's too closely related to the stud. Before your queen visits the stud, make sure you know what conditions, if any, the stud owner will impose. A common requirement is to have male kittens registered as non-active. Ask what the stud owner's policy is if the queen doesn't conceive; many stud owners offer one free repeat mating (usually within a given period), but this is a courtesy and not an entitlement. You should expect all stud owners to ask for your queen to be tested for Feline Leukaemia Virus (FeLV) and Feline Immunodeficiency Virus (FIV).

When you have finally chosen your queen's stud and made advance arrangements with the owner, sit back and wait for the next exciting stage – the calling!

Note: If your queen has been on any form of contraceptive (pill or injection) don't take her to stud until she's had at least one complete call without the contraceptive, or you risk the health of your queen and the life of the kittens.

THE MATING

The oestrus cycle and calling queen

The feline oestrus cycle is approximately 21 days, during which the queen will not permit mating except during the oestrus period.

Anoestrus   The non-receptive period of the oestrus cycle, when the queen is not in season.

Pro-oestrus	2–3 days before onset of oestrus, when she starts to show signs of calling.
Oestrus	5–8 days duration (or up to 14 days if not mated), when she is in season/calling.
Dioestrus	10–14 days following oestrus during which the corpus luteum regresses if the queen is not pregnant.

Most cats are seasonal breeders by nature and, in the northern hemisphere, their breeding season usually runs from January to September. This is less typical in Foreign and Oriental breeds, however, and central heating can prolong the breeding season in cats that live indoors all the time. Tonkinese are sexually precocious; females have been known to start calling as early as four-and-a-half months, but from seven months is more usual. It is referred to as *calling* because that is exactly what the queen does: she bellows with extraordinary clarity for any male in the vicinity to 'Come and get me, boys!' If you've never heard a Foreign queen call you are in for quite a surprise, although there are the rare silent callers.

The signs and duration of oestrus vary considerably from queen to queen, ranging from a short intense period to no obvious signs at all; some queens call regularly, others are quite irregular. The typical signs of a calling queen are increased friendliness and attachment to you to start with, then calling

with increasing intensity and volume, rolling around and along the ground more and more frantically as the days pass. By a couple of days into the queen's season, when you touch her at the base of the spine she adopts the *lordosis* position and paddles with her back feet, sometimes growling gently.

Queen adopting the *lordosis* position.

Blood tests

Once you know your queen is calling, inform the stud owner and make arrangements to take her along. Not more than 24 hours before visiting the stud she must be blood tested for Feline Leukaemia Virus (FeLV) and Feline Immunodeficiency virus (FIV). This is essential to assure the health of your queen and the stud. In a closed cattery where the stud is used only for the breeder's queens it is still advisable to test regularly for FeLV and FIV. Any new queen brought into the household should be isolated and tested to ensure that she is negative before introducing her to the rest of the household. Whether you are required to test your whole feline household or

Chapter 8

SAMPLE ONLY

THE GOVERNING COUNCIL
OF THE CAT FANCY
4-6 PENEL ORLIEU
BRIDGWATER
SOMERSET   TA6 3PG

Tel: 01278 427575

CERTIFICATE OF ENTIRETY

Cat's Name:

Registered No:

Date of Birth:

Breed:

I certify that, at the time of examination, the cat named above had two testicles of normal size and texture correctly positioned within the scrotum.

Micro-chip No. if available ....

Signature of Veterinary Surgeon ....

Date ....

Practice Name and Address

Owners are advised to photocopy this certificate before returning it to the GCCF Office

The owner of a stud should be able to produce his Certificate of Entirety.

just your queen is a matter to be discussed with the stud owner. A stud owner's acceptance of an untested queen who appears perfectly healthy but is actually carrying the virus can result in the stud cat being infected. He can then pass on the virus to other queens who subsequently visit him. Those queens then pass on the virus to their kittens and possibly to other cats in their household. Even if your cats are vaccinated annually against FeLV it is probable that you'll be required to have your queen tested. Some stud owners have arrangements with their own vet to carry out the queen's test.

The day before your queen is to be tested, make an appointment with your vet. Whichever test kit your vet uses it must be removed from storage in time to reach the correct operating temperature to avoid a false reading. Results are usually ready within half an hour of the test. Many breeders prefer to have the blood sample drawn from the leg rather than the queen's throat because the latter leaves the queen with a vulnerable bruised area and the smell/taste of the antiseptic may just be off-putting for the stud.

Off to stud

Make sure your queen is free of fleas, ear mites and worms and that you have clipped her front claws. For the stud owner's information, take along her current inoculation certificate and her blood test certificate. You may also be asked to show her pedigree and registration certificate. In return you should be able to see the same for the stud and a copy of his Certificate of Entirety. It is usual for a queen to remain with the stud for two to four days; be guided by your stud owner, who will let you know when it's time to collect your queen. Once you've got her home again, don't let her outside, as she may be fertile for up to 14 days, even if she is no longer calling, Multiple conception (one litter sired by more than one tom) is possible in cats. The stud owner should provide safe and comfortable accommodation for the queen and cater for her diet. He or she should also provide a mating certificate and a copy of the stud's pedigree, and advise when the kittens are likely to be due. Mistakes can be made, so remember that as the breeder you are responsible for confirming the correct details on the mating certificate. Caring stud owners take an interest and pride in the results of matings with their studs and are prepared to give a novice breeder the benefit of their experience if required.

Example of a Mating Certificate

Stud's Name & Details: Owner's Name & Address:

Queen's Name & Details: Owner's Name & Address:

Were Mated On (dates):   Kittens Due (dates):   Fee (including board): £

Conditions: All male kittens resulting from above mating to be placed on the non-active register, unless by prior agreement.

Signed, Queen's Owner: Date:

Please advise me of the results
in due course.   Stud Owner:

Chapter 8

Running a stud

I would not advise anyone who has not had several years of experience in breeding cats to run a stud. Even then, it is not a decision to take lightly. Do not expect to make profits from stud fees – to keep a stud happy and well you will spend more money than you receive in fees. Remember that first and

Samkabar Pleides (blue). To keep a stud happy and healthy requires
more money than you will recuperate in stud fees.

foremost your stud is a pet, not a breeding machine. The life of a stud can be extremely boring and desperately lonely if he doesn't have enough company, live in the correct environment and receive enough care and attention. How much company will your stud have? Cats are social animals and studs are usually especially friendly toward their owners, possibly because they don't see them often enough to take their company for granted. Are you prepared and willing to spend a minimum of two to three hours each and every day with your stud, even if you are unwell or have had a trying day?

Besides his inoculations, a stud needs an annual (minimum) blood test, as do the rest of your household if they are to keep him company. This is a significant addition to your annual veterinary bill. Are you prepared to lay out a great deal of money to provide the necessary accommodation for him, furnish it with the best quality bedding and fixtures and maintain it to a very high standard? Studs need extra care and attention and, as working cats, full and well-balanced diets supplemented with fresh-cooked food like chicken, fish and rabbit to stimulate their appetites. This too can be expensive.

How will you run your stud – will he be *Public* (available to all and sundry), *Limited* (available to selected queens only) or *Closed* (available to your queens only)? Can you be sure that your stud will get enough work? He will need several queens a year to keep him happy and healthy; four to six may be sufficient if he isn't overworked to begin with. Some studs are very vocal whether a queen is with them or not. Do you have neighbours who are prepared to put up with the noise? What will you do with your stud once his working life is completed?

If you are happy that you have considered these points carefully, the next step is to consult the experts. Get some literature from the Feline Advisory Bureau (FAB) and the GCCF, visit Tonkinese stud owners with good reputations to see their set-ups, and generally collect advice about the pros and cons of running a Tonkinese stud. Find out as much as you can before taking the step of setting up your own stud house.

Companionship

The life of a stud can be very boring and lonely if he isn't cared for properly. A bored cat can become destructive and even aggressive; a lonely cat will become depressed. These conditions should not be imposed on any cat. It is important that he is used to the regular companionship of your cats as well as having as much attention from the human members of the household as possible, especially if your long-term plan is to bring him back into your home at the end of his working life.

Romantica Tiramisu (choc) with her five-month-old son Tonkaholics Arabian Knight (left).
Photo: Alan Robinson

Chapter 8

The young cat should introduced to his new home at about the age of six months, with one or more members of the feline family he has grown up with, ideally neutered cats. Some young cats are sexually aware as early as five months of age; others may show no interest in a calling queen until their early adulthood. This affects the age at which you allow him to mate for the first time, but about nine months is a reasonable age for him to begin his career. Ideally, his first mating should be with an experienced queen who accepts mating easily. Once her visit is over he can be rejoined by his cat companions so that he learns that he isn't always expected to mate his visitors. This reinforces important social relationships with his companions.

The stud house

A suitable stud house will cost upwards of £1500, a cost you should not expect to recoup. There are several manufacturers of stud houses, but bear in mind that they cover only the minimum requirements for stud accommodation. Cat houses made of PVC are now available; they are very expensive (about three times the cost of an equivalent wooden house) but they have the advantage of being easy to maintain. Watch out for gaps and seams that may harbour infectious material, however.

It is up to you to enhance your cat's environment and provide a stimulating and comfortable home. The FAB recommend that a stud house, with queen's quarters, should be a minimum of 2m x 1.5m x 1.8m (7ft x 5ft x 6ft), plus a good sized pen. Your stud will live outside all year round, so connection to the mains power supply is necessary. The power cables must be enclosed within approved conduits and both cabling and sockets must be placed out of range of the cat and his spray. Lighting is necessary inside and outside the house; you will make early morning and late evening visits throughout the year. Good ventilation is necessary and bedding

must be kept free from damp (such as sprayed urine) and warmed by a thermostatically-controlled overhead heater. You may also wish to install an under-bed heater. The house should be lined with washable surfaces and insulated, with all seams sealed to ensure completly hygienic conditions. There should be enough room for you to move around comfortably to clean the house, supervise matings and sit with your cat for long periods.

Stud pen with queen's quarters and separate run.

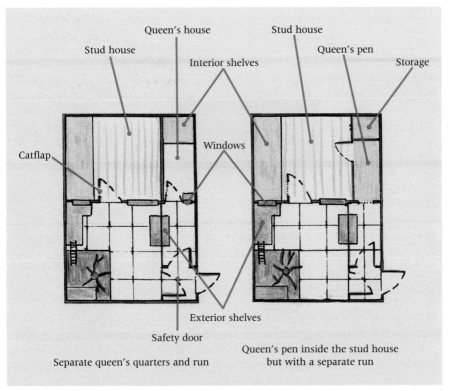

Queen's house   Stud house

Stud house   Queen's pen

Interior shelves   Storage

Catflap

Windows

Exterior shelves

Safety door

Separate queen's quarters and run

Queen's pen inside the stud house but with a separate run

Examples of stud quarters.

The fixtures and furnishings should be of the best quality. This will be the cat's home for several years, and it isn't acceptable to make do with just adequate bedding, a simple cat flap and a bit of wood for a scratching post. A good-quality, well-fitting cat flap should be installed so that your stud doesn't suffer from draughts or a noisy loose flap but still has the option to go into his pen, even if the weather is bad. There should be enough different levels to exercise your stud and to give him somewhere to avoid an outraged queen. In the pen this can incorporate a strong tree branch, firmly set in place, for him to strop his claws and climb on. There should also be non-slip flooring or a suitable heavy mat for the cats' feet to grip when mating.

A separate house, or good sized partitioned area of at least 1.2m x 1m x 1m (4ft x 3ft x 3ft) within the stud house, must be provided for the visiting queen. She needs a sleeping area in which she can feel safe from the unknown and possibly over-amorous stud while they are getting to know each other. It should be large enough to accommodate her bed, food bowls and litter tray while allowing her to stretch out comfortably. It should be partitioned with small-gauge wire to allow the two cats to see and smell each other without being able to paw or claw each other.

Chapter 8

The stud house should lead out to a pen with a sunny aspect, large and secure enough to give your cat exercise, relief from boredom and outside access in the poorest of weather conditions. The pen should be roofed with a shaded area and the walls should have sneeze barriers of glass or solid plastic at ground level to prevent infection. Again, there should be a variety of levels for the stud's exercise. All surfaces should be easy to clean and disinfect. The floor of the pen must be paved for scrubbing and the exterior shelves must be easy to clean. The pen should be at least 1.8m (6ft) high to allow you to move around comfortably. A safety run is absolutely essential. Both the house and pen need thorough daily cleaning and an extra cleaning before and after a queen's visit, using only products suitable for use with animals.

Advertising your stud

It is wrong to take a stud from a queen to attend a show. It's unhealthy and disturbing for the stud and especially so for the queen. It's also morally wrong to accept a fee for the period in question when the stud is not even with the queen all the time – not to mention the extra risk of bringing back infection from the show. However, showing your stud is probably the best form of advertising until word of mouth takes over, which it does rapidly within a breed fancy such as the Tonkinese, where good studs are still limited in number. Breeders like to see a stud at shows to make their own assessment of him without feeling obliged to consult the owner. It isn't necessary to continue showing a stud once he has proved himself on the bench, but you may enjoy the experience of showing your beautiful cat, and there is no harm in continuing to do so if he is happy to be shown. If you want your stud to be seen at shows without having him handled, why not put him on exhibition? It's less expensive, and exhibition pens can be decorated to show him to the best advantage. You can also place an advertising board on the pen. Other places to advertise are in cat magazines, show catalogues and the Tonkinese Breed Club's stud book, which gives useful advice and information on what is expected of the stud and queen's owner.

Clarinath Nightshadow (lilac).

Certificate of Entirety

From 1 January 1996, every GCCF-registered male cat used at stud for the first time must have a

Certificate of Entirety (CoE) deposited with the GCCF before the registration of his first litter of kittens. Established studs must have had their CoEs deposited with the GCCF by 31 December 1996. Certificates are not issued for male cats on the non-active register. If your stud is registered with the GCCF, the visiting queen's owners will expect you to have complied with these regulations, so I recommend that you keep a copy of your stud's CoE for their information.

Fees

If you charge a great deal more or less than the average fee for a Tonkinese stud you are likely to lose work for him. If the fee is too high breeders will not pay it unless your stud is acknowledged by others to be outstanding; if the fee is too low breeders may believe that there is a problem with him and avoid using him. It's acceptable to charge a little more than average if you have sought-after bloodlines in his pedigree and if he and his progeny have been extraordinarily successful on the show bench. An exhibited stud that has had little or no success on the bench is not a good enough example of the breed to be a stud. It's normal for stud fees to be paid in advance, and the fee is for the services of the stud, not for the results. Before the queen is left with you make it clear to the owner whether you offer a free repeat mating (within a reasonable time limit) if the queen doesn't conceive after visiting your stud and what fee, if any, you will charge for the queen's board. You should also make it clear what, if any, conditions you impose upon the resulting litter. Many stud owners now require that male kittens from their stud are registered as non-active, so that they will not be used for breeding. This gives stud owners some control over the use of their bloodlines.

Introducing the queen

Before your stud is regularly used by other breeders you should know what colours he carries. Test matings with dominant colours are the surest way to prove this genetically. You need to know what his faults and strong points are and what bloodlines to avoid. Running a limited or open stud can be quite difficult at times, as each queen's temperament varies seasonally and non-familiarity with any cat can be hazardous. Nevertheless, as the stud owner you have a responsibility to provide the queen with the best possible care and comfort and to ensure her safety and health while on your premises.

Before the visiting queen arrives, make sure that your stud's feline companions are removed from his quarters and clean the quarters thoroughly. When the queen arrives, check her carefully for parasites, dirt, lesions and any sign of illness. If you are in any in doubt about her health you shouldn't accept her. If any of your cats, or cats from the household of the visiting queen, have had an infectious disease within the past month you should not accept her, because the stress of oestrus and mating could be enough to reveal latent infection.

Chapter 8

If there are no problems, take the queen to the stud house in her carrier. Confine the stud until she is comfortable and secure in her own quarters. Before the owner leaves, agree a time for them to telephone you for a progress report. Some queens will not eat much while they are in your care, but offer them whatever they would normally eat at home. Favourite treats make them more comfortable in unfamiliar surroundings.

It is preferable for a maiden queen to be mated with an experienced stud, and vice versa. A bad first experience of mating has been known to put a stud off work or to cause a queen to become unapproachable by future studs. A queen shouldn't be introduced to the stud immediately; she may take a day or so separated from him, especially if she is a maiden, before she is ready to mate. Some queens remain in their bed for several hours. Maiden or nervous queens may even stop calling, while more experienced queens might happily encourage the stud immediately. Once the queen has made her initial investigations through the wire partition, and she and the stud are talking to each other with little chirruping sounds, you can allow them to join each other. The queen will normally want to sniff around him before allowing him to approach her.

The mating and separation can be quite violent. The stud's penis is covered with minute spines, and the effect of these spines stimulates ovulation. On separation, the short, sharp pain causes the queen to lash out at the stud; hence the need for his escape shelf. Leave her pen door open, as she too may wish to head for cover. The queen then spends up to half an hour rolling around and washing herself; only after she has finished this should she be handled; otherwise you may well be scratched.

Try to maintain a record of all matings. This is much easier said than done, as many less experienced studs prefer to work in private or only at night, so you will have to balance the need for supervised matings with the need to allow the two cats to run freely together according to their experience and temperament. It has been recommended that, once there have been at least three supervised matings to ensure ovulation and conception, you can allow them to run together; on the other hand, many successful stud owners feel that once the queen has been introduced to the stud there should be as little human intervention as possible, as it is both unnatural and counter-productive to the mating process

Adouzsh Zachariah Zeus (lilac).
Photo: Alan Robinson

to have periods of enforced separation. Cats are individuals and must be treated accordingly.

You may have heard that it is untrue that more matings produce more kittens (or that less matings produce less kittens), but the fact that cats are capable of producing kittens from dual-mating contradicts this. It is unnecessary and unwise to 'over-mate' a queen, so generally the queen is kept for just three to four days. Queens may be fertile for up to fourteen days, even if they have stopped calling, so advise the owner that the queen should be kept away from entire males for a couple of weeks once she is back home. I've been given several examples of queens mated over a period of more than five days who have had litters in which the kittens are obviously several days apart in development – the earlier ones well developed and the later ones premature. In other instances of queens mated over a long period, kittens have been born several days apart, which is very hard on the queens and usually results in kitten fatalities.

Two Tonkinese from New Zealand:
Zeotrope Boris (lilac) and Zeotrope Inuk (choc).

Before the visiting queen is taken home, be sure to give the owner a copy of the mating certificate, indicating the dates of mating and due dates of kittens. Then make sure that you clean out the quarters thoroughly before re-introducing your stud's feline companion/s.

Retirement

How long is the working life of a stud? Unfortunately, I can't give you a simple answer to this question, as many factors are involved. Recommended ages for retirement from stud work are between four and eight years, but I have known of, and indeed very successfully used, Siamese studs twelve years old. The main priority and guide must be the physical and mental health of your cat.

After he is neutered, your stud's life must continue as normally as possible in his own surroundings for a while. Unless he has had the company of your cats regularly he will be unused to living in company; this must be taken into consideration.

Chapter 8

Some stud owners make a practice of re-homing their studs once they are neutered, which means considerable upheaval for the cat, psychologically and physically. New owners must be chosen very carefully and, sadly for him, he may need to be an only cat. The ideal and kindest situation is for him to live with you for the rest of his life; after all, you have been his only constant companion for many years. Getting used to indoor life will take time and patience, but it is easier for your cat family if they have had regular contact with him. There may be problems with spraying but they can be limited with the use of chemical anti-spray preparations. It is worth the effort – your Tonkinese has earned your trust, affection and a comfortable retirement.

DECIDING NOT TO BREED

The most efficient method of feline contraception is to spay or neuter your cat. This is obviously not an option for breeding animals and the only other alternative is the use of a contraceptive tablet or injection for the calling queen. A queen in full oestrus is an awesome sight as she throws herself around in frustration and ecstasy, not to mention the very loud invitations that she issues to anyone within hearing distance. A silent Tonkinese caller is a rare creature.

Contraception

The feline contraceptive pill has been available since the 1960s. It is still treated with suspicion by some breeders because the doses recommended by the manufacturers have been found to be far higher than necessary for their queens and side effects have included failure to return to oestrus, inflammation of the uterus and pyometra (infected uterus), which often necessitates spaying. The contraceptive pill most routinely used for cats is Ovarid 5mg (Megastrol Acetate), and many breeders who use this drug find that they need far less than the recommended dose. I have used this drug successfully with my queens after consultation with my vet. I give them just a quarter of a tablet as soon as I suspect that they are coming into season. This usually takes them off call within 48 hours, and I have not had any problems with them returning to call or with uterine infection. I have discussed this with many breeders, of a variety of breeds, and it appears that a quarter of a tablet administered at the right time is commonly a satisfactory dosage.

Contraceptive injections are longer lasting. However, it has been known for queens not to return to a normal oestrus cycle once the effects of the injection have worn off. Be sure to consult with your vet before embarking upon any form of contraception, and ask the breeder of your queen whether there is any history of difficulties with contraception in the bloodline.

Artificially-induced ovulation may be viewed as a practical form of contraception. Some breeders keep vasectomized toms for this purpose. However, this invariably results in a phantom pregnancy, which can be distressing for the queen. Furthermore, the repeated production of eggs that are not fertilised can lead to uterine infection. Obviously, any practice that could be detrimental to your queen's health in the long run is to be avoided.

Neutering

Unless it is to be bred from your kitten should be neutered at about six months, or up to nine months for a male. The neutering or spaying of show cats is often delayed to allow their full physical development. If necessary, be guided by your vet. It is quite untrue that a female needs to have a litter of kittens.

When sexually mature, and with Tonkinese this can happen as early as four to five months, females come into season as often as every three weeks and the danger is that, if they are allowed freedom outside, they can easily get into a regular, deleterious cycle of kitten production. If they are not bred from they may become frustrated and possibly difficult to handle. Neutering overcomes these problems and reduces the risk of mammary tumour development. If left unspayed, entire males soon start marking their territories by spraying. They also stray further afield, and often fight

Bonzer Jam Puff (brown tabby) has just been spayed and is wearing an elizabethan collar.

to compete for territories and female cats. A free-ranging unneutered tom is a considerable nuisance to your neighbours and a real danger to the local feline population. Through indiscriminate mating he can contract, carry and spread several diseases, including FeLV and FIP. Neutering takes care of these problems and neutered cats make clean, affectionate and easier-to-care-for pets.

Both operations are carried out under general anaesthetic and the cats are usually eating, drinking and sometimes even playing within a few hours of the operation. In a female, a mid-line spay (see below) may take up to 48 hours' recovery time.

Females: The site of the operation is shaved to prevent infection from dust and dirt from her fur entering the wound. In Europe and Australasia, it is more common to operate through a small incision in the flank. The ovaries and uterus are removed, and the incision is closed with two or three stitches, which will be removed about a week later. In the United States, the preference is for the mid-line operation, in which the incision is made along the middle of the abdomen from the naval toward the hind legs. A female may be spayed from four months. If she is not to be used for breeding early spaying is preferable, as the organs are smaller. A female should *not* be spayed while she is calling.

Males: Males are neutered by castration. A small incision is made in the scrotum and the testicles are removed. Stitches are not needed except in the case of complications. The operation is very quick and usually carried out when the kitten is between six and nine months of age. Males are neutered at a later age than females to allow more growth and development, because lack of development of the penis and urethra can be a contributing factor of urinary problems such as FUS (see chapter 7).

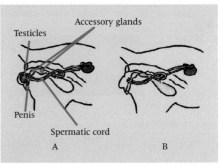

A: Male reproductive system. B: *Castration* is the surgical removal of the testicles (orchidectomy).

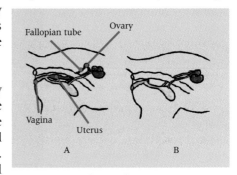

A: Female reproductive system.
B: *Spaying* is the surgical removal of ovaries, fallopian tubes, and uterus (ovario-hysterectomy).

Termination

It is not possible for a cat to have a surgical abortion without the removal of the womb, and there are no safe drugs to prevent conception after mating. If you have a queen who has been mated accidentally you should allow the kittens to be born normally. Although it is possible for a queen to be spayed two to three weeks after mating, even if she is pregnant, the operative risks are considerable because her womb is larger than usual.

TONKINESE PEDIGREES

On the following pages are some examples of first, second and third generation pedigrees, as well as the pedigrees of some of today's Tonkinese studs. I am grateful to all concerned for permission to include them.

MYMYSTIC PHAROAH (First Generation)

DoB: 30 January 1997, Male, Blue Tabby (74at) Owner and Breeder: Mrs Linda Vousden

Parents	Grandparents	Great-grandparents	Great-great-grandparents
Sire:	**Sire:**	**Sire:**	
		Gr Ch Okesha Star Galaxy (24)	S: Gr Ch Amberseal Electo
			D: Okesha Prima
	Sup Gr Ch Zachary Apollo	**Dam:**	
	Choc Tabby Point (32/3)	Simone Bat Cat (32/1)	S: Ch Simone Zeberdee
Gr ChZeppelin Wellington			D: Newmoon Pandora
	Dam:	**Sire:**	
		Gr Ch Harlyquin (24a)	S: Ch Maytime Angelo
Seal Tabby Point (32/1)	Zenobia Misty Fairytale		D: Tinqua
	Blue Point (24a)	**Dam:**	
		Gracelands Zamandra (24c)	S: Ch Maytime Landucci
			D: Honeycrest Appalato
Dam:	**Sire:**	**Sire:**	
		Ch Cataumet Commander (27)	S: Gr Ch Octavian
			D: Gr Ch Arkenstone Fantasia
	Gr Ch Emer Murphys Law	**Dam:**	
	Brown (27)	Bambino Khananlace (27)	S: Gr Ch Kayserling Khan
Predator Minnie Themoocher			D: Gr Ch Bambino Silver Lace
	Dam:	**Sire:**	
		Gr Ch Bambino Mr Mistofilees (27b)	S: Ch Bambino Servalan
Brown (27)	Gr Ch Mainman Caribbean Kiss		D: Bambino Chocolate Martina
	Chocolate (27b)	**Dam:**	
		UK Gr Ch Mainman Pinkissimo (27c)	S: Gr Ch Emer Murphys Law
			D: Sugarsweet Crimson Kiss

ROHESE TEXAS GOLD (Second Generation)

DoB: 18 August 1993, Female, Chocolate (74b) Owner: Mrs Jean Adams, Breeder: Mrs Diana Waters

Parents	Grandparents	Great-grandparents	Great-Great-Grandparents
Sire: Rohese Duke Ofearl (74b) — Chocolate (74b)	**Sire:** Ch Saborna Just Jasper — Blue (27a)	**Sire:** Gr Ch Lusara Charlie Brown	S: Ch Patriarcha Pickapepper
			D: Piccador Patroneze (27)
		Dam: Ch Brizlincoat Toomai	S: Bambino Chinchintarrou
			D: Ch Brizlincoat Fleur (27a)
	Dam: Dering Electra — Ch Tabby Point (32/3)	**Sire:** Locharidge Abacus	S: S Gr Ch Soria Sanjo Panzer
			D: Rantree Donna (24b)
		Dam: Dering Strawberry Sprite	S: Gr Ch Simone Strawberries
			D: Dering Bijou Briony (32/3)
Dam: Alaking Honkytonk Cowgirl (74) — Brown (74)	**Sire:** Ch Monclair Moviestar — Brown (27)	**Sire:** Ch Adreebu Ocala Filbert	S: Gr Ch Cassiobury Beechnut
			D: Tabana Tallahassee (27d)
		Dam: Junari Pollyanna	S: Neptune Chocolate Chalazois
			D: Hygeia Clementine (27e)
	Dam: Adreeam Imperial Jade — Lilac Point (24c)	**Sire:** Adueam Baba Louis	S: Lessur Grand Goya
			D: Azurbeth (24)
		Dam: Summerfolde Jacinth	S: Baskan Prince Charming
			D: Joie De Vie (24c)

TONKAHOLICS REDSUN RYEZING (Third Generation)

DoB: 3 October 1996, Male, Red (74d) Owners and Breeders: Mrs Christine and Miss Jo Richards

Parents	Grandparents	Great-grandparents	Great-great-grandparents
Sire: Tajens Jackademus (74a)	**Sire:** Addeish Arrons Nibbs Brown (74)	**Sire:** Adhuish Yankee Doodledandy (74)	S: Ch Monclair Movie Star
			D: Adreeam Imperial Jade
		Dam: Damilee Hot Chocolate (74b)	S: Nethermist Mister Smee
			D: Damilee Elinore
	Dam: Adhuish Pearl Princess Lilac (74c)	**Sire:** Gr Ch Typha Silverwinged Xplorer (27c)	S: Gr Ch Kathima Prince Rambo
			D: Mijit Gypsy Girl
		Dam: Adraysh Prudence (74c)	S: Ch Saborna Just Jasper
			D: Adraysh Hanover Holly
Dam: Tonkaholics Taloola Moon (74d)	**Sire:** Romantica Remus Red (74d)	**Sire:** Adraybu Dream Knight (27a)	S: Adhuibu Speedy Gonzales
			D: Adkribu Iza Dream
		Dam: Summerdown Angel Eyes (32a)	S: Summerdown Sundancer
			D: Darling Arcadia
	Dam: Romantica Bianca Lilac Tortie (74jv)	**Sire:** Romantica Rodrigo Redsun	S: Adraybu Dream Knight
			D: Summerdown Angel Eyes (74d)
		Dam: Sylvakib Ashemo Swan	S: Sylvakib Tibble Tyrant
			D: Jax Rebecca (74c)

165

TONKABELLA BENEDICT BRUNO

DoB: 24 August 1991, Male, Brown (74) Owner and Breeder: Mrs Jean Sharratt

Parents	Grandparents	Great-grandparents	Great-great-grandparents
Sire: Gr Ch Sleekine Fame (27)	**Sire:** Gr Ch Cassiobury Beechnut Brown (27)	**Sire:** Chezchats Incogniteau (27)	S: Ch Braeside Red Toreador
			D: Chezchats Nanoo (27)
		Dam: Ch Cassiobury Jeenie Brown (27)	S: Lunaris Ortheus
			D: Cassiobury Nightingale (27)
	Dam: Kathima Crown Jewel Brown (27)	**Sire:** Ch Elidor Le Roi (27c)	S: Samantoni Borzoi Boy
			D: Typha Ultra Violet
		Dam: Kathima Ahmeda Buti (27)	S: Gr Ch Typha Dark Enigma
			D: Kathima April Weddingbells (27)
Dam: Adraysh Tinkabella (74b)	**Sire:** Ch Tammeko Toffilees Chocolate (74b)	**Sire:** Gr Ch Bambino Mr Mistofilees (27b)	S: Ch Bambino Servalan
			D: Gr Ch Bambino Lilac Willow (27b)
		Dam: Ch Tammeko Tiger Lily (27c)	S: Bambino Chinchintarrou
			D: Bambino Lucy Locket (27c)
	Dam: Lellybel Chanele Lilac (74c)	**Sire:** Ch Tammeko Toffilees (27b)	S: Gr Ch Bambino Mr Mistofilees
			D: Ch Tammeko Tiger Lily (27b)
		Dam: Wylat Fantasque (24a)	S: Tilenja Commanche
			D: Wylat Josceline (24a)

SAMKABAR PLEIDES

DoB: 21 July 1995, Male, Blue (74a) Owner and Breeder: Mrs H Barnes

Parents	Grandparents	Great-grandparents	Great-great-grandparents
Sire: Rocheros Emperor (24c)	**Sire:** Eirrem Blue Fircone Blue Point (24a)	**Sire:** Gr Ch Eirrem Smart Alec (24a)	S: Ch Eirrem August Moon D: Tinkers Baby
		Dam: Eirrem June Roses (24c)	S: Gr Ch Chao Fa Leo D: Eirrem May Flowers
	Dam: Rocheros Zdenka Blue Point (24a)	**Sire:** Puritan Rival Pashan (24a)	S: Gr Ch Zenobia Fast Mover D: Zenobia Sophisticated Miss
		Dam: Rocheros Odessa (24c)	S: Ailsa Tinku Kambuku D: Widgerwood Janna
Dam: Wilowispa Kharma Kameo (27a)	**Sire:** Wilowispa Kerari Chocolate (27b)	**Sire:** Ch Bambino Kandibar Kid (27b)	S: Ch Bambino Chinchintarrou D: Ch Bambino Lucy Locket
		Dam: Chantaine Nicolina (27b)	S: Kamberri Falcon D: Kamberri Aqualina
	Dam: Wilowispa Columbine Brown (27)	**Sire:** Rocheros Rasputin	S: Ch Kalos Castor D: Ronas
		Dam: Kamberri Kryzti Solitaire (27c)	S: Kamberri Falcon D: Bambino Pink Pastel

TONKAHOLICS ARABIAN KNIGHT

DoB: 10 April 1996, Male, Chocolate (74b) Owners and Breeders: Mrs Christine and Miss Jo Richards

Parents	Grandparents	Great-grandparents	Great-great-grandparents
Sire:			
Rohese Duke Ofearl	**Sire:** Ch Saborna Just Jasper Blue (27a)	**Sire:** Gr Ch Lusara Charlie Brown (27)	S: Ch Patriarca Pickapepper
			D: Piccador Patroneze
		Dam: Ch Brizlincoat Toomai (27a)	S: Bambino Chinchintarrou
			D: Brizlincoat Fleur
Chocolate (74b)	**Dam:** Dering Electra Choc Tabby Point (32/3)	**Sire:** Locharidge Abacus (24a)	S: S Gr Ch Soria Sanjo Panzer
			D: Rantree Donna
		Dam: Dering Strawberry Sprite (32/3)	S: Gr Ch Simone Strawberries
			D: Dering Bijou Briony
Dam:			
Romantica Tiramisu	**Sire:** Adraybu Dream Knight Blue (27a)	**Sire:** Adhuibu Speedy Gonzales (27f)	S: Ch Kamberri Champagne Charlie
			D: Adivebu Madonna
		Dam: Adkribu Iza Dream (27)	S: Sambarbi Amazon Warrior
			D: Sambarbi Lotus Flower
Chocolate (74b)	**Dam:** Widgerwood Joella Choc Point (24b)	**Sire:** Gr Ch Shermese Oberon (24b)	S: Gr Ch Lovinamist Talisman
			D: Tzu Pippistrella
		Dam: Widgerwood Champagne (27c)	S: Simone Arronmist
			D: Widgerwood Kottinor

CLARINATH NIGHTSHADOW

DoB: 24 April 1995, Male, Lilac (74c) Owner and Breeder: Mrs Carol Poole

Parents	Grandparents	Great-grandparents	Great-great-grandparents
Sire: Gr Ch Silverbreeze Lordsananda (24a)	**Sire:** Gr Ch Cachet Tabbeoca Tiptoes Lilac Tabby Point (32/4)	**Sire:** Ch Simone Ragged Robin (24b)	S: Zenobia Blue Urchin
			D: Simone Sanfairyanne
		Dam: Ch Silverbreeze Marimikko (32/4)	S: Simone Semolina Silkpaws
			D: Silverbreeze Eloise
	Dam: Roysterer Cartier Lilac Point (24c)	**Sire:** Gr Ch Roysterer Lord Catmando (24c)	S: Gr Ch Popplebee Tigi Wigi
			D: Aqweam Coco Snowdrop
		Dam: Styeperson Petit Fleur (24c)	S: Gr Ch Sanpaku Admeus
			D: Styeperson Bramble
Dam: Clarinath Lilis Ceridwen (27b)	**Sire:** Gr Ch Emer Murphys Law Brown (27)	**Sire:** Ch Cataumet Commander (27)	S: Gr Ch Octavian
			D: Gr Ch Arkenstone Fantasia (27)
		Dam: Bambino Khananlace (27)	S: Gr Ch Kayserling Khan
			D: Gr Ch Bambino Silver Lace (27)
	Dam: Artro Lilac Lilibet Lilac (27c)	**Sire:** Pegavi Lilac Tequila (27c)	S: Neptune Chocolate Chalazois
			D: Phthazzar Hrya Chitchit (27c)
	Chocolate (27b)	**Dam:** Artro Chocolate Nesta (27c)	S: Gralnoge Blarney
			D: Pegavi Silva Crystal (27b)

Producing Tonkinese kittens

PREGNANCY

Three to four weeks after mating a pregnant queen's nipples become slightly swollen and deepen in colour; this is referred to as *pinking-up*. From three to six weeks into pregnancy she begins to change shape as the kittens develop. The normal gestation period for a cat is 63–65 days (see page 173), during which time usually the queen should be treated quite normally. Take extra care when handling a heavily pregnant queen, making sure that her weight is fully supported when she is picked up. Children should not be allowed to pick up or carry a pregnant queen. Don't be surprised if she suffers from morning sickness occasionally in the early days; some cats suffer this, just as humans do; it is a reaction to the effects of hormonal activity.

Provided that she is given a good, balanced diet, the queen shouldn't need supplements. However, some queens use more of their body's reserves than others, and I find that one daily pinch of a vitamin A and D preparation (such as Stress by Phillips Pet Care, which also contains calcium and phosphorus) in their food helps to keep them on top form. It is very important not to over-supplement the diet. Later in pregnancy, the queen's meals should be little and often rather than the usual two or three larger meals a day. She will probably want more food when she starts to produce milk. In the last couple of weeks of pregnancy a little raw liver or oily fish helps to prevent

Tonkaholics Taloola Moon (red) at seven weeks pregnant.

constipation. Don't give liquid paraffin as it lines the walls of the digestive tract, preventing the absorption of essential nutrients. Normal exercise helps to maintain good muscle tone, which is desirable when she is giving birth.

If in doubt, treat the queen for worms about three weeks before she is due to give birth and again when the kittens are about six weeks of age. Consult your vet about the best treatment for a pregnant cat. Young kittens may be severely retarded in growth and display abdominal distension and loss of appetite because of worm infection. They may also suffer from the presence of the larval form of the worm, which migrates through the liver and lungs.

By the time she is six weeks into pregnancy your queen will be quite distended either side of her belly. Two to three days before she gives birth this bulk will 'drop' towards the rear of her abdomen. At this stage she may appreciate some help with her toilet as she will find it very difficult to wash herself. Clean her anus gently with cotton-wool

A few days before giving birth to seven kittens.

balls dampened in lukewarm water, then carefully dry her. Gently wipe around her nipples with a little warm olive oil to keep them clean and supple. During the last two to three weeks of pregnancy the movement of her kittens will be quite visible. This often ceases during the final couple of days of pregnancy. Two or three days before giving birth, the queen's mammary glands may secrete a little milk.

The kitten pen

Some breeders like to use a large cardboard box with plenty of bedding. Cardboard is relatively sterile, warm and disposable. Others have especially designed kitten pens with removable flooring and a queen's hatch at the top, to allow the queen to get in and out but keep the kittens in. I like to have the kitten pen raised off the floor slightly at first. If I have to help her deliver her kittens or keep her company at any time a raised pen is more practical. My queens have never had problems with this, and a raised pen is less susceptible to draughts. I also prefer to have regulated underbed heating (not hot water bottles, which can burn the kittens) in the kitten pen, which is recognised as being the most efficient form of keeping kittens warm. Whatever type of kitten pen you decide is best for your queen bear in mind these requirements:

- It must be easily cleaned without disturbing the queen and kittens too much.
- It must be large enough for the queen to move around comfortably, to give birth in and to nurse her growing kittens. 60cm x 60cm x 60cm (2ft x 2ft x 2ft) is a fair start.
- It must be kept at 22°C (74°F) 24 hours a day.
- It should be arranged so that in the first few weeks the growing kittens can't get out but the queen can get in and out easily and comfortably.

Place the pen in a warm, dimly-lit, quiet area, preferably within earshot during the night. Some breeders prefer to have the pen in their bedrooms. Many queens like their owner's company during birth and regularly during the long initial days of nursing their kittens. Have the pen in place and ready a couple of weeks before the kittens are due; let your queen 'discover' it and make it her own. Line it with clean towels, newspaper or kitchen roll; some queens like to shred this for themselves. If your queen doesn't want to use the pen, don't force her to; it's more likely that you will motivate her to have her kittens in secret or hide them from you later. Let her have them where she feels most secure and then, if necessary, move her into the pen with her kittens when they are all born and suckling.

BIRTH (Parturition)

During the week before the birth the queen may become restless and spend more time grooming and less time eating. Some queens obligingly have their kittens on the expected date and during the day – others don't. The average term of pregnancy is 63–65 days (see gestation chart opposite), but some queens go a little longer. If the kittens are a day or two late, don't worry as long as the queen is comfortable and not distressed. Most cats have their kittens without any help (interference), but quietly keep an eye on her in case help is needed – many queens prefer their owners to be nearby, especially for a first litter. Contact your vet a day or so before the kittens are due to make sure that he or she will be available if any problems occur, especially if the kittens are due over a weekend.

For this section, refer to the Stages of Labour diagram on page 174. About 12 hours before delivery, the cervix dilates and the kittens are moved towards the pelvis by muscular contractions, often visible along

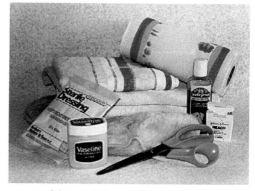

Useful items to have to hand during birth.

	1	2	3	4	5	6	7	8	9	10	11	12	13	14	15	16	17	18	19	20	21	22	23	24	25	26	27	28	29	30	31
Mated Jan	1	2	3	4	5	6	7	8	9	10	11	12	13	14	15	16	17	18	19	20	21	22	23	24	25	26	27	28	29	30	31
Due Mar/Apr	7	8	9	10	11	12	13	14	15	16	17	18	19	20	21	22	23	24	25	26	27	28	29	30	31	1	2	3	4	5	6
Ready May/Jun	30	31	1	2	3	4	5	6	7	8	9	10	11	12	13	14	15	16	17	18	19	20	21	22	23	24	25	26	27	28	29
Mated Feb	1	2	3	4	5	6	7	8	9	10	11	12	13	14	15	16	17	18	19	20	21	22	23	24	25	26	27	28*			
Due Apr/May	7	8	9	10	11	12	13	14	15	16	17	18	19	20	21	22	23	24	25	26	27	28	29	30	1	2	3	4			
Ready Jun/Jul	30	1	2	3	4	5	6	7	8	9	10	11	12	13	14	15	16	17	18	19	20	21	22	23	24	25	26	27			
Mated Mar	1	2	3	4	5	6	7	8	9	10	11	12	13	14	15	16	17	18	19	20	21	22	23	24	25	26	27	28	29	30	31
Due May/Jun	5	6	7	8	9	10	11	12	13	14	15	16	17	18	19	20	21	22	23	24	25	26	27	28	29	30	31	1	2	3	4
Ready Jul/Aug	28	29	30	31	1	2	3	4	5	6	7	8	9	10	11	12	13	14	15	16	17	18	19	20	21	22	23	24	25	26	27
Mated Apr	1	2	3	4	5	6	7	8	9	10	11	12	13	14	15	16	17	18	19	20	21	22	23	24	25	26	27	28	29	30	
Due Jun/Jul	5	6	7	8	9	10	11	12	13	14	15	16	17	18	19	20	21	22	23	24	25	26	27	28	29	30	1	2	3	4	
Ready Aug/Sep	28	29	30	31	1	2	3	4	5	6	7	8	9	10	11	12	13	14	15	16	17	18	19	20	21	22	23	24	25	26	
Mated May	1	2	3	4	5	6	7	8	9	10	11	12	13	14	15	16	17	18	19	20	21	22	23	24	25	26	27	28	29	30	31
Due Jul/Aug	5	6	7	8	9	10	11	12	13	14	15	16	17	18	19	20	21	22	23	24	25	26	27	28	29	30	31	1	2	3	4
Ready Sep/Oct	27	28	29	30	1	2	3	4	5	6	7	8	9	10	11	12	13	14	15	16	17	18	19	20	21	22	23	24	25	26	27
Mated Jun	1	2	3	4	5	6	7	8	9	10	11	12	13	14	15	16	17	18	19	20	21	22	23	24	25	26	27	28	29	30	
Due Aug/Sep	5	6	7	8	9	10	11	12	13	14	15	16	17	18	19	20	21	22	23	24	25	26	27	28	29	30	31	1	2	3	
Ready Oct/Nov	28	29	30	31	1	2	3	4	5	6	7	8	9	10	11	12	13	14	15	16	17	18	19	20	21	22	23	24	25	26	
Mated Jul	1	2	3	4	5	6	7	8	9	10	11	12	13	14	15	16	17	18	19	20	21	22	23	24	25	26	27	28	29	30	31
Due Sep/Oct	4	5	6	7	8	9	10	11	12	13	14	15	16	17	18	19	20	21	22	23	24	25	26	27	28	29	30	1	2	3	4
Ready Nov/Dec	27	28	29	30	1	2	3	4	5	6	7	8	9	10	11	12	13	14	15	16	17	18	19	20	21	22	23	24	25	26	27
Mated Aug	1	2	3	4	5	6	7	8	9	10	11	12	13	14	15	16	17	18	19	20	21	22	23	24	25	26	27	28	29	30	31
Due Oct/Nov	5	6	7	8	9	10	11	12	13	14	15	16	17	18	19	20	21	22	23	24	25	26	27	28	29	30	31	1	2	3	4
Ready Dec/Jan	28	29	30	31	1	2	3	4	5	6	7	8	9	10	11	12	13	14	15	16	17	18	19	20	21	22	23	24	25	26	27
Mated Sep	1	2	3	4	5	6	7	8	9	10	11	12	13	14	15	16	17	18	19	20	21	22	23	24	25	26	27	28	29	30	
Due Nov/Dec	5	6	7	8	9	10	11	12	13	14	15	16	17	18	19	20	21	22	23	24	25	26	27	28	29	30	1	2	3	4	
Ready Jan/Feb	28	29	30	31	1	2	3	4	5	6	7	8	9	10	11	12	13	14	15	16	17	18	19	20	21	22	23	24	25	26	
Mated Oct	1	2	3	4	5	6	7	8	9	10	11	12	13	14	15	16	17	18	19	20	21	22	23	24	25	26	27	28	29	30	31
Due Dec/Jan	5	6	7	8	9	10	11	12	13	14	15	16	17	18	19	20	21	22	23	24	25	26	27	28	29	30	31	1	2	3	4
Ready Feb/Mar	27	28	1	2	3	4	5	6	7	8	9	10	11	12	13	14	15	16	17	18	19	20	21	22	23	24	25	26	27	28	29
Mated Nov	1	2	3	4	5	6	7	8	9	10	11	12	13	14	15	16	17	18	19	20	21	22	23	24	25	26	27	28	29	30	
Due Jan/Feb	5	6	7	8	9	10	11	12	13	14	15	16	17	18	19	20	21	22	23	24	25	26	27	28	29	30	31	1	2	3	
Ready Mar/Apr	30	31	1	2	3	4	5	6	7	8	9	10	11	12	13	14	15	16	17	18	19	20	21	22	23	24	25	26	27	28	
Mated Dec	1	2	3	4	5	6	7	8	9	10	11	12	13	14	15	16	17	18	19	20	21	22	23	24	25	26	27	28	29	30	31
Due Feb/Mar	4	5	6	7	8	9	10	11	12	13	14	15	16	17	18	19	20	21	22	23	24	25	26	27	28	1	2	3	4	5	6
Ready Apr/May	29	30	1	2	3	4	5	6	7	8	9	10	11	12	13	14	15	16	17	18	19	20	21	22	23	24	25	26	27	28	29

* Make necessary adjustments in leap years.

Gestation chart.

the queen's flanks (B in diagram). She pants and may purr strongly and loudly (cats don't just purr in pleasure). She may tremble, whimper, become very restless and appear to be unsure what is occurring, looking often at her flanks and trying to wash herself. She may also discharge a little watery fluid. Give her calm and quiet reassurance, speak soothingly and stroke her gently. Once the contractions begin in earnest she will normally lie on one side or sit forward on her chest. She may expel a mucus plug before the birth of the first kitten. As the abdominal contractions increase the kitten is pushed into the pelvic canal. It is common to see a 'bubble' of the amniotic sac emerging from

Chapter 9

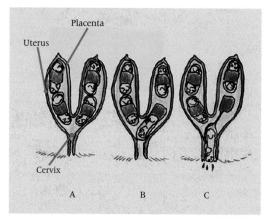

Stages of labour.

the vulva first. This membrane covering the kitten is normally broken by the effects of the contractions, releasing the amniotic fluid that lubricates the birth passage (C). Once the kitten has started to emerge it will be born within a few minutes. If it isn't born within 10 minutes of first emerging, help is needed (see **Possible Problems**).

As soon as the kitten is born, the queen will wash off the membrane. Her rough tongue warms the kitten and stimulates it to breathe. She will chew at the umbilical cord, severing it from the placenta. The placenta is usually passed at the same time as the kitten or shortly afterwards. (It looks like a piece of liver about 4cm long.) It is quite usual for the queen to eat several placentas, and she gains valuable nutrients and hormones from them. There should be one placenta for each kitten (kittens sharing the same placenta are rare). A placenta retained in the uterus can lead to infection. If you are in doubt about the delivery of all the placentas, ask your vet to check your queen 8–12 hours after the birth of the kittens. If the queen does not sever the umbilical cord after a few minutes, you must do so. First make sure that the kitten's nose and mouth are clear of mucus and it is breathing; then, taking your time, grip the cord firmly about 5cm from the kitten and either cut the cord on the side nearest to the placenta, using scissors sterilised in antiseptic, or shear the cord with clean fingernails, pulling towards the kitten's body. Remember that no pressure should be put on the kitten's abdomen, because that could result in a hernia.

There is then a period of uterine rest before the contractions resume and the next kitten is delivered. In a healthy queen the common interval is 15–30 minutes; if she is overweight, old or has a large litter the uterus may become tired and the intervals could be much longer. From the time the contractions begin, the kittens are usually all delivered within 2–4 hours, but occasionally it may be longer. Kittens conceived several days apart may be born days apart. You don't need to do anything if the queen appears well and isn't distressed but, if in doubt, consult your vet. In a large litter there is often a longer interval after about half of the kittens are delivered. This is because the queen delivers the kittens from one horn of the uterus and then rests before delivering the kittens in the other horn.

This is the time-table of one of my queen's deliveries; it is fairly typical of a normal delivery:

Yesterday Shadow began tentative nesting behaviour: today she was much more positive. In the late afternoon she became particularly friendly, tactile and there was much fast purring. As we watched a late night film, Shadow was sitting close into my neck and purring hard. Although she was not expected to have her kittens for two more days she was definitely showing signs of preparing to give birth.

12.20am	*She became very agitated, unsettled and washed herself a great deal.*
12.23am	*Sitting on my lap, she passed a small quantity of watery fluid and there were signs of minor contractions.*
12.24am	*She was very carefully carried to her delivery bed in the kitten pen in our bedroom.*
12.32am	*Contractions started, mucous plug expelled.*
12.43am	*Head presentation, male kitten delivered with placenta, cord sheared by queen.*
12.48am	*Contractions, hind limb presentation, female kitten delivered with placenta, cord sheared by queen.*
12.58am	*Contractions started.*
01.02am	*Full breech presentation, female kitten delivered with placenta, cord sheared by queen.*
01.19am	*Contractions.*
01.20am	*Hind limb presentation, male kitten delivered, cord sheared by my hand, queen busy cleaning herself.*
01.23am	*Placenta expelled.*
01.23am	*Start of rest period, Shadow giving kittens an extra cleaning.*
01.44am	*Contractions started.*
01.45am	*Head presentation, female kitten delivered, cord sheared by queen.*
01.46am	*Placenta expelled.*
01.47am	*Extra cleaning of kittens, two start to suckle.*
02.12am	*Contractions started.*
02.15am	*Head presentation, male kitten delivered, cord sheared by queen.*
02.25am	*All kittens suckling well.*
02.40am	*Final placenta expelled.*

All but the last placenta were eaten, and all cords but one were severed by Shadow. The kittens were delivered after 63 days gestation.

Once all the newborn kittens are suckling you can clear the kitten pen of soiled paper, tissue debris such as uneaten placentas, and wet bedding, but don't worry too much about slightly soiled bedding; it is more important for the queen to be able to rest and nurse her kittens. Too much disturbance at this stage may distress the queen, so it is acceptable to leave the bedding for a day or so before changing it. I recommend that you keep the pen in dim, not dark, light until a day or so after the kittens eyes have opened; after all, in nature a mother cat finds a dimly-lit place in which to give birth.

Chapter 9

Possible problems

This section is only included to alert you to possible problems, not as a guide to obstetrics! Birth is a normal, natural function. Remember that fit, healthy cats free from genetic deformities have little or no trouble in giving birth. If you are in doubt about what is occurring or what you should do, get experienced and/or professional help. A reasonable guide is:

- *Wait no longer than 20 minutes* (less if the queen is distressed): if fluids have been expelled but no kitten has been presented; if a kitten is partially presented but no further progress is made; if a kitten is partially presented but disappears back into the queen.
- *Wait no longer than 2 hours* (less if the queen's condition deteriorates): if the queen is exhausted and panting; if she occasionally lies on her side, neglecting her kittens.
- *Wait at least 2 hours*: if more kittens are expected but there are no contractions and the queen is bright, comfortable and suckling contented kittens.

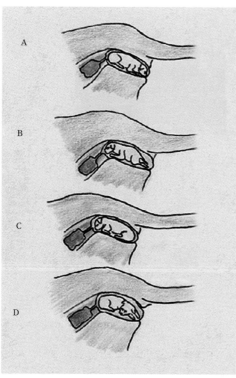

Birth positions: A: Normal, head first; B: Normal, hind feet first; C: True breech presentation; D: Head first, but head has turned.

Abnormal presentation: The easiest delivery position is when the kitten is presented head-first with the front paws alongside the head. However, many kittens are born hind legs first with no problems. The most difficult position for delivery is the true breech position, where the hindquarters are presented first. If a kitten is still only partly delivered after 10–15 minutes from the time it was first presented, it may be stuck. Your queen needs help. If you cannot get to your vet quickly, grasp as much of the kitten as possible (preferably with a piece of clean towelling); then, in time with her contractions, very carefully pull downwards and outwards. By slightly rocking or rotating the kitten you may find it comes out more easily. Be careful, and never try to help a birth by pulling on the kitten's head or legs.

Bleeding umbilical cord: This is an uncommon problem but it might occur if the queen severs the cord too near to the kitten's body. The blood flow must be stopped quickly; tie the cord off, near its end, with cotton dipped in antiseptic or with dental floss.

Kitten not breathing: Clear the mouth and nose of any membranes and gently rub the kitten vigorously with a piece of towelling to warm it and stimulate breathing. If it is still not breathing, hold it carefully (bearing in mind that newborn kittens can be very slippery) head down in the palms of your hands, supporting the head and neck. Stand and raise your arms to shoulder height. Then, in one smooth movement, swing your arms down firmly. The motion and force of gravity should help to clear out any mucus blocking the kitten's lungs and airways. This may be repeated two or three times if necessary.

No contractions: If the queen ceases to have contractions through exhaustion or for any other reason, veterinary attention is needed. Your vet may be able to induce contractions with drugs or, if for example a kitten is stuck, a caesarian section may be necessary.

NURSING
Cats have eight nipples, which are small and pale pink in males and non-pregnant/non-lactating females. In pregnant and nursing queens the nipples are much larger and darker, often with a definite breast. Sometimes one or two nipples don't develop fully (usually the pair nearest the forelimbs), but it is quite normal for nursing queens to have an irregular breast pattern: each kitten chooses a specific breast and any not chosen stop producing milk. A tender or abnormally swollen nipple or breast indicates a problem, requiring veterinary consultation.

The first milk produced by the queen, the colostrum, contains less lactose than usual and is particularly rich in nutrients and antibodies, so it is very important that each kitten receives this first milk.

POST-NATAL CARE OF THE QUEEN
It is most important to keep the pen warm, clean and dry; otherwise uterine infections and mastitis might occur. Mastitis is an infection or inflammation of one or more of the mammary glands, and can be caused by injury, blocked teats or bacterial infection. Symptoms include refusal to feed the kittens and hot and painful breasts with abnormal secretions. Urgent treatment is required. Uterine infection is serious. It can be caused by unhygienic conditions or the retention of a placenta or foetus. Treatment may involve spaying.

Up to several days after giving birth it is normal for the queen to discharge a thick, reddish-brown fluid from the vulva, but it should not be

Chapter 9

much more than a teaspoon full in total. If the discharge is abnormal in quantity, colour and/or foul smelling consult your vet straight away.

Although the queen might not be interested in food directly after giving birth she will soon begin to eat with a voracious appetite, as her reserves of energy are channelled into feeding her kittens. She should be given as much good quality food as she wants and have constant access to fresh water. Give her a good multi-vitamin/mineral supplement as well. By the time the kittens are about four to five weeks old she may be eating as much as three or four times her normal meals. You cannot over-feed a nursing queen!

KITTEN DEVELOPMENT

During the first six weeks of a kitten's life it is totally dependent upon its mother. It is usually weaned during the sixth week and, at the same time, enters a critical socialisation period. A kitten should not be taken from its mother and litter-mates before it is twelve weeks old. To remove a kitten from maternal care at six weeks of age is roughly the same as removing a two-and-a-half-year-old child from its mother.

1–5 days

At birth Tonkinese kittens weigh 85–140g (3–5oz), according to the number of kittens in the litter. They are born blind and quite pale in colour, with pink nose leathers and paw pads. The colour starts to appear in a few days. The ears are flat to the sides of the head and the limbs and joints are very flexible.

5 days–2 weeks

The eyes begin to open and are normally fully open by the time the kitten is about two weeks of age. The colour on the nose leather and edges of the ears

Brown and brown tabby kittens, one day old.

starts to appear. By the end of this period the claws have hardened and the milk teeth start to show under the gums. The limbs are stronger and the ears are more pricked.

Brown and brown tabby kittens, two weeks old.

2–4 weeks

At two weeks the kittens are more active, crawling around their bed and tentatively washing themselves. They become more aware of their environment as their eye-sight improves. By three weeks they are learning at a staggering speed, copying each new skill learned by a litter-mate. They follow you with their eyes and almost as quickly with their feet. This is when they begin to climb out of their pens and explore their surroundings. At three weeks you can start to supplement their diet with a good brand of powdered kitten milk (Cimicat or Lactol, for example). Teach them to lap by placing them in front of a flat dish and, with clean hands, wiping their lips with some of the milk. If they like the taste, encourage them closer to the bowl by letting them lick a little more from your fingers until your fingers are almost in the bowl. Do not force their heads down to the milk. This may take several attempts on your part, and bear in mind that some kittens never take to the milk, but continue to suckle from their mothers until they are old enough to eat solid foods.

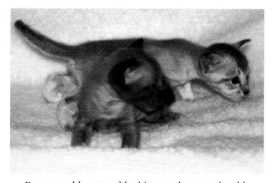
Brown and brown tabby kittens, three weeks old.

By four weeks of age their legs, tails and ears stand up and their neck muscles are much stronger. They begin to wash themselves and play fight. Now you can start them on solid foods especially produced for kittens. The easiest way to get them interested in food is to feed them with their mother from a large flat plate so that they can all get to the food at the same time. While it is fine for your queen to eat kitten food (provided that she doesn't eat the kitten's share), you should prevent the kittens from eating the adult cat food as it isn't sufficient for their nutritional requirements and is probably too strong for their young digestive systems. They are likely to walk through their food, so a plastic sheet, mat or towel under the plate is advisable to start with. Don't use newspaper if you

Chapter 9

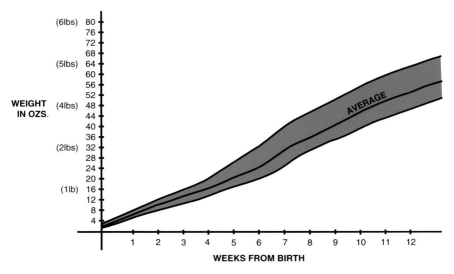

GROWTH RATE OF TONKINESE KITTENS

WEIGHT IN OZS.

(6lbs) 80
76
72
68
(5lbs) 64
60
56
52
(4lbs) 48
44
40
36
(2lbs) 32
28
24
20
(1lb) 16
12
8
4

AVERAGE

1 2 3 4 5 6 7 8 9 10 11 12

WEEKS FROM BIRTH

This diagram shows the normal range of growth of Tonkinese kittens. It has been observed that kittens from subsequent generations appear larger than first-generation kittens, but there is not yet enough evidence to draw any firm conclusions. (To convert to metric, 1oz = 28.3g.)

have placed their litter trays on newspaper. In their litter trays a relatively fine litter is better initially; litter such as wood pellets is likely to be too large for kittens to scratch in properly. Don't forget that they will probably start by trying to eat the litter! Every time the kitten is fed, put it straight into the litter tray afterwards. It will soon pick up the habit for itself.

4–6 weeks

The kittens should now be eating solid food, about 30g of food per 450g of kitten per day, divided into three meals, plus a milk meal. Unlike puppies, kittens only eat what they need at the time, so it is better to put out a little too much food than not enough. They are now well into the exploratory stage, far more steady on their feet, and very active – climbing, running and playing with objects. Their milk teeth are coming through and their future colour is far

At six weeks this kitten has all its milk teeth.

Kittens bred by Sandra Miller, red and blue tortie. Their eyes are beginning to change colour.

more apparent, especially the nose leather, the paw pads, the edges of the ears, the tails and possibly along the spine. Their eyes are beginning to change colour.

During the weaning period it is quite common for the queen to develop diarrhoea for a while. The kittens are beginning to take in nourishment other than that produced by their mother and they are using the litter tray to empty their bowels. As she is still cleaning them, she is ingesting bacteria foreign to her system, and her body may also be having to cope with her unused milk. Don't panic, but by all means have her checked out by your vet.

6–7 weeks

You should consider worming the kittens at this age, using a wormer intended specifically for kittens, obtainable from your vet. They will be stropping their claws, so provide a suitable scratching post. Continue to feed four meals a day, including a milk meal if they will take it. This is a very critical time for the socialisation of kittens. Gently introduce them to all the usual household noises: washing machines, tumble dryers, vacuum cleaners and hair dryers. If a kitten is frightened by anything at this age it may remain fearful of it for the rest of its life. Socialisation with people is also very important. Constant contact just with yourself is fine, but limiting, and likely to ensure that the kittens become fixated upon you. I find that leaving a television or radio on in their presence from a young age is beneficial, but they still need to see, smell and be handled by several people. This is especially advantageous if the kitten is going to be shown.

7–10 weeks

By this time you will probably be sure of their sex and fairly certain of their coat pattern and colour. Don't be concerned about the eye colour; it will still be changing, unless it is clear blue. They should be on four solid meals a day, which may be supplemented with suitable cat biscuits. They should be feeding from separate bowls. The males weigh more than the females and are usually bigger overall. Kittens, like all babies, grow in a Christmas-tree pattern – length/height, then girth (up and out, up and out). As long as they continue to put on weight, don't be too concerned if they look long and lanky

Chapter 9

at this stage. Their ears are now higher on their heads and quite large. Their ears, face masks, tail, feet and legs are displaying distinct colour, even though their body colour may still be very pale – this is often the case with chocolates, lilacs, reds and creams. By eight weeks, the kittens have learned the basics of hunting and killing, even if it's only a twig, toy mouse or sock. They know that other cats are not always potential enemies, and have advanced litter-tray habits.

Mymystic Pasha (blue tabby) exploring his new world.

From left to right:
Samkabar's Metaphor (choc), Mephisto (brown), Mila (choc) and Methinks (blue).

Zeotrope Chiquita, first New Zealand Tonkinese to win Breeder's Award of Merit. Note changing eye colour.

10–12 weeks

The kittens have developed a full set of social and hunting skills and are ready to put them into practice. At 12 weeks they are ready to leave home, free of worms and fleas, fit and active, and used to being handled. Some breeders keep their kittens for 13 weeks, giving them time to recover from the inoculations.

7–9 months

A full set of adult teeth have erupted; kittens not required for breeding should have been spayed or neutered. Their eye and coat colours may still be developing. For show purposes, kittens officially become adult cats at the age of nine months in Great Britain and eight months in the United States.

SORTING OUT YOUR KITTENS
Sexing a kitten

Sexing a kitten, especially a very young kitten, is more difficult than sexing an adult cat because the anus and genitalia are so much closer together. Even the most experienced breeder may occasionally make an error. The anus should be easy to discern in either sex, as the fur stops short of it, forming a circular bald area the size of a small button. In some kittens the genitalia are quite difficult

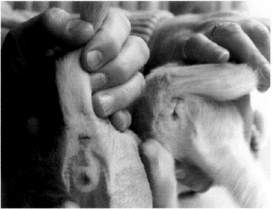

At seven weeks: (left) male, (right) female.

to see. This problem may be eliminated by wetting the area so that the shape of the genital organ itself can be seen: a round dot for males and a short line for females.

183

Chapter 9

In six-week-old male kittens, the testicles are internal and the scrotum is often undeveloped. The sheathed penis is typically about 13mm below the anus, increasing to 40mm by ten weeks of age. The scrotum, containing the testicles, is directly below the anus and, in a mature male Tonkinese, the scrotum is usually the same colour as the cat's lower limbs. In neutered males, the scrotum may be smaller, but is usually still obvious. Normally by twelve weeks the kitten's testicles have descended and sexing is as for an adult cat.

In six-week-old female kittens, the vulva is seen as a short line about 6mm below the anus. In appearance, the anus and vulva form an upside-down exclamation point.

What colours do you have?

As far as the Tonkinese are concerned this is some question! An experienced Tonkinese breeder once told me that it may take three litters before you can be sure what colours your queen will produce. By studying the queen's and sire's pedigrees you should have a good idea of what she is able to produce but, until you've had those kittens, you cannot be sure that she is carrying the colours you expect. Test matings with dominant colours are the surest way to prove what your new queen, or stud, carries.

Kittens with the tonkinese coat pattern vary in the way their colour develops according to what

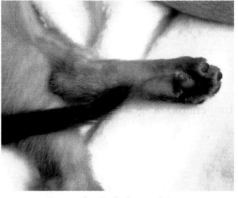
Foot and tail of a brown kitten.

colour they are, possibly which generation they are and whether they have a poor or good tonkinese coat pattern. First generation (Burmese x Siamese) kittens are the easiest to sort out since there are no variants from such a mating. The first positive indications of the actual colour are seen on the edge of the ears (like a seam joining the inside and outside of the ears together) and the nose leather. Tabby nose leathers are generally a shade of

Foot and tail of a blue kitten.

Foot and tail of a chocolate kitten.

pink with the significant colour appearing as a pencil line around the nose. Tortie nose leathers may be a solid colour or mottled with shades of pink. The colour on the tail, ears, paw pads and mask then gradually develops – often in that order.

Siamese kittens are born completely white, and their points colour up gradually. Burmese kittens are born with colour all over the body, and this gradually deepens. Tonkinese variant kittens normally follow the equivalent development pattern. A distinct separation of point colour from body colour is typical for Siamese, a lack of distinction for Burmese, but this is not so clear with the sex-linked reds, creams and torties. In general, a good tonkinese coat pattern is associated with good eye colour, and variant coat pattern with strong associated eye colour, so the development of eye colour is another useful guide as to whether or not your Tonkinese

Foot and tail of a lilac kitten.

has a variant coat pattern. By 10 weeks a kitten that still has clear blue eyes (in other words, eyes with no pigmentation other than shades of blue) is more likely to have a variant (Siamese) coat pattern; a kitten with yellowish-green eyes is more likely to have a variant (Burmese) coat pattern. A kitten with indistinct eye colour at that age (for instance, bluish in the middle changing to dark yellowish green at the outer edge, or vice versa) has a good chance of developing correct Tonkinese eye colour eventually.

Tip: In some kittens the strongest colour first appears on the 'seam' along the edge of the kitten's ears and on the nose leather.

Development patterns can vary from litter to litter and I have heard breeders say that their kittens have 'changed colour' at around the age of five, six or even seven weeks. I've had such a mortifying experience myself: my 'blue' kittens, confirmed as blue by other breeders, settled into a definite

Chapter 9

brown. Don't be disheartened by the apparent difficulties of sorting out your colours; just think of it as yet another aspect of the breed that makes it unique and interesting. You will soon learn to recognise the colours of your kittens and be able to concentrate on differentiating between your coat patterns. Remember there are always other breeders who are happy to help you. If you are uncertain just don't register your kittens too soon. For more detail on individual colours see chapter 3.

VACCINATION

For information on the basic principles of immunity and the difference between *live* and *killed* vaccines, see **Vaccination** in chapter 7 (page 112–113).

Normally, kittens are protected against cat flu and enteritis by antibodies passed to them from their mother's first milk, the colostrum. As this immunity also has the effect of preventing the kitten from manufacturing its own antibodies while still suckling, it is usual to wait until it is fully weaned from its mother's milk at eight to nine

'What are you doing?' A Trampuss litter.

weeks before vaccination. Arrange with your vet to vaccinate your kittens against cat flu and enteritis when they are nine weeks old, with the second dose three weeks later. After this the kitten will only need an annual booster to maintain necessary antibody levels.

Many cats are now vaccinated against FeLV, but it is worth noting that many breeders prefer not to have their kittens vaccinated against FeLV at the same time as they are vaccinated against cat flu and enteritis. The potent combination of vaccines usually makes kittens very unwell for a period. It may be preferable for the new owners to wait until the kittens have settled with them for a couple of weeks (by which time the cat flu and enteritis vaccinations are optimally effective) before they are vaccinated against FeLV. An annual booster is necessary, and now a three-in-one vaccine is available (cat flu, enteritis and FeLV).

After their first stage vaccinations you may find that some of the kittens react more than others. If this is the case, consult your vet. There may be a bump the size and shape of a penny under the skin. This is just where the oily fluid is taking time to disperse and is nothing to worry about.

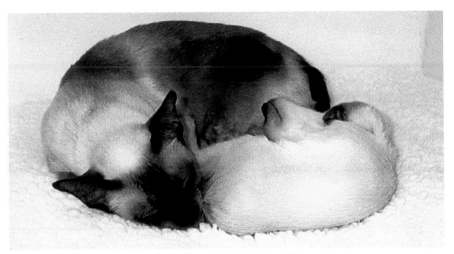

Ishokats Bianka (choc) with her kitten.

BREEDING PROBLEMS
Abortion
This is the abnormal expulsion of a foetus, alive or dead. Abortion may occur as a result of bacterial or viral infection, hormonal imbalance or accident during pregnancy. Abortions due to hormonal imbalance usually occur around the seventh week of pregnancy. In the event of abortion, take the following steps to ensure that problems are not passed on to other queens:

- Isolate other queens from the area in which the abortion occurred. This area must be disinfected.
- Take the queen to the vet (with the foetus and foetal membrane) for any necessary treatment, tests or post mortem to establish the cause of abortion.
- Keep the queen isolated in an easily-disinfected area until the results of the tests are known, but give her plenty of care and reassurance.
- Scrupulous hygienic conditions must be maintained, especially around other pregnant queens.

Abnormalities
Abnormalities may be congenital (present from birth, either inherited or due to an event occurring during pregnancy) or acquired as a result of infection or injury after birth. There are few genetically inherited problems in the Tonkinese breed and those that do occur are, unfortunately, known problems brought into the breed from either the Burmese or Siamese lines. Those that may occasionally arise include bent or kinked tails, flattened chests, hooked sternums and crossed eyes. A cat that exhibits any deformities should not be bred from. Congenital abnormalities in kittens may be caused by a number of

187

factors: incompatibility of the queen and stud, genetic factors, accidents to the queen during pregnancy, administration of vaccines or other drugs that are dangerous for the developing kittens during pregnancy, or many other possibilities. It is not advisable to try to rear a seriously deformed kitten; it should be put to sleep as quickly and painlessly as possible by a vet. Unfortunately, seriously deformed kittens, such as one with a pronounced umbilical hernia (where the intestines and even some organs are enclosed in a pouch of skin outside of the body cavity), are often unaware of their deformity and fight to live. This is very upsetting, but such a kitten couldn't possibly survive for long and is likely to cause the queen distress.

Cleft palate A partial opening in, or entire absence of, the roof of the mouth, causing severe breathing and eating difficulties. The first signs may be bubbles coming from the kitten's nose as it tries to suckle. Euthanasia is normally advised. This abnormality is more usual in Persian cats.

(Left) Partial cleft palate, (centre) unilateral cleft palate, (right) bi-lateral cleft palate.

Cryptorchid This refers to a mature male cat whose testicles have not descended. If only one testicle remains undescended it is called *monorchidism*. Breeding from such cats is not recommended.

Eye problems Tonkinese kittens don't usually begin to open their eyes before they are about four days to a week old. If they are **born with open eyes**, seek veterinary advice, as their eyes will be prone to infection and must be kept moist with appropriate treatment. Failure to do this may lead to blindness.

Kittens born with swollen eyes must receive immediate veterinary attention, as this may be due to a condition known as **opthalmia neonatum** or neonatal conjunctivitis. This is an infection that develops within the conjunctival sac before the eyelids open, and often more than one member of the litter is affected. It has been suggested that the trauma of birth may force the eyelids apart temporarily, allowing bacteria from the queen's vagina to enter the eyes, causing the infection. The first sign is a swelling of the fused eyelids with, occasionally, the escape of a small amount of pus. This is a serious condition, as ulceration of the cornea may occur and can lead to permanent blindness. It must be treated promptly, and only by a vet.

Crossed eyes, which are not always immediately apparent but become so as the kitten matures, are not usually more than a cosmetic problem. However, extreme or rapid crossing of the eyes should be checked by a vet. Some kittens who appear to have crossed eyes grow out of it.

Sticky eyes in kittens may be caused by many things: environmental problems such as dust from the litter being used, irritation from the queen's fur when the kitten is suckling, injuries such as a scratch from another kitten or an infection such as conjunctivitis.

Consult your vet if there are any problems with the kittens' eyes. Don't be tempted to wash the eyes out yourself, because damage to the eyeball is permanent.

Flat Chested Kittens (FCK)
This thoracic deformity has been found in most breeds of cat but is seen significantly in Burmese and Burmese-related breeds like the Tonkinese. The defect is not usually apparent at birth but develops during the first weeks of life. It is a flattening of the thoracic cavity, which causes angulation of the rib cage and often an abnormal spinal curve, seen as a dip over the shoulder blades (*kyphosis*, referred to as *hunchback* in humans). The severity of the deformity varies considerably, and kittens that

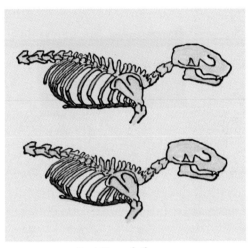

(top) Normal rib cage.
(bottom) Flattened rib cage.

survive often develop a normal chest shape by adulthood. Studies at the Feline Centre at Langford have indicated that the condition may be inherited or result from other non-heritable, environmental factors. No specific treatments have been shown to be effective. Euthanasia should be considered for severely affected kittens. If they survive, most FCKs have a normal life expectancy, but they should not be bred from. As both the stud and the queen contribute to the FCK syndrome, avoid mating queens who produce FCKs with studs who produce FCKs. It has been observed by some breeders of Burmese that often it is only the queen's first litter that includes one or more FCKs.

Hare lip This may be associated with a cleft palate, but not necessarily. The upper lip does not join in the middle, which causes severe difficulties in breathing and eating. Euthanasia is normally advised.

(left) Normal head-on view of rib cage.
(right) Ribs flattened beneath, constricting chest cavity.

189

Hernia Fatty tissue or intestines pass through a hole in the muscles of the abdominal wall and press against the skin, forming a visible swelling. If the hole is large enough, a loop of intestine may become twisted, affecting the blood supply and causing severe infection. An umbilical hernia may be caused by the cord being broken or pulled too vigorously by the queen or a helper. Many small umbilical hernias resolve themselves over a period of about eight months. In all cases of hernia, consult your vet, as surgery may be necessary. If the hernia is congenital the kitten shouldn't be bred from.

Hooked sternum The small section of cartilage (xiphoid sternum) at the lower end of the sternum lies forward facing instead of in line with the sternum. It is seen as a hard lump in the middle of the lower chest. This is a purely cosmetic abnormality and causes no problems for the cat, but cats with this fault shouldn't be bred from.

Tail faults These range from an invisible and almost imperceptible 'pip' on the end of the tail to the more obvious kink in a joint near the end of the tail. Neither of these is likely to affect the cat's quality of life; indeed cats of many breeds with a tail pip are successfully shown. However, when a tail kink occurs at the root of the tail, it is considered to be a serious defect, as it may be the effect of spinal and possible organ deformities, so veterinary advice should be sought.

(left) Detail showing xiphoid sternum in hooked position.
(right) Xiphoid sternum in correct position.

FALSE PREGNANCIES (phantom pregnancies)

It is quite possible for a female cat to go through the usual changes associated with pregnancy but not actually have kittens. This may happen if the kittens are naturally aborted or she is artificially induced to ovulate (see **Contraception**), but there may also be psychological reasons. She may produce milk, although this is uncommon, and she will become enlarged and build her kittening nest. In extreme cases she may adopt a surrogate kitten in the form of a small toy or even steal a kitten from the litter of another queen. Drugs are available from your vet to dry up any milk produced and cases of phantom pregnancies generally sort themselves out spontaneously after about 40 days. Just be patient with her.

DUAL-MATING

Cats have the ability to carry kittens in the same litter from more than one sire (super-fecundity). This is a biological peculiarity they share with ferrets and mink. For this reason you must ensure that your queen doesn't leave the house after she has been to stud. Firstly there is the risk that she may still be calling and will mis-mate with a local tom; secondly, there is the ever-present risk of her contracting disease.

MONGREL LITTERS

Surprisingly, many people used to think that, if their pedigree queen was mated by the local tom, she would be spoiled and so would her future litters. This supposed influence of the sire is called *Telegony*, and is not correct. Once the queen has had her mongrel kittens, which are usually very striking, she can be mated again in due course. If this should happen to you, for the sake of both your queen and her developing kittens, it is wise to have her blood-tested as soon as possible after the mating to be sure that she has not contracted any disease from the stray tom. Keep her separated from the rest of your cats until you have a safe result.

TONKINESE REGISTRATION IN GREAT BRITAIN (GCCF)

As the breeder, you may register your kittens with the GCCF as:

- Active – indicating that you are permitting them to be bred from and any progeny may be registered.
- Non-Active – indicating that you do not wish them to be bred from. Any progeny from such a cat will not be registered by the GCCF.

A breeder with a GCCF prefix who does not wish to register all of the kittens in the litter (for instance, omitting those that are never going to be bred from or shown) is required to declare the sex, breed number and colour of the non-registered kittens. There is no fee for declaring kittens and no kitten names are required. The reason for the declaration is to

Chocolate kitten. Photo: Animals Unlimited

191

Chapter 9

GCCF registration form.

GCCF registration certificate.

enable the genetic make-up of the cat to be recorded for future reference. Declared cats may be registered at a later date by the breeder *or* owner so, if you wish to safeguard a cat from being bred from, it is advisable to register it non-active.

GCCF registration forms are obtainable from the GCCF offices (see **Useful Addresses**). Once the completed forms are received by the GCCF they may take up to four weeks to process, so I recommend that you send off the completed forms as soon as you are sure of the kitten's coat patterns and colour. The new owners are entitled to expect their Tonkinese to be properly registered and to receive the registration papers when they collect their kittens from you. The GCCF will return a white registration certificate and a pink ownership transfer form for each kitten; keep the certificate and give the transfer form to the new owner, duly signed and dated by yourself.

Cats may be transferred from the active to the non-active register by the legal owner, but only the breeder may transfer a cat from the non-active to the active register.

Note: The GCCF requires that any litter comprised solely of red and red-tabby kittens, or cream and cream-tabby kittens, is registered as an all-tabby litter. This is because the red and cream colours normally show some tabby barring, which may be quite heavy and indistinguishable from a tabby pattern.

Registration bodies

The first body to set up a register of cats was the National Cat Club, which handed over its functions to the newly-created Governing Council of the Cat Fancy (GCCF) on 11 March 1910. The GCCF is still the principal body for the registration of cats in Great Britain. For a cat to be registered as a Tonkinese with the GCCF its breeding must comply with an approved registration policy. A sound registration policy is crucial for any new breed as this is what defines and regulates the breed. The GCCF recognises all three Tonkinese coat patterns and for registration it uses the abbreviations TKSMVA for a Tonkinese variant with a pointed (Siamese) coat pattern and TKBUVA for a Tonkinese variant with a solid (Burmese) coat pattern.

The Tonkinese Breed Advisory Committee

On 26 October 1994 the Tonkinese Breed Club was granted affiliation with the GCCF. This was a significant and important step for the Tonkinese because it meant that the breed would thereafter be represented by an independent Breed Advisory Committee (BAC), governed by the rules of the GCCF. Each GCCF-recognised breed has only one BAC, comprising representatives from relevant GCCF-affiliated breed clubs (referred to as constituent clubs). At present, the Tonkinese Breed Club is the Tonkinese BAC's only constituent club. All changes to the breed's Registration Policy, Standard of Points and matters relating to the exhibition of Tonkinese under the GCCF are the province of the Tonkinese BAC. In agreement with Tonkinese breeders the Tonkinese BAC has since refined the registration policy to ensure that the Tonkinese progresses as a distinct breed rather than continuing to back-cross with the Burmese and Siamese breeds. The new policy was approved by the GCCF Council on 28 February 1996.

Chapter 9

Breeds permitted in the pedigree of Tonkinese cats

- *Tonkinese*: Tonkinese with the typical coat pattern expressed in any of the following colours: brown, blue, chocolate, lilac, these colours in tortie and tortie-tabby, red, cream and all six colours in tabby.
- *Tonkinese variant*: a cat from the mating of a Tonkinese to a Tonkinese, a Tonkinese variant, a Burmese or a Siamese whose coat pattern is of either Burmese or Siamese appearance in any of the colours and/or patterns described above.
- *Burmese and Siamese*: On their respective Full Registers but only in accordance with the requirements of the Tonkinese registration policy given below.

Note: All offspring of Tonkinese variants mated to similar breed of origin will be registered as the appropriate coat pattern Tonkinese variants (ie progeny from Tonkinese variant (Burmese coat pattern) x Burmese, or Tonkinese variant (Siamese coat pattern) x Siamese).

Breed numbers permitted in the pedigree of Tonkinese

- Tonkinese breed numbers: all
- Burmese breed numbers: 27, 27a–27h, 27j
- Siamese breed numbers: 24, 24a–24c, 32/1–32/6, 32a, 32b/1–32b/4, 32c, 32t1–32t4

Note: Siamese colours Cinnamon (24k), Caramel (24n) and Fawn (24r) are not acceptable. See chapter 4 for further information.

Tonkinese breed numbers (GCCF)

Colour	Tonkinese	Variant (Bu)	Variant (Si)
Brown	74	74qv	74v
Blue	74a	74aqv	74av
Chocolate	74b	74bqv	74bv
Lilac	74c	74cqv	74cv
Red	74d	74dqv	74dv
Brown Tortie	74e	74eqv	74ev
Cream	74f	74fqv	74fv
Blue Tortie	74g	74gqv	74gv
Chocolate Tortie	74h	74hqv	74hv
Lilac Tortie	74j	74jqv	74jv
Brown Tabby	74t	74tqv	74tv
Blue Tabby	74at	74atqv	74atv
Chocolate Tabby	74bt	74btqv	74btv

Lilac Tabby	74ct	74ctqv	74ctv
Red Tabby	74dt	74dtqv	74dtv
Brown Tortie-Tabby	74et	74etqv	74etv
Cream Tabby	74ft	74ftqv	74ftv
Blue Tortie-Tabby	74gt	74gtqv	74gtv
Chocolate Tortie-Tabby	74ht	74htqv	74htv
Lilac Tortie-Tabby	74jt	74jtqv	74jtv

GCCF registration policy

Full Register: Tonkinese with Championship or Provisional status that have only Tonkinese in their pedigree within three (3) generations.

Supplementary Register: Tonkinese with Championship or Provisional status that have in their pedigree, within three (3) generations, only Tonkinese on the Full, Supplementary or Experimental Register, Tonkinese Variants and

i   The progeny of Tonkinese or Tonkinese Variants mated with either Burmese or Siamese (on their respective Full Registers), born on or before 31 December 1996.

ii   The progeny of Burmese on the Full Register mated with Siamese on the Full Register, born on or before 31 December 1998.

Experimental Register: Tonkinese with Preliminary Recognition which have in their pedigree, within three (3) generations, only Tonkinese or Tonkinese Variants and

i   The progeny of Tonkinese or Tonkinese Variants mated with either Burmese or Siamese (on their respective Full Registers), born on or before 31 December 1996.

ii   The progeny of Burmese on the Full Register mated with Siamese on the Full Register, born on or before 31 December 1998.

Reference Register: All Tonkinese Variants plus

i   Tonkinese that have in their pedigree, within five (5) generations, any breeds other than those permitted in the Tonkinese pedigree. This includes Burmese or Siamese not on the Full Register, cats with unknown background and cats that have not been registered.

ii   Tonkinese or Tonkinese Variants from the mating of a Tonkinese or Tonkinese Variant to a Burmese or Siamese on the Full Register (born on or after 1 January 1997) or the progeny from these cats, that have in their pedigree, within three (3) generations, Burmese or Siamese.

iii   Tonkinese from the mating of a Burmese on the Full Register to a Siamese on the Full Register (born on or after 1 January 1999) or the progeny from these cats that have in their pedigree, within three (3) generations, Burmese or Siamese.

Chapter 9

Note: The three (3) generation requirement for the Full Register to be increased to five (5) generations as soon as is practicable.

Breed progression

As far as breed progression is concerned, what the registration policy means to Tonkinese breeders is that:

Kittens born with these parents:	Will be placed on this register:	If their date of birth is:
Tonkinese x Burmese (or Siamese)	Reference	1997 onwards
Tonkinese Variant x Burmese (or Siamese)	Reference	1997 onwards
Burmese x Siamese	Reference	1999 onwards

Kittens and cats may be registered only between the ages of two months and two years. Once they have been registered it will make no difference to them if the registration policy changes because registration is not retrospective. For instance, if your Tonkinese kitten is born before 1997 from a Tonkinese x Siamese mating, it is eligible to go on the Experimental register and there it will remain. This will not prevent it from being shown when the breed is promoted.

Some breeders are of the opinion that, once we are only breeding with Tonkinese and Tonkinese variants, we should cease to breed with our first-generation cats. This option may be considered, but hopefully not until some years into the 21st century. There would be little point in continuing to enlarge our gene pool up until 1999 if we then eliminate the use of those new first-generation lines.

REGISTRATION WORLD-WIDE

This is a subject of considerable diversity so I have included just a few examples for information. However, regardless of each authority's specific requirements for registering a Tonkinese, the common factor, wherever the Tonkinese is being bred, is to achieve a cat with health, vigour, subtlety of colouring and clarity of eye colour.

Europe

The Fédération Internationale Féline (FIFe), established in 1949, is now the largest cat body, with affiliates in many countries of the world. The FIFe is a chartered body managed by an executive board of experts who are elected to serve a term of three years. In Europe many countries have more than one registering body, at least one of which is likely to be affiliated to the FIFe. The British member of the FIFe is the Cat Association of Britain (CA).

The Tonkinese breed is not recognised by the FIFe: it is categorised as XSH (unclassified Short-hair) with the registration codes TON non, 32, 66 (TONkinese non-recognised, coat pattern in the pointed series, Tonkinese eye-colour). Before its affiliation with the FIFe, the CA granted the Tonkinese provisional recognition as a new breed and it was granted a

A Tonkinese from Germany: Anderwelt Isabelle (brown).

dispensation to keep the provisional status for the Tonkinese. The recognised colours are the six non-agouti basic colours (brown, blue, chocolate, lilac, red and cream) and their four corresponding tortoiseshell colours (brown, blue, chocolate and lilac), but only in the tonkinese (cbcs) coat pattern. Before the Tonkinese can be promoted under the CA they must be officially recognised by the FIFe.

Many other bodies in Europe register cats and license cat shows, among them the World Cat Federation, in which Tonkinese may achieve championship status.

United States of America and Canada

There is no central co-ordination of cat clubs in the United States, but there are nine bodies of national scope. The largest of these is the Cat Fanciers Association (CFA), which registers about 90% of all registered cats in that country. Each body has its own registration system, none of which uses breed numbers as we do in Great Britain. Instead, the registration numbers indicate the breed, colour and, in the case of the CFA, the sex of the cat.

Chapter 9

A Tonkinese from the United States of America: Gr Ch Shanfoo's Shampagne of Sulltan (choc).

The recognition of breeds differs from body to body. Some breeds may not be recognised, or are recognised differently by the various bodies. For example, the red-point Siamese is also registered as a red Colourpoint short-hair. Certain breeds are recognised by all registering bodies but the permissible colours vary. For instance, the Burmese may only be brown (sable) according to most bodies, but a few of the smaller bodies also recognise blue and/or champagne (chocolate) and/or platinum (lilac). Elsewhere these colours are registered as the Himalayan cat. The Cat Fanciers Association (in common with the Canadian Cat Association) recognises four breed categories:

Natural: Both parents and all ancestors to be of the same breed as the cat to be registered. Thus, only seal, blue, chocolate and lilac are allowed in the Siamese, and even then a seven-generation pedigree may be necessary. Other cats in this group are the Abyssinian, Domestic (American) Short-hair,

Another American Tonkinese:
Pendragon Lily's Equinox (choc).

Persian, Manx, Russian Blue, Maine Coon, British Short-hair, Turkish Angora, Egyptian Mau and Japanese Bobtail.

Established: Cats that are the result of breeding with two or more Natural breeds. They may only continue as an Established breed by breeding with each other; in other words, without further outcrosses to the original Natural breeds. The Burmese (brown only) is classified under this group, as are the Korat and the Balinese.

Mutations: These are offspring of Natural breeds that have distinct or different characteristics, which may be perpetuated by breeding specimens of the Natural breed and/or the Mutation. Rex and Somali are in this group.

Hybrids: These are cats resulting from the cross-breeding of two or more Natural breeds. They differ from Established breeds only in that future outcrosses to the original Natural breeds are allowed to continue in their breeding programmes to maintain desirable characteristics and colours. Breeds in this group are the Tonkinese, Himalayan (Burmese of any colour other than brown), Havana and Colour-point.

It is interesting to consider that, had the Burmese been introduced to the West before the arrival of the Siamese, it may have been the Burmese that was classified as a Natural breed and the Siamese as an Established breed. The Burmese appears to be regarded as a Natural breed where the classification of the Tonkinese as a Hybrid is concerned.

New Zealand

In New Zealand the registration system is founded on Breed/Type rather than colour or hair length. The Tonkinese is Breed/Type number 35. However, first generation Tonkinese, resulting from either an outcross or a back-cross mating, are registered as Breed 26V, which is Any Other Variety Short-hair (Siamese/Burmese Hybrid, First Generation). In other words, the breed is only recognised as such when it results from a Tonkinese x Tonkinese breeding programme.

A Tonkinese from New Zealand:
Utopia Kachaturian (lilac).

10
The Tonkinese at GCCF shows

SHOWING YOUR TONKINESE

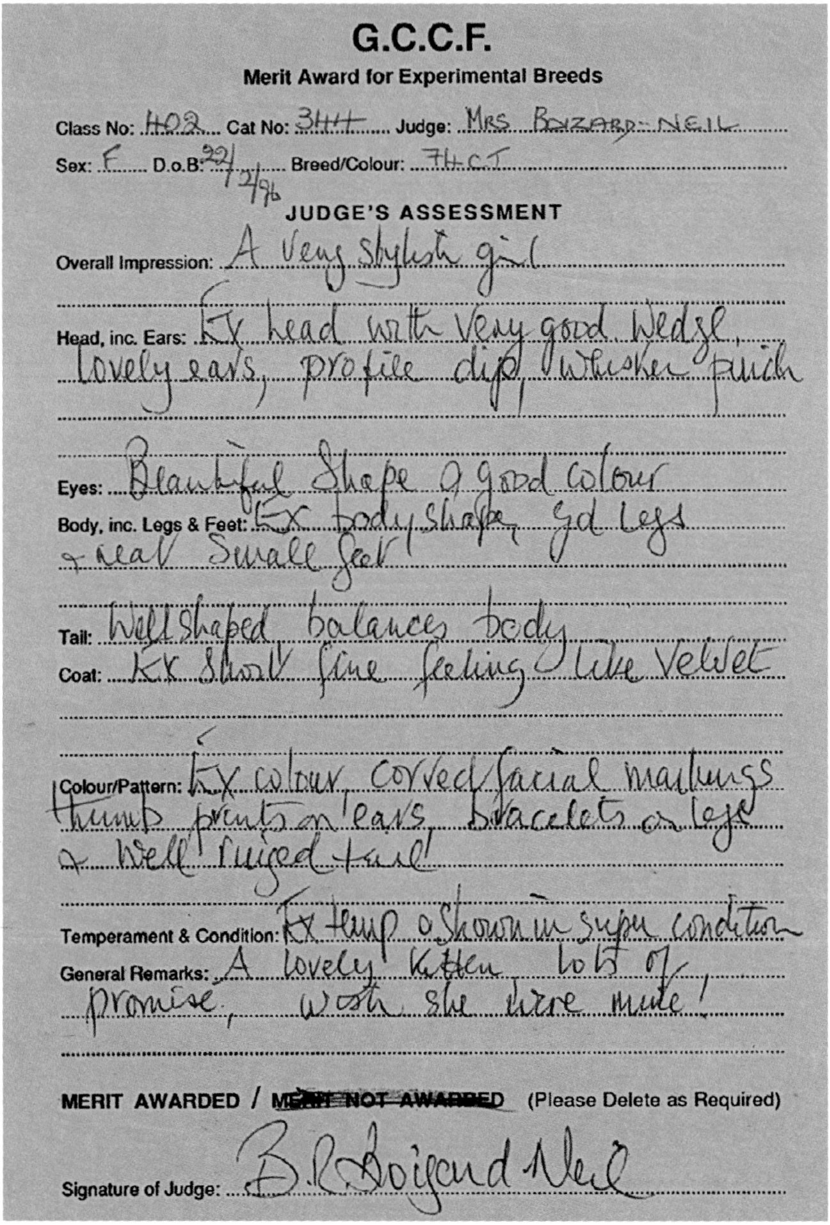

G.C.C.F.
Merit Award for Experimental Breeds

Class No: ..H02.... Cat No: ..3444.... Judge: ..MRS BOIZARD-NEIL..........

Sex: ..F.... D.o.B: ..22/12/96.... Breed/Colour: ..THCT......

JUDGE'S ASSESSMENT

Overall Impression: ..A very stylish girl....

Head, inc. Ears: ..Ex head with very good wedge, lovely ears, profile dip, whisker pinch....

Eyes: ..Beautiful shape & good colour....

Body, inc. Legs & Feet: ..Ex body shape, gd legs + neat small feet....

Tail: ..Well shaped balances body....

Coat: ..Ex short fine feeling like velvet....

Colour/Pattern: ..Ex colour, correct facial markings thumb prints on ears, bracelets on legs + well ringed tail....

Temperament & Condition: ..Ex temp o shown in super condition....

General Remarks: ..A lovely kitten lots of promise, wish she were mine!....

MERIT AWARDED / ~~MERIT NOT AWARDED~~ (Please Delete as Required)

Signature of Judge: ..B R Boizard Neil.........

Judge's critique of a Tonkinese in an assessment class.

Showing your Tonkinese can be frustrating as well as uplifting, and it is also time-consuming and relatively expensive. However, it is most satisfying when the judges show that they agree with your own opinion by awarding your beautiful cat a certificate and rosette. If you are a breeder then the awards and attention that your Tonkinese receive are the best possible advertisements for you.

Curiously enough, some people consider neuters to be second-class citizens. This is definitely not so; in fact, since 1945, there has even been a club specifically catering for neuters (the Kensington Kitten and Neuter Cat Club). It the constancy of the neuters on the show bench, while our queens and studs are at home breeding, that keeps Tonkinese in the public eye, proving their worth in competition with other breeds and thus ultimately ensuring the breed's promotion. Breeders and exhibitors must share any credit for the popularity of the breed.

Whatever the breed, a breeder probably cannot guarantee you a show-quality kitten. This is certainly so with Tonkinese, because they can take several months to show their competition potential, especially the blues and the browns. Nevertheless, do heed the advice of your cat's breeder, who should be able to tell you if a kitten is definitely not suitable to put on the bench and should explain both the good points and any faults your cat may have according to the show standard.

At GCCF shows there are two types of main class related to the breed's recognition status:

- *Open class:* Breeds with either Provisional or full Championship recognition enter these classes. Cats compete with other cats of the same breed, colour and sex for first place, Best of Breed and certificates. Breeds with Provisional recognition compete for Intermediate Certificates (ICs); breeds with full Championship recognition compete for Challenge Certificates (CCs) and Premier Certificates (PCs). Kittens may be shown but are not eligible to compete for certificates.
- *Assessment class:* As a breed with Preliminary recognition the Tonkinese are shown in Assessment classes. This means they are not competing with each other but are assessed individually against the Tonkinese Standard of Points. If the judge decides that a kitten or cat meets the breed standard a Merit Certificate is awarded. This is the only class for which you receive a copy of the judge's critique (a pink paper), which is placed on your kitten/cat's pen before the show closes. If your Tonkinese wins a Merit Certificate it is eligible to enter the GCCF Supreme Cat Show.

A good Tonkinese is likely to win its Merit Certificate. Naturally, the more often such a cat is shown the more Merits it will win, so a highly-merited Tonkinese is not necessarily better than one shown less and therefore awarded fewer Merits. For this reason, we should not regard any Tonkinese bloodline as being better than another on the basis of Assessment class results.

First things first

Do you have a Tonkinese that is suitable for showing? Remember that Tonkinese variants cannot be shown. Does your Tonkinese have good type, a good coat pattern and good eye colour? Does your Tonkinese have a good temperament? Has your cat been registered with the GCCF and transferred into your name as the owner? If your answer to all of these questions is 'yes', your next step is to select the correct shows. Here are the basic steps, 1997 prices being quoted throughout:

1 Send a cheque for £3 to the GCCF (see **Useful Addresses**) for a copy of the latest show calendar. This lists all GCCF-licensed shows for the show season (1 June to 31 May) and provides the names and addresses of the show managers. Even if you're not going to be showing for a while it will give you a good idea of what shows there are within your chosen travelling distance. It's also worthwhile sending off for a couple of schedules, as they contain all the rules and requirements and give you a good idea of the classes held. Go along and see a few shows, chat with other Tonkinese exhibitors, get an idea of the procedures and pick up hints and tips from the old hands. Shows are the best (and often only) places to buy the equipment you'll need.

Deelando Rachels Angel (choc).
Photo: Alan Robinson

2 Choose your shows. It's probably best for the kitten's sake, and your own, to start with something close to home. Write to the show manager for a schedule and be sure to enclose a C5 stamped, self-addressed envelope. Plan your own show diary well in advance because the closing date for receipt of entry forms is usually six to eight weeks before the show date. There are three types of GCCF show:

Exemption The first shows that GCCF affiliated clubs are licensed to hold. They are usually quite small and often more relaxed than Sanction or Championship shows. At present this is the only type of show in which the Tonkinese compete in Open classes against each other, winning First, Second and Third places instead of Merits.

Sanction After running three Exemption shows to get their hand in and prove to the GCCF that there is sufficient support for their shows, affiliated clubs may be granted a Sanction show licence. Assessment breeds were placed in Open classes but in 1994 the GCCF ruled that Assessment classes would be held at these shows enabling Assessment breeds to win their Merit Certificates.

Championship After running three Sanction shows a club may be granted a Championship show licence. Assessment breeds may win their Merit Certificates, Provisional breeds compete for Intermediate Certificates (ICs) and Championship breeds compete for Challenge and Premier Certificates (CCs and PCs). The **GCCF Supreme Show** (the only show actually run by the GCCF) is a Championship show with unique rules and awards, so be sure to read the schedule carefully.

3   When your schedule arrives, study the rules very carefully. This would be a good time to consult with an experienced exhibitor or your cat's breeder about picking classes. You must enter your cat in the relevant Assessment class (or Open class when the breed recognition status progresses) but the choice of miscellaneous classes is up to you. Make sure you enter the correct minimum number of classes. When completing the entry form, copy your cat's details exactly from its registration form. One possible pitfall is the name of the breeder, who is not specifically referred to on the registration forms. The breeder is the person (or persons) who is the registered owner of the queen when the kitten is born.

Note: The classes your Tonkinese is eligible to enter depend what it has won up to, and including, the day you send off your entry form. The exceptions are classes related to the age and sex status of your Tonkinese, which are in accordance with your Tonkinese's status on the day of the show. When the age or sex status of your Tonkinese changes (in other words, when a kitten becomes an adult at nine calendar months of age or when a kitten or adult is neutered) it becomes eligible to enter classes as if it were a debutante again. This is because all previous show results are invalid for the new status. This means you can enter your cat as a debutante up to three times during its show career: as a kitten, as an adult and as a neutered adult.

4   Having selected your classes, completed the correct entry form (the schedules normally contain both a non-pedigree and a pedigree entry form), signed it and made out an appropriate cheque, be sure that you also enclose a copy of your Standard of Points (SOP) and a stamped,

addressed envelope for your entry to be acknowledged. Don't forget to order your catalogue and, if necessary, an admission ticket. Believe it or not, there are some shows that charge you extra to get in even if you are entering cats in the show! If you can, it's a good idea to keep a photocopy of your entry form.

Equipment

To show your Tonkinese you will need a limited amount of equipment, none of which must show any distinguishing marks or labels :

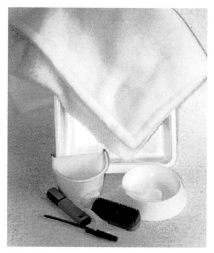

Basic show equipment.

- White blanket or vet bed, non-cellular
- White litter tray, small (pens are normally 60cm x 60cm x 60cm (2ft x 2ft x 2ft)
- White water bowl (the 'D' shaped bowls are best, as they can hang on the side or back of the pen to avoid being knocked over)
- White food bowl
- White tape to tie the pen tag around the cat's neck

In addition, you should take:

- Your cat's Vaccination Certificate (this is compulsory)
- Vet wipes (such as Formula H)
- Spare SOP
- Your copy of the entry form
- A pen to mark up your catalogue
- Food, water and litter for your cat (usually obtainable at the larger shows)
- A purse full of pennies – there's always something to buy at these shows!

Most of this equipment can be bought either at a show or from companies advertising in cat magazines. The SOP for your particular colour of Tonkinese is available from the Hon Secretary of the Tonkinese Breed Advisory Committee (BAC) on receipt of a stamped, addressed envelope (see **Useful Addresses**).

Preparing your Tonkinese for the show

Regular grooming (see chapter 6) reduces the effort needed for that extra special show preparation, but it's always worthwhile to make sure of the following points:

- The ears should be clean and the eyes free of dirt.
- The folds of skin around the nose should be clean.
- The anus and genital area should be clean.
- The coat should be free of loose fur (difficult during the moulting seasons, but not impossible).
- The feet should be clean and the claws trimmed.
- There should be no wounds or lesions on the cat, and there should be no fleas or flea-dirt in the coat, or you will be turned away from the show and may have to undergo veterinary clearance procedures before you can show your cat again.

If you trim the claws a couple of days before the show your Tonkinese will have blunted them nicely by show day. It's usual to trim the front claws only but if, like me, you have a cat that uses its back claws for balance or has a habit of walking backwards up your arm, trim the back claws too. It will be appreciated by judges and stewards. I've even had *well trimmed claws, much appreciated* in a write-up on my backward-walking Burmese.

Mymystic Goldenshadow (brown). Photo: Alan Robinson

Chapter 10

With proper regular grooming it isn't really necessary to bathe your cat. However, we all know about those accidental rolls in the mud or flying leaps into a particularly gooey dessert. From personal experience, I know that curry sauce is especially colourful on a lilac coat! A stud owner in particular might feel that their Tonkinese would benefit from a bath before the show. Try to avoid bathing your cat the night before a show, as shampoo removes the coat's natural oils, leaving it fluffy. If you must do so, use the minimum of shampoo. Only use shampoos produced especially for cats, and definitely not ones that alter the colour of the cat's coat.

Generally speaking, cats loathe being bathed, so make everything as easy as possible for yourself and, before you start, clip your cat's claws. Use a sink or bowl large enough to stand the cat in with about 10cm of lukewarm water. Use a jug to pour the water over the cat from the neck towards the tail, taking care to avoid the face and ears. A good tip is to tie a large towel around yourself, sarong-style, so that, when you have finished thoroughly rinsing out the shampoo, you can hold the cat to yourself and wrap it in the towel for immediate drying. With careful handling and gentle reassurance, your cat may respond very well to being bathed and dried. My own cats have been used to the sound and feel of a hair-dryer from birth and my boy Fable positively revels in having his fur gently blow-dried. As a final touch I recommend that you give your Tonkinese a thorough stroking with a chamois-leather and/or a silk cloth, to give the fur that extra sheen.

Unless you are prepared to prevent your cat from going outside at all, be aware that sunlight, especially in the summer, lightens and may brindle the coats of Tonkinese, particularly the brown and blue cats. This effect is intensified by the cat's saliva when it washes itself in the sunshine.

A last word on show preparation: keep all show equipment spotless. This is not just for the sake of hygiene: there is no point in placing a beautifully-prepared cat on a grimy blanket.

The big day arrives

Showing can be very hard on the feet and back, so wear something comfortable. Arrive in good time for your cat to go through the vetting-in procedures and for you to set up the pen without flustering either yourself or your cat. Vetting-in times are indicated in the schedule.

Show pens are generally dipped in disinfectant after each show, but disinfection doesn't necessarily equate with cleanliness – on one occasion I wiped dry faeces from the lining of a pen. Pens are not only used for cat shows but may be used for poultry or rodent exhibitions among others, so it's worth wiping down the inside of the pen walls with a vet wipe before you set up your cat's equipment.

All GCCF shows (with the exception of the GCCF Supreme and the National Cat Club shows) require exhibitors to leave the show hall at 10.00 am when Open class judging begins.

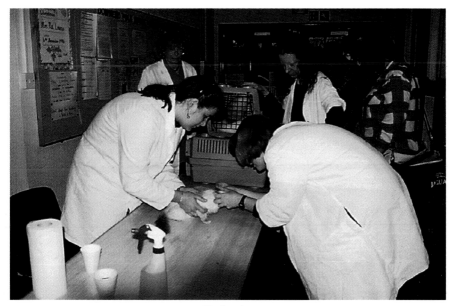

Vetting-in.

Make sure you have tied your pen identification tag either around the neck of your cat or, as most exhibitors do nowadays, onto the front of the pen. Be sure that all your carriers and spare equipment are safely tucked out of the way under your pen and that you have removed food bowls, but not water bowls, from the pen itself. Now make sure that you have your catalogue voucher, entry card (which lists the classes you've entered your cat in) and handbag/wallet with you before you leave the hall. This is the time to join the queue for catalogues, coffee or the toilet! You'll be permitted to re-enter the hall at 12.30 pm to check your cat's water, tidy its pen and give it some food.

Throughout the afternoon you are likely to be going back and forth between your cat's pen and the results board, marking up your catalogue and collecting your rosettes, for which you need to take along your entry and place cards. Some shows deliver rosettes to the pens. Remember that if a judge is at, or in the close vicinity of, your pen, the protocol is to remain at a distance (at least out of earshot) until he or she has finished judging. You may not pack up and leave the hall until the show manager declares that the show is over, usually at 5.00 pm.

You might need a reasonably thick skin. Everyone analyses the judges' reports according to their own perception of the ideal cat. Some of the 'constructive' criticisms are well meant but can be less than sensitive. Just play at being a duck and let it all roll off your back. Don't let me put you off; it's great fun to come home with a beautiful rosette having had a good long day chatting about nothing but cats and knowing that your Tonk really is the most beautiful cat in the world.

Chapter 10

When you finally get home, excited and exhausted, give your cat a big hug and a bowl of food, bung the show blankets in the washing machine and clean the bowls and litter tray ready for the next show. Then, sit down with a cup of tea, your merit critique and your marked-up catalogue and enjoy a review of the day!

THE STANDARD OF POINTS

Today's Standard of Points (SOP) still incorporates the scale of points, totalling 100, originally established by Harrison Weir. He called it the Standard of Excellence. However, now it is normally used by judges as a guide to what emphasis should be placed on the various aspects of any breed rather than strictly to award points, which would otherwise average out the qualities of the cats being judged, and might even cause a good average cat to be placed above a very good cat.

The following Tonkinese SOP is in use at the time of writing this book. It contains amendments approved by the GCCF in October 1996. You can see that the greatest emphases are expected to be placed on the head and body shape (the type) and the coat pattern and colour. Since GCCF recognition of the Tonkinese, breeders and the Tonkinese Breed Advisory Committee (BAC) have worked together to tighten up the standard by which Tonks are judged so that it describes more accurately the ideal Tonkinese. This work continues.

Tonkinese Standard of Points (Breed 74)

General type standard: The Tonkinese should be a beautifully balanced cat of medium build and foreign type. The head has a gently rounded top shaping to a medium wedge with a slight nose break. The body should be firm and muscular with the head, body, legs and tail in proportion to give a well balanced appearance. The coat pattern, which derives from the incomplete dominance of the Burmese and Siamese alleles, should be paler in tone on the body shading to a darker expression of the same colour on the legs, ears, mask and tail. The cat should be of equable temperament and good weight for its size. Tonkinese can be late developers, coming to their best when two years old.

Head: A gently rounded top with good width between the ears. Moderate wedge of medium proportions, neither pointed nor square muzzled. Definite but not exaggerated whisker pinch. In profile there should be a slight nose break leading down to a level bite and chin of medium depth.

Ears: Medium size, slightly taller than wide, pricked forward, with broad base and oval tips. Base equally balanced between side and top of head, with outer line continuing line of wedge.

Eyes: More open than oriental but not round. Medium sized, oriental top slanting towards the nose, with the lower line rounded, and set well apart.

Eye colour: Greenish-blue or bluish-green preferred with a range from green to light blue allowed but orange, yellow and deep or vivid blue are not acceptable. Incomplete development of eye colour may be found in kittens.

Body: Medium to long in length, well balanced, firm, and muscular. Chest slightly rounded in profile, flanks level, back rising gently from shoulders to rump. Neck medium in length.

Legs and feet: Legs slim, well muscled and in proportion to the body, the hind legs slightly longer than the front. Feet neat and oval.

Tail: Preferably reaching to the shoulder, neither thick nor whippy.

Coat: Close-lying and short. Fine, soft, silky with a lustrous sheen.

Colour: The Tonkinese coat pattern requires that the points colour of the mask, ears, legs and tail should present an unmistakably darker expression of the body colour, merging gently and not sharply contrasted. The legs may be paler in tone than the other points and the body colour should shade gradually to a slightly lighter hue on the underparts.

Temperament: Lively, inquisitive, yet relaxed and very friendly.

Scale of points:

Type and Shape	(50)	Coat and Colour	(50)
Head	15	Eye colour	10
Ears	05	Coat colour and pattern	20
Eye shape	05	Coat texture	10
Body	15	Temperament	10
Legs and paws	05		
Tail	05		
Total	**100**		

Withhold all awards for:

1 Variant coat pattern, ie solid coat colour or pattern, or sharp contrast between the points and body colour. NB: Coat pattern in kittens may develop slowly.

2 Miniaturisation.

3 A cluster of white hairs or a white patch.

Withhold certificates or first prizes in Kitten Open Classes for:

1 Barring on the body in non-tabby pattern colours. Note: Ghost tabby markings may be present in all non-tabby kittens, young cats of all colours and in red and cream adults (see note under Solid Colours).

2 Orange, yellow, dark blue or vivid blue eye colour (incomplete development of eye colour in kittens should be allowed for).

3 Round eyes.

4 Exaggerated elongation of the wedge or short wedge.
5 Straight profile or exaggerated nose break.
6 Any defect as listed in the preface to the SOP booklet.

Faults:
1 Scattered white hairs.

For details of the individual colours, see chapter 3.

HOW TO BECOME A JUDGE (UNDER THE GCCF)

It is an honour to be a judge in the Cat Fancy, not because of any assumed status but because loving cat owners grant you the privilege of handling their cats.

If you have an ambition to become a judge remember that, when you have achieved your goal and are still learning your craft, exhibitors always have the right to choose whether or not to enter their cats in your classes. Note the statement above and keep it firmly in mind – all the best judges do.

It will take a first-time applicant to the GCCF Judge Appointment Scheme at least 11 years to become a Full GCCF judge, including a minimum of four years' breeding experience. There are two routes to becoming a Tonkinese judge. As a first-time applicant you can apply for nomination as a probationer judge via the Stewarding Scheme, or you can apply for nomination as a probationer judge of the Tonkinese breed having been a full judge of another breed.

A first-time applicant

You must apply to the GCCF Hon Secretary to register into the Judge Appointment scheme with respect to the Tonkinese Breed Advisory Committee (BAC). There is a single fee of £10 (non-refundable) and there are also minimum conditions to be met:

- You must be a GCCF prefix holder.
- You must have at least four years' experience of breeding Tonkinese, from the registration date of your first litter.
- You must be a member of a constituent club of the Tonkinese BAC and remain so throughout your involvement with the Judge Appointment Scheme.
- You must have exhibited Tonkinese regularly for at least three consecutive years. This will give you time to observe closely the whole pageant of cat showing, the way in which judges and stewards handle the cats and the various critique styles of judges (seen in *Cats* magazine). Most importantly it will give you the chance to look at examples of the breed that you are hoping to judge, to see how they change as they mature and to hear what the breeders expect to see in the cats.
- You must present GCCF slips as evidence of at least five stewarding

engagements. The GCCF produces a leaflet (*Notes On Stewarding*), which will tell you how to obtain a stewarding engagement and what is required of a steward, both generally and in detail. It is quite an enlightening document for exhibitors, too.

• You must present GCCF certificates as evidence of at least two engagements as a table-worker at Championship or Sanction shows, to show you have gained a working knowledge of show rules and procedures.

On receipt of your application to join the scheme, the GCCF will send you a package of relevant rules and documentation and inform the Tonkinese BAC of your registration into the scheme.

Once you have registered into the GCCF Judge Appointment Scheme you can join the Tonkinese BAC's Stewarding Scheme by sending the appropriate completed form and £10 fee (non-refundable). In return you will receive a set of relevant procedures, requirements and documentation plus the current Tonkinese Standard of Points.

The Stewarding Scheme for each breed's BAC is breed-related, but otherwise the BACs follow the same GCCF rules. The Tonkinese BAC requires 20 GCCF stewarding certificates from the applicant to show that they have handled cats, including one Russian Blue, one Abyssinian, one Rex, one Asian, one Burmese, one Siamese and one Longhair – a good representative group from the Foreign section plus a Longhaired cat for comparison. Applicants must attend breed seminars and submit evidence of veterinary tuition to show that they understand and can identify veterinary defects. They must also submit all certificates and documentation required by the Scheme to the Tonkinese BAC, which continues to observe the applicant's progress.

After a minimum of three years stewarding within the Tonkinese Stewarding Scheme the applicant may apply to the BAC for nomination as a probationer judge of Tonkinese. The BAC will nominate the candidate as a probationer judge, defer nomination until certain requirements have been met or reject the application. In each case the GCCF Hon Secretary and the candidate will be fully informed.

Serving as a probationer judge

Until the Tonkinese is in Provisional recognition it cannot compete in Open classes at Sanction or Championship shows. This means that anyone enrolled in the Tonkinese Stewarding Scheme must wait for breed promotion until they can apply for nomination as a probationer judge but, until then, full judges of other breeds may apply to become a full judge of the Tonkinese.

The probationary period is a maximum of four years of on-going tuition and continuous assessment. During this time probationer judges must copy their show reports to the BAC Secretary within four weeks of the show, including all Tonkinese judged by them in Open and other Tonkinese breed-specific classes, Tonkinese to which they have awarded places in other miscellaneous classes, and any other Tonkinese they feel are worthy of comment. Probationer judges are also expected, among other things, to consult with and consider the opinions of full Tonkinese judges, attend Tonkinese seminars and judge a minimum of six Open classes generating, overall, reports on at least 20 kittens in a range of colours and patterns.

When all the conditions of the probationary period have been met the Probationer judge may apply to the BAC for promotion to Full judge. The BAC nominate the candidate for promotion, defer nomination until certain requirements have been met or reject the application. In each case the GCCF Hon Secretary and the candidate are fully informed.

The appointment and dismissal of GCCF judges are the sole prerogatives of the GCCF Council.

TONKINESE STATISTICS AND ACHIEVEMENTS

The following statistics relate solely to GCCF-registered Tonkinese and I am grateful to members of the Governing Council for their help while I was compiling this information.

Tonkinese at the National Cat Club Show 1996.

Although cats were registered with the GCCF as Tonkinese rather than Burmese/Siamese hybrids as early as 1976, the first Tonkinese to be registered with fully recognised Burmese/Siamese parentage were Adreesh Ming Thedancer, a chocolate tortie Tonkinese born on 9 March 1985 (Dam: brown tortie Burmese x Sire: seal point Siamese) and Rhampaws Minkie Mouse, a brown Tonkinese born on 21 February 1986 (Dam: brown Burmese x Sire: seal-point Siamese).

This table shows the first Tonkinese in each coat colour (excluding variant coat patterns) to be registered following breed recognition in May 1991. No tortie-tabbies registered at the time of writing.

Colour (Breed No)	Name, Sex and DoB
Brown (74)	Thaimar Nicsmi Northstar, M, 1/2/91
Blue (74a)	Seansuki Timothy Silver, M, 22/2/91
Chocolate (74b)	Keoni Kalvin Klein, M, 6/5/91
Lilac (74c)	Adraysh Soft Lilac, F, 9/3/91
Red (74d)	Coerulea Regent, M, 11/4/91
Brown Tortie (74e)	Adraysh Thumbelina, F, 22/6/91
Cream (74f)	Adraysh Ozymandias, M, 22/6/91
Blue Tortie (74g)	Sylvakib Tinkerbell Tart, F, 16/5/91
Choc Tortie (74h)	Coerulea Chloe Blaze, F, 11/4/91
Lilac Tortie (74j)	Allming Jasmin, F, 4/7/91
Brown Tabby (74t)	Rohese Mystiko, M, 15/5/91
Blue Tabby (74at)	Treedancer Suhba, F, 29/11/92
Choc Tabby (74bt)	Bonzer Lorelei, F, 24/2/91
Lilac Tabby (74ct)	Treedancer Ishtar, F, 29/11/92
Red Tabby (74dt)	Wychwind Fella, M, 17/5/95
Cream Tabby (74ft)	Bonzer Tangerine Cream, M, 18/9/96

Once they had a GCCF breed number the Tonkinese could be entered in competition. By August 1991 the GCCF had assigned the breed number 74. That month the Tonkinese were seen for the first time at a GCCF-licensed show – the Mid-Somerset Agricultural Society (exemption) Show.

The table below shows the first Tonkinese in each coat colour to win a Merit certificate. No cream-tabbies or tortie-tabbies have been shown yet, and Tonkinese with variant coat patterns are not eligible to be shown.

Colour	Cat's Name
Brown (74)	Nicsmi Treacle Pud
Blue (74a)	Keoni Kully Kulvinder
Chocolate (74b)	Keoni Kalvin Klein
Lilac (74c)	Sylvakib Chinca Toi
Red (74d)	Adraysh Oli Tu
Brown Tortie (74e)	Keo Princess Blossom
Cream (74f)	Adhuish Atlas
Blue Tortie (74g)	Beakerfolk Blue Medley
Choc Tortie (74h)	Rohese Sugarandspice
Lilac Tortie (74j)	Allming Jasmin
Brown Tabby (74t)	Bonzer Glenmorangie
Blue Tabby (74at)	Bonzer Blu Tigre
Choc.Tabby (74bt)	Bonzer Octopussy
Lilac Tabby (74ct)	Mymystic Pagan
Red Tabby (74dt)	Bonzer Red Rum

Chapter 10

To be promoted from Preliminary to Provisional recognition, the Tonkinese breed must meet a number of GCCF requirements. One of these requires the Tonkinese Breed Advisory Committee to provide a list of least 15 Tonkinese cats that have been awarded their four qualifying Merits. The four Merits must be given under four different judges and only two of them may have been won as a kitten.

From recognition in 1991 until the end of 1996 over 250 Tonkinese have been awarded a Merit Cerificate, of which more than 70 have won their qualifying Merits. Nearly 1000 Merits have been awarded to the Tonkinese in that period, which represents a staggering success for any new breed of cat.

Many cats are shown just once, usually by enthusiastic new owners with the prompting of their breeders, so the number of Merits won is not an accurate reflection of the number of cats shown or the frequency with which they are shown. Nevertheless, it is a useful guide to the presence of Tonkinese on the show bench. Here is a breakdown of Merits won between 1991 and the end of 1996: 1 Merit (91 cats), 2 Merits (43 cats), 3 Merits (30 cats), 4 Merits (24 cats), 5–10 Merits (43 cats), 11–20 Merits (17 cats), 21 or more Merits (3 cats).

This table lists the increasing number of Tonkinese shown since 1991, based solely on the number of cats which have won Merits over the years.

Mymystic Pagan (lilac tabby).

Mymystic's Addeish Lansdale Fable (blue).

Year	No of Tonkinese Winning Merits	Total No of Merits Won
1991	22	26
1992	52	125
1993	54	123
1994	65	184
1995	90	243
1996	106	290

With any popular breed of cat the ratio of colours shown may be affected by several factors, including the general popularity of a certain colour at any time, the numbers of each colour actually being bred and, most significantly in a new breed, the colours of the studs available.

The following table shows the first Tonkinese in each coat colour to win four qualifying Merit certificates and the first to win ten Merit certificates:

Colour	Qualifying Merits	Ten Merits
Brown (74)	Keo Arabella	Mymystic Goldenshadow
Blue (74a)	Keoni Kully Kulvinder	(Mymystic) Addeish Lansdale Fable
Chocolate (74b)	(Talofapuss) Adraysh Rickytix	Deelando Rachels Angel

215

Chapter 10

Lilac (74c)	(Clarinath) Adraysh Stormbringer	(Clarinath) Addeish Clarinath Oberon
Red (74d)	(Tonkitu) Addinsh Wong Mei	(Tonkitu) Addinsh Wong Mei
Brown Tortie (74e)	Melusine Bellaclova	Tonkaholics Speckled Star
Cream (74f)	Episcopuss Caesar	Episcopuss Caesar
Blue Tortie (74g)	*	*
Choc Tortie (74h)	Rohese Sugarandspice	*
Lilac Tortie (74j)	Episcopuss Europa	Episcopuss Europa
Brown Tabby (74t)	Bonzer Glenmorangie	*
Blue Tabby (74at)	Bonzer Moody Blues	*
Choc Tabby (74bt)	Bonzer Octopussy	Mymystic Nimrod
Lilac Tabby (74ct)	Mymystic Mischa & Mymystic Pagan	Mymystic Pagan

* = None at time of writing

Senior judge Norma Robinson at the Havelock North (New Zealand) Cat Show. Photo: Earl Reay

Chapter: 11
Tonkinese tail-ends

In any book there are various topics which, although of interest, do not seem to fit in comfortably in other sections. I have collected these 'Tonkinese tail-ends' together at the end of the book.

PHOTOGRAPHING YOUR TONKINESE

A photographic record is of great value to any breeder, especially for a breeder of Tonkinese. It's so useful to be able to check on the development of coat colour, eye colour and coat-patterns of previous litters for reference, particularly if you are trying to decide whether a kitten's coat pattern is slow to develop or whether it is a variant.

There are several difficulties in photographing cats, particularly cats as naturally active and inquisitive as the Tonkinese. It is usually easier to photograph your own cats than someone else's, simply because your cats know you well enough to be completely relaxed and behave naturally in your presence.

The success of your feline photography also depends a great deal upon how well you know your camera. An all-singing, all-dancing single lens reflex

Kittens yawn on waking up, as demonstrated by Mymystic Pharoah.

Chapter 11

camera (SLR) is no better for photography than the most simple point-and-click camera if the photographer doesn't know how to use it. Take time to get to know your camera functions and limitations so that, when you see that ideal opportunity for a photograph, you don't have to think too much about the technicalities. Try to keep the backgrounds as simple as possible and watch out for those stray flashes of colour. Many photographs are spoiled by the inadvertent inclusion of a distracting colour, which you may not notice if you are concentrating on the cat. Cluttered backgrounds, busy wall papers or materials, unnoticed shadows and the stray item that seems to be coming out of the cat's ear spoil what could have been a wonderful photo if only you had checked before taking it. Practise with your camera so that you know instinctively how to use it. This will give you that fraction of extra time to check the background details.

Above all, you need patience and time to watch and wait for the right moment. It helps to know something of your subject's habits. Does your cat wash itself immediately after eating or wait a while? Where is its favourite sleeping place? Does it always yawn and stretch when it wakes up? Does it have any curious habits? Does it answer when you speak to it? What is its favourite food or toy? What is likely to hold its attention for the longest period? Does it watch television?

If you're keen on getting good studies of your cat there are some excellent (and relatively inexpensive) compact auto-focus cameras, many of which include a lens suitable for wide-angle and portrait shots and the invaluable anti-red-eye function. This is a double flash function, which causes the cat's pupils to contract on the first flash, thus minimising the red-eye when the second flash goes off seconds later with the release of the shutter. These cameras are especially useful for indoor photos. The only drawback that I have found with them is that in those few seconds the subject may well have changed its pose.

Unless you are lucky enough to have the equipment to control the lighting you are probably better off taking 'natural' photos rather than formal studio-type portraits. Many of the best photographs of cats come into the natural category. Photographs taken in natural light are usually easier for the amateur but, if you have to take your photos indoors,

Shotonks Lady Camilla on a pedestal.

218

give yourself a helping hand by using one of the faster speed films (200 or 400 ASA), which will give you a little extra lee-way in poor light conditions.

I have listed below some of the questions commonly asked by those trying for that perfect shot.

Q: *How do I keep my subject still long enough to focus properly?*

A: I'm afraid the simple answer to this question is that generally you can't. However, knowledge of the cat's habits and idiosyncrasies helps you to anticipate certain photographic situations. There are also a few tricks. For instance, young kittens are not too confident with heights, so try isolating them by putting them on a cat-climber, stool, table or ironing board in the middle of the room. This will confine them and raise them to make photographs easier to control, and it may also work with older kittens and cats. Placing young kittens on a heated pad will make them feel more secure and relaxed, and a favourite food is always useful – attract and keep the subject's interest with the odd prawn or piece of chicken.

Lenape Tonkinese kittens (USA), posed on a stand so that they are more likely to keep still.

Q: *How can I avoid the red-eye effect?*

A: I've already mentioned cameras that have the anti-red-eye function but, if you don't have such a camera, you can often overcome this problem with the most simple of devices. Tape a piece of plain white paper or heavy grease-proof paper over your flash to diffuse the flash-light. This reduces the red-eye effect significantly, without the loss of too much light

219

Chapter 11

Red-eye, caused by direct flash.

from your flash. If you have a flash with a swivel head then use it indirectly. For instance, aim it at the ceiling so that the light is bounced back onto the subject. Be careful when using the camera on its side as you will end up with a semi-lit subject if the light is bounced in the wrong direction. Experiment to see what best suits you and your camera.

Q: *How can I avoid a silhouette photo?*

A: This usually occurs if your subject is lit from behind, either by the sun or a bright window. If you are outside, avoid facing into the sun or having the cat looking directly into the sun, as bright light makes it squint. When photographing a cat

Camera on its side: flash-light unbalanced.

sitting in a window, remember that the camera cannot adjust its reaction to light as sensitively as your eyes can, so the light from the window will

Trampuss Trail Blazer, nicely photographed in strong sunlight.

dominate the picture. This is when you should use a fill-in flash – even in bright daylight you'll be amazed at the clarity it will give your picture. Alternatively, you could hold a sheet of white card in front of yourself, below the level of the picture, to reflect the window light back onto the subject.

Q: *Why do indoor photos sometimes look yellow?*

A: Normal film is balanced to give the best results in natural midday sunlight, which is a very strong bluish light. Our household bulbs, including fluorescent strips, are far weaker and much warmer in tone. Our eyes compensate a great deal for different quality of lighting. However, film is not adjustable so, if your subject is only lit with household lamps, the result is a yellowish wash called a colour cast. The colour cast varies a little according to the dominant colour of the room reflected by the light source. To avoid a colour cast, use your camera flash; this adjusts the light quality to the equivalent of natural midday sunlight.

Don't be afraid to use up your film. If you get one really good photograph from a reel you can consider yourself fortunate. If you regularly get several you should consider taking up photography for a living!

Chapter 11

Example of colour cast from fluorescent lighting.

CATS AND THE LAW

For centuries cats have had a raw deal, and it wasn't until 1988 that in the eyes of the law cats (along with other animals) ceased to be second-class creatures compared with dogs. Here are just some of the laws relating to cats.

The Protection of Animals Act (1911) is the main source of protection for cats. Cruelty to animals is an offence under that Act and those found guilty of cruelty may be punished by a fine, or up to six months imprisonment, or both. An offender may also be disqualified from owning an animal for a specified period. To prosecute an offender successfully the courts must have proof that unnecessary suffering has been caused. This is usually given by the examining veterinary surgeon. If you should have the misfortune to need to use this Act you should have your cat examined by a vet as soon as possible after the incident of cruelty. Under this Act there are three basic ways in which offenses may be caused to cats:

- Acts of commission, committed by any person, whereby a cat is caused physical or mental suffering by a positive/deliberate act, eg beating, kicking, torturing or the improper killing of an animal, such as the drowning of kittens. If an animal has to be killed it should be carried out by a vet or the RSPCA.
- Acts of omission, committed by any person, whereby a cat is caused unnecessary suffering, for instance by failing to provide a cat with food, water, adequate shelter or veterinary treatment.
- The owner permitting acts of commission or omission. This includes companies, businesses and corporations that own cats.

The Abandonment of Animals Act (1960) makes it an offence for any person owning, or having control of, an animal to abandon it, permanently or otherwise. For the purposes of this act it's sufficient to prove that suffering is likely to have been caused. Examples of abandonment are leaving a cat in its basket in a car on a hot day or leaving it at home to fend for itself for a couple of days.

The Theft Act (1968) states that *a person is guilty of theft if he/she dishonestly appropriates property belonging to another with the intention of permanently depriving the other of it.* A convicted thief can be imprisoned. Unfortunately many an owner reporting their cat missing or stolen has been fobbed off by the authorities, who claim that no action can be taken by them because cats are not classed as property. However, the legal definition of property includes all creatures that by habit or training live in association with man. Furthermore, pets are recognised as belongings within the provisions of Section 48 of the National Assistance Act (1948) in conjunction with Section 79 of the National Health Services Act (1946). Unless the cat is adopted or rescued the owner of a Tonkinese has registration and/or transfer documents to prove ownership, so the authorities cannot deny that your cat is your property.

The Criminal Damages Act (1971) is your ally against threats and/or damage to your cat. Within the meaning of this Act it is an offence to *deliberately or recklessly kill or injure domestic and captive animals which belong to or are in the care, control or charge of others.* It is also an offence to threaten to kill or injure such an animal as long as it can be shown that the threat was made in such a manner that the threatened person believed that the threat would be carried out. In such cases the court can order compensation to be paid.

Section 48 of **The National Assistance Act (1948)** in conjunction with Section 79 of **The National Health Services Act (1946)** requires that local authorities *take reasonable steps to prevent or mitigate loss or damage to property* of anyone admitted as a patient to any hospital. If you are admitted to hospital in an emergency and have no-one to care for your cat you should arrange for the Social Services Department to be informed. They have a duty to care for all 'goods and chattels' belonging to anyone admitted to hospital or an institution, and animals are classed as belongings. Local council officials are empowered to enter the home of a person confined in hospital and are also able to claim reasonable expenses for doing so as a civil debt.

The Breeding of Cats Act – sorry, there's no such thing. There is a Breeding of Dogs Act but, sadly, there is no protection against the indiscriminate breeding or sale of cats.

Anyone who owns, controls or has charge of an animal has a legal duty to take reasonable care that the animal does not cause injury or damage; otherwise they may be sued. In the case of an owner/keeper who is under 16 years of age, the head of the household is liable for any injury or damage caused by the animal. The burden of proof is placed on the injured party. Cats don't have a special status under the law, but owners of cats are rarely held responsible for damage. It's so difficult to prove the owner's negligence if, for

Chapter 11

instance, a cat ruins a neighbour's flower bed or empties his pond of prize fish. At one time, if someone was injured by an animal while trespassing he or she was considered to be partly to blame and any damages that might have been awarded were reduced; if the injured party was entirely to blame no damages would have been awarded. Now, **The Occupiers Liability Act (1984)** *imposes a duty on an occupier to take such care as is reasonable in all circumstances to see that any uninvited entrants do not suffer injury by reason of any risk of which he is aware or has reasonable grounds to believe exists.* Hence the number of cases of people being prosecuted for defending their home against intruders. For the cat owner this means that the cat may be considered to be a trespasser and, as such, should be safe from harm imposed by the occupier.

It's an offence for a driver to fail to stop at the scene of an accident if a horse, cow, ass, mule, sheep, pig, goat or dog (but not a cat) is injured outside the vehicle.

Any pet that attacks people or has a disease that could affect humans is considered in law to be dangerous, as is any pet likely to cause severe harm because it has characteristics not normally found in others of the same species. Owner/keepers aware of such an abnormality are liable for any harm done even if they are not to blame for it.

Many councils have by-laws stating that it is an offence to keep a persistently noisy animal, such as a barking dog, so it would be wise to be on good terms with your neighbours if you intend to run a stud. Tenants who have animals that cause persistent disturbance may risk eviction.

IMPORTING AND EXPORTING TONKINESE

It is an offence to bring a cat into the country without complying with the quarantine regulations. The penalties for evading quarantine are an unlimited fine and up to a year's imprisonment. As a further precaution against rabies the cat may be destroyed.

It is only common sense to insure any cat travelling to another country. It is the owner's responsibility to ensure that the cat is securely contained and comfortable. Carrying agents are not normally held responsible for cats escaping from their containers. Unless a cat is unable to be handled it is inadvisable to sedate it for the journey because it's now generally known that sedatives and tranquillisers have distressing effects on healthy cats. They try to fight the effects of the sedatives, which makes them uncomfortable and miserable.

Importing into the United Kingdom

To prevent the spread of rabies cats, dogs and most mammals must spend six months quarantined in special quarters. This applies both to animals brought into the country for the first time and to animals returning after a visit abroad, however brief the visit. It makes no difference whether or not an animal has been vaccinated against rabies.

You will need an import licence, obtainable from the Animal Health Unit (AHU) of the Ministry of Agriculture, Fisheries and Food (see **Useful Addresses**). This will not be issued until you have made the quarantine arrangements. To help you, Division 1B of the AHU can provide the official list of approved quarantine catteries and approved carrying agents.

- You must book accommodation for your cat at one of the approved catteries.
- You must employ an approved carrying agent to collect your cat on arrival – you are not permitted to take the cat to the quarantine cattery yourself.
- You must apply for an import licence on form ID1, obtainable from the AHU. You will state your port of entry, which must have facilities for keeping an animal for up to 48 hours if necessary until it can be taken to the quarantine cattery (Dover, Harwich, Hull, Liverpool, Southampton sea-ports and Ramsgate hoverport have such facilities; Birmingham, Edinburgh, Gatwick, Glasgow, Heathrow, Leeds, Manchester and Prestwick airports also have the necessary facilities).

Your application form must be returned at least four weeks before the cat's journey begins. The Ministry will issue a boarding document to be presented at the departure point before the cat is allowed to board the ship or plane. Cats must travel in a nose-, paw- and tongue-proof kennel and, on arrival, will be transferred by the carrying agent to the quarantine cattery previously booked. On arrival they must be examined by a vet and vaccinated against rabies, a second injection to be given 28 days afterwards. To allow the cat to settle down into its temporary home it is usually recommended that you do not visit for two weeks, although rules do vary from cattery to cattery.

GCCF requirements for registering imported cats

If you wish to register an imported cat with the GCCF you will be required to send the following documents, with a fee of £6, to the GCCF Office:

1 An original (photocopy not acceptable) four-generation Certified Pedigree from the relevant overseas Cat Fancy, which must show breed colours for at least three generations.
2a For cats coming through the European Union without quarantine: a copy of the Certificate of Importation and the microchip number.
2b For cats coming through quarantine: the Import Licence number, a copy of the Certificate of Quarantine and the microchip number if there is one.
3 If the cat is male: a Certificate of Entirety or Certificate of Neutering as appropriate.
   Note: As of 21 June 1995, no imported Burmese, or their progeny, shall be registered with a GCCF Burmese breed number.

Chapter 11

Exporting from the United Kingdom

British Tonkinese are becoming increasingly desirable around the world. Their standard is maintained by careful breeding programmes and there is the great added incentive that our cats are guaranteed rabies-free. Recent problems in the United States with the lethal 'contemporary' gene affecting certain Burmese bloodlines has further enhanced the desirability of British Tonkinese, who do not have such lines in their backgrounds; indeed the GCCF have now taken steps to try to prevent these lines affecting our cats (see **Note** above).

GCCF requirements for exporting GCCF-registered cats

As usual, the ownership of the cat must be transferred but, in this instance, Transfer Application forms may be signed by the present owners on behalf of the new owner who is resident abroad. The GCCF also requires that the following documentation is provided for the new owners.

1 If the cat is male: a Certificate of Entirety or Certificate of Neutering as appropriate.
2 A Certified Pedigree to enable the new owners to register the cat with the relevant overseas Cat Fancy. The number of generations to be shown is determined by the rules of the relevant overseas registering authority. Apply to the GCCF for a Certified Pedigree by sending a copy of the cat's normal pedigree and the appropriate fee (three generations – £20, four generations – £35, five generations – £50).

Legal requirements for exporting cats

As international quarantine regulations are frequently amended it is advisable to check with the embassy of the country to which you intend to export your kitten or cat before you confirm a sale, as you may decide that the restrictions are such that you do not want to subject a kitten of yours to them. Here is a guide to some of the current (1996) quarantine regulations:

Australia Three months' quarantine for cats travelling by air, direct from country of origin in a sealed nose-, tongue- and paw-proof kennel. The cat must be certified healthy, fit to travel and free of clinical signs of disease and parasites by an approved vet at the airport, before being officially sealed into its air-kennel. If the seal is broken in transit the cat will be returned to its country of origin. Besides the import permit (which must be forwarded to Assistant General, Animal Quarantine Branch, Commonwealth Department of Health, PO Box 100 Wooden ACT 2606, Australia) and official declarations, a certificate must be provided to prove that the cat has been vaccinated against feline-enteritis, feline-calicivirus and feline-rhinotracheitis, which must have been administered at least 30 days, and not more than 12 months, prior to travelling.

Austria No quarantine, but a bilingual certificate of health must be provided and rabies vaccination is necessary.

Belgium No quarantine, but rabies vaccination is necessary.

Canada No quarantine, but a certificate of health and an export certificate must be provided.

Denmark No quarantine, but entry is restricted for unaccompanied animals.

Finland No quarantine, but a special certificate of health and an import permit must be provided.

France No quarantine, but an import permit is usually required. Cats under one year of age require a certificate of vaccination against feline enteritis, which must have been administered at least 30 days prior to travelling, and either an export certificate or a certificate of vaccination against rabies, which must have been administered at least 30 days prior to travelling.

Germany No quarantine, but an import permit is usually required and a bilingual certificate of vaccination against rabies is required, which must have been administered at least 30 days prior to travelling.

Gibraltar No quarantine, but an import permit and a bilingual vaccination certificate against rabies, a certificate of health and a ministry certificate must be provided.

Greece No quarantine, but a certificate of health must be provided and rabies vaccination is necessary.

Italy No quarantine, but an import permit is required for unaccompanied animals; rabies vaccination is necessary.

Netherlands No quarantine but a certificate of health and an authenticated certificate of vaccination against rabies must be provided.

New Zealand No quarantine, but otherwise the conditions are generally as per Australia. The completed import application form should be sent to Animal Health Division, Ministry of Agriculture and Fisheries, Private Bag, Wellington, New Zealand.

Norway No quarantine, but an import permit and health certificate must be provided.

Tajens Fast Foreward (brown), now living in Dusseldorf.

Portugal No quarantine, but an export certificate and an authenticated certificate of health must be provided.

South Africa No quarantine, but an import permit is required, which also covers the health and export certificates (must be obtained from The Director of Veterinary Services, Private Bag X138, Pretoria, Transvaal, SA). Various other official declarations are required.

Spain Twenty days quarantine, unless rabies vaccinations are in order. An authenticated health certificate and export certificate must be provided, plus a visa (granted immediately prior to departure).

Switzerland No quarantine, but health and rabies vaccination certificates are usually required.

United States of America No quarantine, but a health certificate is required by the relevant airline.

THE WAY AHEAD FOR THE TONKINESE
Tonkinese and the GCCF

As far as showing the Tonkinese is concerned, the next step for the breed, under the authority of the GCCF, is promotion from Preliminary to Provisional recognition. The Tonkinese Breed Advisory Committee (BAC) must provide sufficient evidence of the progress of the breed to warrant its promotion, both in our breeding programmes and on the show bench, especially in competition with other breeds. The Tonkinese BAC must show that the breed is significantly different from existing breeds and confirm that at least 20 breeders who have held a GCCF prefix for more than three years are working actively with the breed. Once the Tonkinese has been granted Provisional status the cats will be in competition with each other rather than assessed against the breed standard alone. They will compete for Intermediate Certificates (ICs), and any cat winning an IC will be eligible to compete for the Best In Show (Foreign) award at that particular show.

So far well over 70 breeders with a GCCF prefix are interested in, and consistently breed, these lovely cats. I doubt that any 'new' breed of cat has created such an overwhelming interest in such a short period of time.

Following Provisional recognition, the Tonkinese will obviously be aiming for Championship status. To achieve this the Tonkinese BAC must provide evidence of the popularity of the breed in terms of its attendance at shows nationally; and will also have to provide a list of at least 20 cats that have

Mymystic's Nimrod (choc tabby) and Mischa (lilac tabby). Photo: Animals Unlimited.

been awarded three ICs under three different judges. Once Championship status is granted the Tonkinese will compete with each other for Champion/Premier and Grand Champion/Grand Premier titles.

As this book goes to press the Tonkinese BAC, and all those who show their Tonkinese under the GCCF, await the decision on our application for promotion. Promotion will be a considerable stride forward for the breed. However, if we are not granted promotion, at this early stage it is not a set-back but an opportunity to re-enforce good breeding practices and spend more time working together through the generations without the pressure that competition places on so many breeds. I believe that there is absolutely no advantage to racing ahead, especially if it is to the detriment of the health and reputation of the breed as a whole. Let promotion take as long as it needs to: after all, the overall future of our Tonkinese is far more important than any individual claiming the glory of having the first GCCF Champion Tonkinese. I have no doubt that the Tonkinese are here to stay and the breed will ultimately achieve GCCF Championship status.

Ultra-Tonkinese

It is so easy for us to say that there will never be a Tonkinese of extreme, or ultra, type, particularly since we value moderation of type in the breed at the moment. Sadly, the same could well have been said of the Siamese, Persians and Burmese of yesteryear. Breeders on both sides of the Atlantic could not possibly have foreseen just how exaggerated some examples of their breeds would become as a result of a combination of breeding and exhibition reward. Tonkinese breeders and judges have the great advantage of seeing these examples of breed development and, with the benefit of such knowledge, we can work together to avoid manufacturing the Ultra-Tonkinese.

Many lovers of Tonkinese have an abiding interest in learning about this genetically unique breed of cat rather than concerning themselves with its competition status. In April 1997, I joined Rosemary Harper and Brenda Rawlinson in establishing a Tonkinese Research Group with the aim of encouraging and supporting the study of such aspects as specific colour and pattern development, clarity of type and coat pattern as the breed progresses, and the physical development of Tonkinese kittens, which are recognised by many breeders as precocious. The purpose of such work is to be able to offer objective and well-informed advice to any individual or organisation who may require it and, thereby, help to protect the integrity of the breed. Although the group is still in its infancy it has already aroused considerable interest and support.

I hope that our combined aim is to see this beautiful and affectionate breed of cat move forward in health, stability of type and abiding good nature, with a range of clean bloodlines on which we will be able to look back with pride.

Appendix A
Cat photographs

This is a list of cats whose photographs appear in this book, with information supplied by the owners. The key is B: Breeder, O: owner, P: Photographer, M: Male, MN: Male Neuter, F: Female, FN: Female Neuter, and []: parents. Numbers in parentheses after names refer to GCCF Breed Numbers (see pages 194–195), and the date given is Date of Birth.

Addeish Katey Clare (74bqv) O/P: L Aldous, B: H M Carter, 7.4.92, F, *[Ch Kamberri Champagne Charlie (27b) ex Kataczinka Clarice (74b)]*.

Adhirsh Cato Redbaron (74d) O/P: S A Ward, B: P Jenkinson, 21.3.93, MN, *[Addeish Arrons Nibbs (74) ex Tajens Unesco (74e)]*.

Adkrish Sittana (74) O/P: H Barnes, B: B J Reid, 13.5.88, F, *[Rocheros Rasputin (27) ex Adreesh Ming Thedancer (74e)]*.

Adouzsh Zachariah Zeus (74c) O: J Sharratt, B: B Lowndes, P: A Robinson, 28.9.94, M, *[Tonkabella Frisco Francis (74b) ex Rohese Child Ofthemist (74a)]*.

Alice (74) O/P: Julie Hanson, B: Gaynor Sharko, 26.9.92, F, *[Tonkabella Benedict Bruno (74) ex Ayesha (24)]*.

Anderwelt Isabelle (74), Germany, O/B: G Wolf, P: J Westrich, 31.12.94, F, *[Ch Anderwelt El Sareei (24) ex Traig Mor's Edna Eiliv (27)]*.

Beau (74), Samson (74b) & Ellie (74t) O/P: J Mischker.

Black hybrid O/B/P: J Clark, 25.4.96, F, *[Lilly (74c) ex William (15, British Black)]*.

Bonzer Jam Puff (74t) O/P: J Mischker, B: J Ponsford, 11.2.96, FN, *[Bonzer Seal Ofapproval (74b) ex Bonzer Duskey Dawn (74t)]*.

Caesar (74a) O/P: Sheila Evans.

Chamboza Maiway (27a) O/P: L Vousden B: D Burnard.

Clarinath Nightshadow (74c) O/B: C Poole, P: L Vousden, 25.4.95, M, *[Gr Ch Silverbreeze Lordsananda (24c) ex Clarinath Lilis Ceridwen (27c)]*.

GC, RW Connacht's Caramel Quinn of Lenape, DM (74b), USA, O/P: P Mullin, B: F Yaccino/L Rhinard, 10.4.90, F, *[GC, RW Connacht's Shenanigan, DM (74c) ex GC Sonham's Anna Livia of Connacht, DM (74b)]*.

Cornwood Charlie Barkalot (74b) O/P: G Webster, B: J Cornish, 22.10.91, MN, *[Adrayam King Louis (24b) ex Adkribu Thursis Moonmist (27c)]*.

Deelando Rachels Angel (74b) O: R Toth, B: Z Shacklady, P: A Robinson, 21.3.95, MN, *[Gr Ch Shermese Sonofatiger (24) ex Bonzer Blue Lagoon (27a)]*.

Herkatz Milliflora (74bqv) O/P: E Lowe, B: J Logan & B Lee, 26.7.96, F, *[Ishmal Darling Budofmay (74b) ex Romantica Anastasia (74b)]*.

Ishokats' Beki Saffron (74e) & Biba Belle (74h) O/B/P: H Forshaw, 15.2.92, F, *[Typha Phantom Oarsman (27) ex Grimspound Yasmin (32b2)]*.

Ishokats Bianka (74b) O/B: H Forshaw, P: L Vousden, 15.2.92, F, *[Typha Phantom Oarsman (27) ex Grimspound Yasmin (32b2)]*.

Ishokats Bijan Valentino (74) B: H Forshaw, P: Linda Vousden, 15.2.92, MN, *[Typha Phantom Oarsman (27) ex Grimspound Yasmin (32b2)]*.

Ishokats Dizzy Deirdre (74aqv) O/B: H Forshaw, P: L Vousden, 5.3.93, FN, *[Iamsiam Noble Valentino (32/1) ex Ishokats Bianka (74b)]*.

Ishokats Geisha Girl (74e) O/B: H Forshaw, P: L Vousden, 23.2.95, F, *[Tajens Red Hotpoker (74d) ex Ishokats Bianka (74b)]*.

Imperial Medallist (CA) Katalyst Munchinella (74) O: P Wild, B: A & J Fraser, P: B Sillitoe, 10.6.90, FN, *[Ch Tamourie Tuffnut (27a) ex CA Medallist Mindy Scoffalot of Katalyst (74b)]*.

Kipper (74b) O/P: H Smith, B: A Power, 12.9.84, FN, *[Burmese ex Siamese]*.

Appendix A

Kittykus Lottie Loveheart (74c) O: M & K Leaver, B: S Davison, 31.7.95, F, *[Rohese Dukeofearl (74b) ex Adouzbu Bluestone (27a)].*

Laryna's Lucy Locket (74) & Lindy Lou (74bt) O/P: A & J Heys, B: J Vardon, 20.4.96, FN, *[Gr Ch Bambino Performing Art (27) ex Mishanash Mariah Celine (32/3)].*

Learoyd Heidi (74c) O/P: S Pearson & M Thompson, B: P Rayner, 29.12.92, FN, *[Adhuish Yankee Doodledandy (74) ex Learoyd Opal (74c)].*

Learoyd Serendipity (74a) O: A I Hunter, B: P Rayner, P: S A Ward, 24.1.94, MN, *[Addeish Arrons Nibbs (74) ex Learoyd Opal (74c)].*

Lenape Tonkinese Kittens, USA, O/B/P: P Mullin.

Mandu (24) O: A Barnes-Henley, P: L Vousden.

Melusine's Aquatay (74b) & Bellaclova (74e) O/P: M Haas, B: B & S Rawlinson, 1.6.96, MN, *[Romantica Rodrigo Redsun (74d) ex Romantica Sheba Noelle (74b)].*

Melusine's Adouzsh Flower Fox (74b) O: M & K Leaver, B: B & S Rawlinson, 9.9.94, MN, *[Romantica Rousseau (74d) ex Romantica Lilith Venezia (74c)].*

Melusine's Adouzsh Hypnos (74a) O/B: B & S Rawlinson, P: M Haas, 9.9.94, MN, *[Romantica Rousseau (74d) ex Romantica Lilith Venezia (74c)].*

Mirber Contessa Zarta (74c) O/P: R Al-Badi, B: M Smith, 13.4.96, F, *[Clarinath Nightshadow (74c) ex Clarinath Lilac Cordelia (74c)].*

Mymystic Goldenshadow (74) O: K Wilkinson, B/P: L Vousden, 22.4.95, MN, *[Fabiola Balladeer (24b) ex Predator Minnie Themoocher (27)].*

Mymystic's Nimrod (74bt) & Mischa (74ct) B: L Vousden, O: K Wilkinson, P: P Cutts, 22.2.96, MN, *[Gr Ch Cachet Tabbeoca Tiptoes (32/4) ex Predator Minnie Themoocher (27)].*

Mymystic Nemesis (74) O: R Toth, B/P: L Vousden, 22.2.96, F, *[Gr Ch Cachet Tabbeoca Tiptoes (32/4) ex Predator Minnie Themoocher (27)].*

Mymystic's Opalshadow (74b) & Snowshadow (74b) O: S Lee-Boone, B/P: L Vousden, 22.4.95, *[Fabiola Balladeer (24b) ex Predator Minnie Themoocher (27)].*

Mymystic Pagan (74ct) O/B/P: L Vousden, 22.2.96, F, *[Gr Ch Cachet Tabbeoca Tiptoes (32/4) ex Predator Minnie Themoocher (27)].*

Mymystic Pasha (74at) O: D Powell, B/P: L Vousden, 22.2.96, MN, *[Gr Ch Cachet Tabbeoca Tiptoes (32/4) ex Predator Minnie Themoocher (27)].*

Mymystic's Addeish Lansdale Fable (74a) & Caspar Lilacflush (74c) O/B/P: L Vousden, 24.12.91, MN, *[Adhuish Atlas (74f) ex Chamboza Maiway (27a)].*

Pendragon Lily's Equinox (74b), USA, O/P: S Bumgarner, 21.3.94, FN.

Predator Minnie Themoocher (27) O/P: L Vousden, B: E Cardy, 20.2.94, F, *[Gr Ch Emer Murphys Law (27) ex Gr Ch Mainman Caribbean Kiss (27b)].*

Rogata's Elrond (74f), Germany, O/B/P: S Ortmann, 23.9.95, M, *[Ch Anderwelt El Sareei (24) ex Aniela Of Velvety Friends (27h)].*

Ch Rogata's Elvyn (74), Germany, O/B/P: S Ortmann, 23.9.95, F, *[Ch Anderwelt El Sareei (24) ex Aniela Of Velvety Friends (27h)].*

Rogata's Grisu (74f), Germany, O/B/P: S Ortmann, 29.5.96, M, *[Int Ch Rogata's Cochise (74a) ex Aniela of Velvety Friends (27h)].*

Romantica Lilith Venezia (74c) O: B & S Rawlinson, B: R Harper, P: S Bellis-Jones, FN.

Romantica Lorenzo (74c) O: Mr & Mrs Howell-Jones, B: R Harper, P: M Haas, 2.7.94, MN, *[Romantica Rodrigo Redsun (74d) ex Sylvakib Ashemo Swan (74c)].*

Romantica Rousseau (74d) O: B & S Rawlinson, B: R Harper, P: M Haas, 1.9.93, MN, *[Adraybu Dream Knight (27a) ex Summerdown Angel Eyes (32a)].*

Romantica Sheba Noelle (74b) O: B & S Rawlinson, B: R Harper, P: S Bellis-Jones, 22.12.94, F, *[Adraybu Dream Knight (27a) ex Widgerwood Joella (24b)].*

Romantica Tiramisu (74b) O: C & J Richards, B: R Harper, P: A Robinson, 22.12.94, F, *[Adraybu Dream Knight (27a) ex Widgerwood Joella (24b)].*

Samkabar Jasper (74qv) O: S Baron & I Forward, B: H Barnes, P: J Siewruk, 13.4.93, MN, *[Ch Kizwozzi Oliver (27) ex Adkrish Sittana (74)]*.

Samkabar's Mephisto (74), Methinks (74a), Metaphor (74b), Mila (74b) O/B/P: H Barnes & J Siewruk, 21.12.93, F, *[Rohese Duke Ofearl (74b) ex Adkrish Sittana (74)]*.

Samkabar Nimbus (74a) O: S Rodgers, B: H Barnes, P: J Siewruk, 1.7.94, M, *[Rocheros Emperor (24c) ex Wilowispa Kharma Kameo (27a)]*.

Samkabar's Odonata (74), Onapromise (74cv), Orache (74cv), Oteetee (74qv) O/B: H Barnes, P: J Siewruk, 14.2.95, F, *[Rohese Duke Ofearl (74b) ex Adkrish Sittana (74)]*.

Samkabar Pleides (74a) O/B/P: H Barnes & J Siewruk, 21.7.95, M, *[Rocheros Emperor (24c) ex Wilowispa Kharma Kameo (27a)]*.

Samkabar Quivical (74bqv) O: M Avison, B: H Barnes, P: J Siewruk, 16.3.96, F, *[Romantica Lancelot (74b) ex Samkabar Novella (74c)]*.

GC Shanfoo's Shampagne of Sulltan (74b), USA, O: N A Sullivan, B: N & S Roy, P: R Cote, 20.7.95, F, *[Ch Spielzeit Kleine Krise of Shanfoo (74c) ex Ch B'ssa Janie Lou of Shanfoo DM]*.

Shotonks Lady Camilla (74b) O/P: N Hector-Thomas, B: M Booth, 20.6.95, FN, *[Ch Bambino Talisman (27a) ex Fletchwood Pasha Bubastis (24)]*.

Simon (74d) & Mymystic's Addeish Blueberry Fortune (74a) O/P: L MacIsaac, B: L Vousden.

Tajens Fast Foreward, Germany, O/P: M Martin, B: P Jenkinson.

Tajens Irredescent Opal (74c) B: Patricia Jenkinson, P: P Cutts.

Tajens Isabella (74e) B: P Jenkinson, P: P Cutts.

Tajens Unesco (74e) B: P Jenkinson, P: P Cutts.

Tomas (74t) O/B/P: E Rowe-Leete, M.

Tonkabella Amata Aurora (74b) O/B: J Sharratt, P: A Robinson, 18.7.91, F, *[Adhuish Yankee Doodledandy (74) ex Adraysh Felibella (74b)]*.

Tonkabella's Daffy Dorothea (74b) & Diggory Dai (74b) O: J Price, B: J Sharratt, P: D Price, 22.5.92, M, *[Tonkabella Benedict Bruno (74) ex Adraysh Felibella (74b)]*.

Tonkabella Questa Quintus (74b) O/P: J Illingworth, B: J Sharratt, 30.12.95, F, *[Adouzsh Zachariah Zeus (74c) ex Tonkabella Cara Christabel (74b)]*.

Tonkabella Thaddeus Titus (74c) O/P: J Illingworth, B: J Sharratt, 20.3.96, MN, *[Adouzsh Zachariah Zeus (74c) ex Tonkabella Dulcie Doll (74c)]*.

Tonkaholics Arabian Knight (74b) O/B: C & J Richards, P: A Robinson, 10.4.96, M, *[Romantica Tiramisu (74b) ex Rohese Duke Ofearl (74b)]*.

Tonkaholics Speckled Star (74e) O/B: C & J Richards, P: A Robinson, 3.10.96, F, *[Tajens Jackademus (74a) ex Tonkaholics Taloola Moon (74d)]*.

Tonkaholics Taloola Moon (74d) O/B/P: C & J Richards, 28.8.95, F, *[Romantica Remus (74d) ex Romantica Bianca (74jv)]*.

Trampuss's Tarragon (74v), Trail Blazer (74), Troubadour (74b), O/B/P: F & C Jolley, 3.3.96, *[Tajens Jackademus (74a) ex Majik Korma (74b)]*.

Treedancer Lilac Korene (74c) O: G Greer, B: A & J Fraser, P: A Robinson, 19.8.93, FN, *[Gr Ch Shybu Darhvel Dandy (24c) ex Treedancer Beaumont Poppy (27c)]*.

Utopia Kachaturian (74c), New Zealand, O: R Giddens B/P: C Riethmann, 11.10.95, F, *[Ch Jomanda Bellamy Quinn (27a) ex Zaffiro Lauren Beaucall (74b)]*.

Zeotrope Boris (74c), New Zealand, O: R & S Barrett, B/P: E & L Reay, 13.9.95, M, *[Ch Nodrog Ritz (24b) ex Ch Pyret Lilac Kaleen (27c)]*.

Zeotrope Chiquita (74), New Zealand, O: Earl & Lois Reay/M Mills, B/P: E & L Reay, 10.3.96, F, *[Ch Nada Solus (24) ex Ch Cannondale Coco (27)]*.

Zeotrope Inuk (74b), New Zealand, O: R & S Barrett, B/P: E & L Reay, 13.9.95, M, *[Ch Nodrog Ritz (24b) ex Ch Pyret Lilac Kaleen (27c)]*.

Appendix B
Breeding colour tables

How to use the colour tables

Each table is headed with a queen's colour. Find the relevant table for your queen and then look down the first column for the colour of the stud you wish to use. In the next column you will see the optimum potential colours resulting from that particular mating. The percentages do not always add up to 100 simply because you cannot have a percentage of a kitten!

If you find the order of red and cream in the tables confusing, remember that they are in the order of their base colours: brown, blue, chocolate, lilac.

Tabby is a pattern, not a colour, so the tables are equally applicable to tabby matings. The pattern is not gender-related, so which of the parents is tabby is irrelevant. If both parents are tabby-patterned all of the kittens will be tabby-patterned; if one parent is tabby-patterned you will get a percentage of tabby-patterned kittens; if neither parent is tabby-patterned, none of the kittens will be (see chapters 3 and 4 for more detail).

Key

( )   Brackets enclose a colour that is carried: that is, a colour that is not visible (expressed) in a cat but that can be passed on to its offspring.

:   The colour following the colon is the base colour of a red or cream cat; in other words, the coat-colour masked by the effects of the sex-linked gene. For example, Red:Brown(bl) is a red cat which would have been brown (carrying blue) if the sex-linked gene was not present.

Note 1 All tortoiseshell kittens are female.

Note 2 When a tortoiseshell, red or cream queen is mated with a brown, blue, chocolate or lilac stud the resulting red or cream kittens are male.

Note 3 When a tortoiseshell, red or cream queen is mated with a red or cream stud the resulting red or cream kittens may be either male or female.

STUD	Possible colours shown as a % of the litter
	QUEEN - BROWN
Brown	100% Brown
Brown(bl)	50% Brown, 50% Brown(bl)
Brown(ch)	50% Brown, 50% Brown(ch)
Brown(bl)(ch)	25% Brown, 25% Brown(bl), 25% Brown(ch), 25% Brown(bl)(ch)
Blue	100% Brown(bl)
Blue(ch)	50% Brown(bl), 50% Brown(bl)(ch)
Chocolate	100% Brown(ch)
Chocolate(bl)	50% Brown(ch), 50% Brown(bl)(ch)
Lilac	100% Brown(bl)(ch)
Red:Brown	50% Brown, 50% Brown Tortie
Red:Brown(bl)	25% Brown, 25% Brown(bl), 25% Brown Tortie, 25% Brown Tortie(bl)
Red:Brown(ch)	25% Brown, 25% Brown(ch), 25% Brown Tortie, 25% Brown Tortie(ch)
Red:Brown(bl)(ch)	12% Brown, 12% Brown(bl), 12% Brown(ch), 12% Brown(bl)(ch), 12% Brown Tortie, 12% Brown Tortie(bl), 12% Brown Tortie(ch), 12% Brown Tortie(bl)(ch)
Cream:Blue	50% Brown(bl), 50% Brown Tortie(bl)
Cream:Blue(ch)	25% Brown(bl), 25% Brown(bl)(ch), 25% Brown Tortie(bl), 25% Brown Tortie(bl)(ch)
Red:Chocolate	50% Brown(ch), 50% Brown Tortie(ch)
Red:Chocolate(bl)	25% Brown(ch), 25% Brown(bl)(ch), 25% Brown Tortie(ch), 25% Brown Tortie(bl)(ch)
Cream:Lilac	50% Brown(bl)(ch), 50% Brown Tortie(bl)(ch)
	QUEEN - BROWN(bl)
Brown	50% Brown, 50% Brown(bl)
Brown(bl)	25% Brown, 50% Brown(bl), 25% Blue
Brown(ch)	25% Brown, 25% Brown(bl), 25% Brown(ch), 25% Brown(bl)(ch)
Brown(bl)(ch)	12% Brown, 25% Brown(bl), 12% Brown(ch), 25% Brown(bl)(ch), 12% Blue, 12% Blue(ch)
Blue	50% Brown(bl), 50% Blue
Blue(ch)	25% Brown(bl), 25% Brown(bl)(ch), 25% Blue, 25% Blue(ch)
Chocolate	50% Brown(ch), 50% Brown(bl)(ch)
Chocolate(bl)	25% Brown(ch), 50% Brown(bl)(ch), 25% Blue(ch)
Lilac	50% Brown(bl)(ch), 50% Blue(ch)
Red:Brown	25% Brown, 25% Brown(bl), 25% Brown Tortie, 25% Brown Tortie(bl)
Red:Brown(bl)	12% Brown, 25% Brown(bl), 12% Blue, 12% Brown Tortie, 25% Brown Tortie(bl), 12% Blue Tortie

235

Appendix B

STUD	Possible colours shown as a % of the litter

QUEEN- BROWN(bl) (Cont'd)

Red:Brown(ch)	12% Brown, 12% Brown(bl), 12% Brown(ch), 12% Brown(bl)(ch), 12%BrownTortie, 12% Brown Tortie(bl), 12%Brown Tortie(ch), 12%Brown Tortie(bl)(ch)
Red:Brown(bl)(ch)	6% Brown, 12% Brown(bl), 6% Brown(ch), 12% Brown(bl)(ch), 6% Blue, 6% Blue(ch), 6% Brown Tortie, 12% Brown Tortie(bl), 6% Brown Tortie(ch), 12% Brown Tortie(bl)(ch), 6% Blue Tortie, 6% Blue Tortie(ch)
Cream:Blue	25% Brown(bl), 25% Blue, 25% Brown Tortie(bl), 25% Blue Tortie
Cream:Blue(ch)	12% Brown(bl), 12% Brown(bl)(ch), 12% Blue, 12% Blue(ch), 12% Brown Tortie(bl), 12% Brown Tortie(bl)(ch), 12% Blue Tortie, 12% Blue Tortie(ch)
Red:Chocolate	25% Brown(ch), 25% Brown(bl)(ch), 25% Brown Tortie(ch), 25% Brown Tortie(bl)(ch)
Red:Chocolate(bl)	12% Brown(ch), 25% Brown(bl)(ch),12%Blue(ch), 12% Brown Tortie(ch), 25% Brown Tortie(bl)(ch), 12% Blue Tortie(ch)
Cream:Lilac	25% Brown(bl)(ch), 25% Blue(ch), 25% Brown Tortie(bl)(ch), 25% Blue Tortie(ch)

QUEEN- BROWN(ch)

Brown	50% Brown, 50% Brown(ch)
Brown(bl)	25% Brown, 25% Brown(bl), 25% Brown(ch), 25% Blue(bl)(ch)
Brown(ch)	25% Brown, 50% Brown(ch), 25% Chocolate
Brown(bl)(ch)	12% Brown, 12% Brown(bl), 25% Brown(ch), 25% Brown(bl)(ch), 12% Chocolate, 12% Chocolate(bl)
Blue	50% Brown(bl), 50% Brown(bl)(ch)
Blue(ch)	25% Brown(bl), 50% Brown(bl)(ch), 25% Chocolate(bl)
Chocolate	50% Brown(ch), 50% Chocolate
Chocolate(bl)	25% Brown(ch), 25% Brown(bl)(ch), 25% Chocolate, 25% Chocolate(bl)
Lilac	50% Brown(bl)(ch), 50% Chocolate(bl)
Red:Brown	25% Brown, 25% Brown(ch), 25% Brown Tortie, 25% Brown Tortie(ch)
Red:Brown(bl)	12% Brown, 12% Brown(bl), 12% Brown(ch), 12% Brown(bl)(ch), 12% Brown Tortie, 12% Brown Tortie(bl), 12% Brown Tortie(ch), 12% Brown Tortie(bl)(ch)
Red:Brown(ch)	12% Brown, 25% Brown(ch), 12% Chocolate, 12% Brown Tortie, 25% Brown Tortie(ch), 12% Chocolate Tortie

STUD	Possible colours shown as a % of the litter
Red:Brown(bl)(ch)	6% Brown, 6% Brown(bl), 12% Brown(ch), 12% Brown(bl)(ch), 6% Chocolate, 6% Chocolate(bl), 6% Brown Tortie, 6% Brown Tortie(bl), 12% Brown Tortie(ch), 12% Brown Tortie(bl)(ch), 6% Chocolate Tortie, 6% Chocolate Tortie(bl)
Cream:Blue	25% Brown(bl), 25% Brown(bl)(ch), 25% Brown Tortie(bl), 25% Brown Tortie(bl)(ch)
Cream:Blue(ch)	12% Brown(bl), 25% Brown(bl)(ch), 12% Chocolate(bl), 12% Brown Tortie(bl), 25% Brown Tortie(bl)(ch), 12% Chocolate Tortie(bl)
Red:Chocolate	25% Brown(ch), 25% Chocolate, 25% Brown Tortie(ch), 25% Chocolate Tortie
Red:Chocolate(bl)	12% Brown(ch), 12% Brown(bl)(ch), 12% Chocolate, 12% Chocolate(bl), 12% Brown Tortie(ch), 12% Brown Tortie(bl)(ch), 12% Chocolate Tortie, 12% Chocolate Tortie(bl)
Cream:Lilac	25% Brown(bl)(ch), 25% Chocolate(bl), 25% Brown Tortie(bl)(ch), 25% Chocolate Tortie(bl)

QUEEN - BROWN(bl)(ch)

Brown	25% Brown, 25% Brown(bl), 25% Brown(ch), 25% Blue(bl)(ch)
Brown(bl)	12% Brown, 25% Brown(bl), 12% Brown(ch), 25% Brown(bl)(ch), 12% Blue, 12% Blue(ch)
Brown(ch)	12% Brown, 12% Brown(bl), 25% Brown(ch), 25% Brown(bl)(ch), 12% Chocolate, 12% Chocolate(bl)
Brown(bl)(ch)	6% Brown, 12% Brown(bl), 12% Brown(ch), 25% Brown(bl)(ch), 6% Blue, 12% Blue(ch), 6% Chocolate, 12% Chocolate(bl), 6% Lilac
Blue	25% Brown(bl), 25% Brown(bl)(ch), 25% Blue, 25% Blue(ch)
Blue(ch)	12% Brown(bl), 25% Brown(bl)(ch), 12% Blue, 25% Blue(ch), 12% Chocolate(bl), 12% Lilac
Chocolate	25% Brown(ch), 25% Brown(bl)(ch), 25% Chocolate, 25% Chocolate(bl)
Chocolate(bl)	12% Brown(ch), 25% Brown(bl)(ch), 12% Blue(ch), 12% Chocolate, 25% Chocolate(bl), 12% Lilac
Lilac	25% Brown(bl)(ch), 25% Blue(ch), 25% Chocolate(bl), 25% Lilac
Red:Brown	12% Brown, 12% Brown(bl), 12% Brown(ch), 12% Brown(bl)(ch), 12% Brown Tortie, 12% Brown Tortie(bl), 12% Brown Tortie(ch), 12% Brown Tortie(bl)(ch)

Appendix B

Red:Brown(bl)	6% Brown, 12% Brown(bl), 6% Brown(ch), 12% Brown(bl)(ch), 6% Blue, 6% Blue(ch), 6% Brown Tortie, 12% Brown Tortie(bl), 6% Brown Tortie(ch), 12% Brown Tortie(bl)(ch), 6% Blue Tortie, 6% Blue Tortie(ch)
Red:Brown(ch)	6% Brown, 6% Brown(bl), 12% Brown(ch), 12% Brown(bl)(ch), 6% Chocolate, 6% Chocolate(bl), 6% Brown Tortie, 6% Brown Tortie(bl), 12% Brown Tortie(ch), 12% Brown Tortie(bl)(ch), 6% Chocolate Tortie, 6% Chocolate Tortie(bl)
Red:Brown(bl)(ch)	3% Brown, 6% Brown(bl), 6% Brown(ch), 12% Brown(bl)(ch), 3% Blue, 6% Blue(ch), 3% Chocolate, 6% Chocolate(bl), 3% Lilac, 3% Brown Tortie, 6% Brown Tortie(bl), 6% Brown Tortie(ch), 12% Brown Tortie(bl)(ch), 3% Blue Tortie, 6% Blue Tortie(ch), 3% Chocolate Tortie, 6% Chocolate Tortie(bl), 3% Lilac Tortie
Cream:Blue	12% Brown(bl), 12% Brown(bl)(ch), 12% Blue, 12% Blue(ch),12% Brown Tortie(bl), 12% Brown Tortie(bl)(ch), 12% Blue Tortie, 12% Blue Tortie(ch)
Cream:Blue(ch)	6% Brown(bl), 12% Brown(bl)(ch), 6% Blue, 12% Blue(ch), 6% Chocolate(bl), 6% Lilac, 6% Brown Tortie(bl), 12% Brown Tortie(bl)(ch), 6% Blue Tortie, 12% Blue Tortie(ch), 6% Chocolate Tortie(bl), 6% Lilac Tortie
Red:Chocolate	12% Brown(ch), 12% Brown(bl)(ch), 12% Chocolate, 12% Chocolate(bl) 12% Brown Tortie(ch), 12% Brown Tortie(bl)(ch), 12% Chocolate Tortie, 12% Chocolate Tortie(bl)
Red:Chocolate(bl)	6% Brown(ch), 12% Brown(bl)(ch), 6% Blue(ch), 6% Chocolate, 12% Chocolate(bl), 6% Lilac, 6% Brown Tortie(ch), 12% Brown Tortie(bl)(ch), 6% Blue Tortie(ch), 6% Chocolate Tortie, 12% Chocolate Tortie(bl), 6% Lilac Tortie
Cream:Lilac	12% Brown(bl)(ch), 12% Blue(ch), 12% Chocolate(bl), 12% Lilac, 12% Brown Tortie(bl)(ch), 12% Blue Tortie(ch), 12% Chocolate Tortie(bl), 12% Lilac Tortie

QUEEN - BLUE

Brown	100% Brown(bl)
Brown(bl)	50% Brown(bl), 50% Blue
Brown(ch)	50% Brown(bl), 50% Brown(bl)(ch)

STUD	**Possible colours shown as a % of the litter**
Brown(bl)(ch)	25% Brown(bl), 25% Brown(bl)(ch), 25% Blue, 25% Blue(ch)
Blue	100% Blue
Blue(ch)	50% Blue, 50% Blue(ch)
Chocolate	100% Brown(bl)(ch)
Chocolate(bl)	50% Brown(bl)(ch), 50% Blue(ch)
Lilac	100% Blue(ch)
Red:Brown	50% Brown(bl), 50% Brown Tortie(bl)
Red:Brown(bl)	25% Brown(bl), 25% Blue, 25% Brown Tortie(bl), 25% Blue Tortie
Red:Brown(ch)	25% Brown(bl), 25% Brown(bl)(ch), 25% Brown Tortie(bl), 25% Brown Tortie(bl)(ch)
Red:Brown(bl)(ch)	12% Brown(bl), 12% Brown(bl)(ch), 12% Blue, 12% Blue(ch), 12% Brown Tortie(bl), 12% Brown Tortie(bl)(ch), 12% Blue Tortie, 12% Blue Tortie(ch)
Cream:Blue	50% Blue, 50% Blue Tortie
Cream:Blue(ch)	25% Blue, 25% Blue(ch), 25% Blue Tortie, 25% Blue Tortie(ch)
Red:Chocolate	50% Brown(bl)(ch), 50% Brown Tortie(bl)(ch)
Red:Chocolate(bl)	25% Brown(bl)(ch), 25% Blue(ch), 25% Brown Tortie(bl)(ch), 25% Blue Tortie(ch)
Cream:Lilac	50% Blue(ch), 50% Blue Tortie(ch)

QUEEN – BLUE(ch)	
Brown	50% Brown(bl), 50% Brown(bl)(ch)
Brown(bl)	25% Brown(bl), 25% Brown(bl)(ch), 25% Blue, 25% Blue(ch)
Brown(ch)	25% Brown(bl), 50% Brown(bl)(ch), 25% Chocolate(bl)
Brown(bl)(ch)	12% Brown(bl), 25% Brown(bl)(ch), 12% Blue, 25% Blue(ch), 12% Chocolate(bl), 12% Lilac
Blue	50% Blue, 50% Blue(ch)
Blue(ch)	25% Blue, 50% Blue(ch), 25% Lilac
Chocolate	50% Brown(bl)(ch), 50% Chocolate(bl)
Chocolate(bl)	25% Brown(bl)(ch), 25% Blue(ch), 25% Chocolate(bl), 25% Lilac
Lilac	50% Blue(ch), 50% Lilac
Red:Brown	25% Brown(bl), 25% Brown(bl)(ch), 25% Brown Tortie(bl), 25% Brown Tortie(bl)(ch)
Red:Brown(bl)	12% Brown(bl), 12% Brown(bl)(ch), 12% Blue, 12% Blue(ch), 12% Brown Tortie(bl), 12% Brown Tortie(bl)(ch), 12% Blue Tortie, 12% Blue Tortie(ch)
Red:Brown(ch)	12% Brown(bl), 25% Brown(bl)(ch), 12% Chocolate(bl), 12% Brown Tortie(bl), 25% Brown Tortie(bl)(ch), 12% Chocolate Tortie(bl)

Appendix B

STUD | **Possible colours shown as a % of the litter**

QUEEN – BLUE(ch) (Cont'd)

STUD	Possible colours shown as a % of the litter
Red:Brown(bl)(ch)	6% Brown(bl), 12% Brown(bl)(ch), 6% Blue, 12% Blue(ch), 6% Chocolate(bl), 6% Lilac, 6% Brown Tortie(bl), 12% Brown Tortie(bl)(ch), 6% Blue Tortie, 12% Blue Tortie(ch), 6% Chocolate Tortie(bl), 6% Lilac Tortie
Cream:Blue	25% Blue, 25% Blue(ch), 25% Blue Tortie, 25% Blue Tortie(ch)
Cream:Blue(ch)	12% Blue, 25% Blue(ch), 12% Lilac, 12% Blue Tortie, 25% Blue Tortie(ch), 12% Lilac Tortie
Red:Chocolate	25% Brown(bl)(ch), 25% Chocolate(bl), 25% Brown Tortie(bl)(ch), 25% Chocolate Tortie(bl)
Red:Chocolate(bl)	12% Brown(bl)(ch), 12% Blue(ch), 12% Chocolate(bl), 12% Lilac, 12% Brown Tortie(bl)(ch), 12% Blue Tortie(ch), 12% Chocolate Tortie(bl), 12% Lilac Tortie
Cream:Lilac	25% Blue(ch), 25% Lilac, 25% Blue Tortie(ch), 25% Lilac Tortie

QUEEN - CHOCOLATE

STUD	Possible colours shown as a % of the litter
Brown	100% Brown(ch)
Brown(bl)	50% Brown(ch), 50% Blue(bl)(ch)
Brown(ch)	50% Brown(ch), 50% Chocolate
Brown(bl)(ch)	25% Brown(ch), 25% Brown(bl)(ch), 25% Chocolate, 25% Chocolate(bl)
Blue	100% Brown(bl)(ch)
Blue(ch)	50% Brown(bl)(ch), 50% Chocolate(bl)
Chocolate	100% Chocolate
Chocolate(bl)	50% Chocolate, 50% Chocolate(bl)
Lilac	100% Chocolate(bl)
Red:Brown	50% Brown(ch), 50% Brown Tortie(ch)
Red:Brown(bl)	25% Brown(ch), 25% Blue(bl)(ch), 25% Brown Tortie(ch), 25% Blue Tortie(bl)(ch)
Red:Brown(ch)	25% Brown(ch), 25% Chocolate, 25% Brown Tortie(ch), 25% Chocolate Tortie
Red:Brown(bl)(ch)	12% Brown(ch), 12% Brown(bl)(ch), 12% Chocolate, 12% Chocolate(bl), 12% Brown Tortie(ch), 12% Brown Tortie(bl)(ch), 12% Chocolate Tortie, 12% Chocolate Tortie(bl)
Cream:Blue	50% Brown(bl)(ch), 50% Brown Tortie(bl)(ch)
Cream:Blue(ch)	25% Brown(bl)(ch), 25% Chocolate(bl), 25% Brown Tortie(bl)(ch), 25% Chocolate Tortie(bl)
Red:Chocolate	50% Chocolate, 50% Chocolate Tortie
Red:Chocolate(bl)	25% Chocolate, 25% Chocolate(bl), 25% Chocolate Tortie, 25% Chocolate Tortie(bl)
Cream:Lilac	50% Chocolate(bl), 50% Chocolate Tortie(bl)

STUD	Possible colours shown as a % of the litter QUEEN - CHOCOLATE(bl)
Brown	50% Brown(ch), 50% Brown(bl)(ch)
Brown(bl)	25% Brown(ch), 50% Brown(bl)(ch), 25% Blue(ch)
Brown(ch)	25% Brown(ch), 25% Brown(bl)(ch), 25% Chocolate, 25% Chocolate(bl)
Brown(bl)(ch)	12% Brown(ch), 25% Brown(bl)(ch), 12% Blue(ch), 12% Chocolate, 25% Chocolate(bl), 12% Lilac
Blue	50% Brown(bl)(ch), 50% Blue(ch)
Blue(ch)	25% Brown(bl)(ch), 25% Blue(ch), 25% Chocolate(bl), 25% Lilac
Chocolate	50% Chocolate, 50% Chocolate(bl)
Chocolate(bl)	25% Chocolate, 50% Chocolate(bl), 25% Lilac
Lilac	50% Chocolate(bl), 50% Lilac
Red:Brown	25% Brown(ch), 25% Brown(bl)(ch), 25% Brown Tortie(ch), 25% Brown Tortie(bl)(ch)
Red:Brown(bl)	12% Brown(ch), 25% Brown(bl)(ch), 12% Blue(ch), 12% Brown Tortie(ch), 25% Brown Tortie(bl)(ch), 12% Blue Tortie(ch)
Red:Brown(ch)	12% Brown(ch), 12% Brown(bl)(ch), 12% Chocolate, 12% Chocolate(bl), 12% Brown Tortie(ch), 12% Brown Tortie(bl)(ch), 12% Chocolate Tortie, 12% Chocolate Tortie(bl)
Red:Brown(bl)(ch)	6% Brown(ch), 12% Brown(bl)(ch), 6% Blue(ch), 6% Chocolate, 12% Chocolate(bl), 6% Lilac, 6% Brown Tortie(ch), 12% Brown Tortie(bl)(ch), 6% Blue Tortie(ch), 6% Chocolate Tortie, 12% Chocolate Tortie(bl), 6% Lilac Tortie
Cream:Blue	25% Brown(bl)(ch), 25% Blue(ch), 25% Brown Tortie(bl)(ch), 25% Blue Tortie(ch)
Cream:Blue(ch)	12% Brown(bl)(ch), 12% Blue(ch), 12% Chocolate(bl), 12% Lilac, 12% Brown Tortie(bl)(ch), 12% Blue Tortie(ch), 12% Chocolate Tortie(bl), 12% Lilac Tortie
Red:Chocolate	25% Chocolate, 25% Chocolate(bl), 25% Chocolate Tortie, 25% Chocolate Tortie(bl)
Red:Chocolate(bl)	12% Chocolate, 25% Chocolate(bl), 12% Lilac, 12% Chocolate Tortie, 25% Chocolate Tortie(bl), 12% Lilac Tortie
Cream:Lilac	25% Chocolate(bl), 25% Lilac, 25% Chocolate Tortie(bl), 25% Lilac Tortie

Appendix B

STUD	Possible colours shown as a % of the litter

QUEEN - LILAC

Brown	100% Brown(bl)(ch)
Brown(bl)	50% Brown(bl)(ch), 50% Blue(ch)
Brown(ch)	50% Brown(bl)(ch), 50% Chocolate(bl)
Brown(bl)(ch)	25% Brown(bl)(ch), 25% Blue(ch), 25% Chocolate(bl), 25% Lilac
Blue	100% Blue(ch)
Blue(ch)	50% Blue(ch), 50% Lilac
Chocolate	100% Chocolate(bl)
Chocolate(bl)	50% Chocolate(bl), 50% Lilac
Lilac	100% Lilac
Red:Brown	50% Brown(bl)(ch), 50% Brown Tortie(bl)(ch)
Red:Brown(bl)	25% Brown(bl)(ch), 25% Blue(ch), 25% Brown Tortie(bl)(ch), 25% Blue Tortie(ch)
Red:Brown(ch)	25% Brown(bl)(ch), 25% Chocolate(bl), 25% Brown Tortie(bl)(ch), 25% Chocolate Tortie(bl)
Red:Brown(bl)(ch)	12% Brown(bl)(ch), 12% Blue(ch), 12% Chocolate(bl), 12% Lilac, 12% Brown Tortie(bl)(ch), 12% Blue Tortie(ch), 12% Chocolate Tortie(bl), 12% Lilac Tortie
Cream:Blue	50% Blue(ch), 50% Blue Tortie(ch)
Cream:Blue(ch)	25% Blue(ch), 25% Lilac, 25% Blue Tortie(ch), 25% Lilac Tortie
Red:Chocolate	50% Chocolate(bl), 50% Chocolate Tortie(bl)
Red:Chocolate(bl)	25% Chocolate(bl), 25% Lilac, 25% Chocolate Tortie(bl), 25% Lilac Tortie
Cream:Lilac	50% Lilac, 50% Lilac Tortie

QUEEN - BROWN TORTIE

Brown	50% Brown, 25% Red:Brown, 25% Brown Tortie
Brown(bl)	25% Brown, 25% Brown(bl), 12% Red:Brown, 12% Red:Brown(bl), 12% Brown Tortie, 12% Brown Tortie(bl)
Brown(ch)	25% Brown, 25% Brown(ch), 12% Red:Brown, 12% Red:Brown(ch), 12% Brown Tortie, 12% Brown Tortie(ch)
Brown(bl)(ch)	12% Brown, 12% Brown(bl), 12% Brown(ch), 12% Brown(bl)(ch), 6% Red:Brown, 6% Red:Brown(bl), 6% Red:Brown(ch), 6% Red:Brown(bl)(ch), 6% Brown Tortie, 6% Brown Tortie(bl), 6% Brown Tortie(ch), 6% Brown Tortie(bl)(ch)
Blue	50% Brown(bl), 25% Red:Brown(bl), 25% Brown Tortie(bl)
Blue(ch)	25% Brown(bl), 25% Brown(bl)(ch), 12% Red:Brown(bl), 12% Red:Brown(bl)(ch), 12% Brown Tortie(bl), 12% Brown Tortie(bl)(ch)

STUD	Possible colours shown as a % of the litter
Chocolate	50% Brown(ch), 25% Red:Brown(ch), 25% Brown Tortie(ch)
Chocolate(bl)	25% Brown(ch), 25% Brown(bl)(ch), 12% Red:Brown(ch), 12% Red:Brown(bl)(ch), 12% Brown Tortie(ch), 12% Brown Tortie(bl)(ch)
Lilac	50% Brown(bl)(ch), 25% Red:Brown(bl)(ch), 25% Brown Tortie(bl)(ch)
Red:Brown	25% Brown, 50% Red:Brown, 25% Brown Tortie
Red:Brown(bl)	12% Brown, 12% Brown(bl), 25% Red:Brown, 25% Red:Brown(bl), 12% Brown Tortie, 12% Brown Tortie(bl)
Red:Brown(ch)	12% Brown, 12% Brown(ch), 25% Red:Brown, 25% Red:Brown(ch), 12% Brown Tortie, 12% Brown Tortie(ch)
Red:Brown(bl)(ch)	6% Brown, 6% Brown(bl), 6% Brown(ch), 6% Brown(bl)(ch), 12% Red:Brown, 12% Red:Brown(bl),12% Red:Brown(ch), 12% Red:Brown(bl)(ch), 6% Brown Tortie, 6% Brown Tortie(bl), 6% Brown Tortie(ch), 6% Brown Tortie(bl)(ch)
Cream:Blue	25% Brown(bl), 50% Red:Brown(bl), 25% Brown Tortie(bl)
Cream:Blue(ch)	12% Brown(bl), 12% Brown(bl)(ch), 25% Red:Brown(bl), 25% Red:Brown(bl)(ch), 12% Brown Tortie(bl), 12% Brown Tortie(bl)(ch)
Red:Chocolate	25% Brown(ch), 50% Red:Brown(ch), 25% Brown Tortie(ch)
Red:Chocolate(bl)	12% Brown(ch), 12% Brown(bl)(ch), 25% Red:Brown(ch), 25% Red:Brown(bl)(ch), 12% Brown Tortie(ch), 12% Brown Tortie(bl)(ch)
Cream:Lilac	25% Brown(bl)(ch), 50% Red:Brown(bl)(ch), 25% Brown Tortie(bl)(ch)

QUEEN - BROWN TORTIE(bl)

Brown	25% Brown, 25% Brown(bl), 12% Red:Brown, 12% Red:Brown(bl), 12% Brown Tortie, 12% Brown Tortie(bl)
Brown(bl)	12% Brown, 25% Brown(bl), 12% Blue, 6% Red:Brown, 12% Red:Brown(bl), 6% Cream:Blue, 6% Brown Tortie, 12% Brown Tortie(bl), 6% Blue Tortie
Brown(ch)	12% Brown, 12% Brown(bl), 12% Brown(ch), 12% Brown(bl)(ch), 6% Red:Brown, 6% Red:Brown(bl), 6% Red:Brown(ch), 6% Red:Brown(bl)(ch), 6% Brown Tortie, 6% Brown Tortie(bl), 6% Brown Tortie(ch), 6% Brown Tortie(bl)(ch)

Appendix B

Brown(bl)(ch)	6% Brown, 12% Brown(bl), 6% Brown(ch), 12% Brown(bl)(ch), 6% Blue, 6% Blue(ch), 3% Red:Brown, 6% Red:Brown(bl), 3% Red:Brown(ch), 6% Red:Brown(bl)(ch), 3% Cream:Blue, 3% Cream:Blue(ch), 3% Brown Tortie, 6% Brown Tortie(bl), 3% Brown Tortie(ch), 6% Brown Tortie(bl)(ch), 3% Blue Tortie, 3% Blue Tortie(ch)
Blue	25% Brown(bl), 25% Blue, 12% Red:Brown(bl), 12% Cream:Blue, 12% Brown Tortie(bl), 12% Blue Tortie
Blue(ch)	12% Brown(bl), 12% Brown(bl)(ch), 12% Blue, 12% Blue(ch), 6% Red:Brown(bl), 6% Red:Brown(bl)(ch), 6% Cream:Blue, 6% Cream:Blue(ch), 6% Brown Tortie(bl), 6% Brown Tortie(bl)(ch), 6% Blue Tortie, 6% Blue Tortie(ch)
Chocolate	25% Brown(ch), 25% Brown(bl)(ch), 12% Red:Brown(ch), 12% Red:Brown(bl)(ch), 12% Brown Tortie(ch), 12% Brown Tortie(bl)(ch)
Chocolate(bl)	12% Brown(ch), 25% Brown(bl)(ch), 12% Blue(ch), 6% Red:Brown(ch), 12% Red:Brown(bl)(ch), 6% Cream:Blue(ch), 6% Brown Tortie(ch), 12% Brown Tortie(bl)(ch), 6% Blue Tortie(ch)
Lilac	25% Brown(bl)(ch), 25% Blue(ch), 12% Red:Brown(bl)(ch), 12% Cream:Blue(ch), 12% Brown Tortie(bl)(ch), 12% Blue Tortie(ch)
Red:Brown	12% Brown, 12% Brown(bl), 25% Red:Brown, 25% Red:Brown(bl), 12% Brown Tortie, 12% Brown Tortie(bl)
Red:Brown(bl)	6% Brown, 12% Brown(bl), 6% Blue, 12% Red:Brown, 25% Red:Brown(bl), 12% Cream:Blue, 6% Brown Tortie, 12% Brown Tortie(bl), 6% Blue Tortie
Red:Brown(ch)	6% Brown, 6% Brown(bl), 6% Brown(ch), 6% Brown(bl)(ch), 12% Red:Brown, 12% Red:Brown(bl), 12% Red:Brown(ch), 12% Red:Brown(bl)(ch), 6% Brown Tortie, 6% Brown Tortie(bl), 6% Brown Tortie(ch), 6% Brown Tortie(bl)(ch)
Red:Brown(bl)(ch)	3% Brown, 6% Brown(bl), 3% Brown(ch), 6% Brown(bl)(ch), 3% Blue, 3% Blue(ch), 6% Red:Brown, 12% Red:Brown(bl), 6% Red:Brown(ch), 12% Red:Brown(bl)(ch), 6% Cream:Blue, 6% Cream:Blue(ch), 3% Brown Tortie, 6% Brown Tortie(bl), 3% Brown Tortie(ch), 6% Brown Tortie(bl)(ch), 3% Blue Tortie, 3% Blue Tortie(ch)

STUD	Possible colours shown as a % of the litter
Cream:Blue	12% Brown(bl), 12% Blue, 25% Red:Brown(bl), 25% Cream:Blue, 12% Brown Tortie(bl), 12% Blue Tortie
Cream:Blue(ch)	6% Brown(bl), 6% Brown(bl)(ch), 6% Blue, 6% Blue(ch), 12% Red:Brown(bl), 12% Red:Brown(bl)(ch), 12% Cream:Blue, 12% Cream:Blue(ch), 6% Brown Tortie(bl), 6% Brown Tortie(bl)(ch), 6% Blue Tortie, 6% Blue Tortie(ch)
Red:Chocolate	12% Brown(ch), 12% Brown(bl)(ch), 25% Red:Brown(ch), 25% Red:Brown(bl)(ch), 12% Brown Tortie(ch), 12% Brown Tortie(bl)(ch)
Red:Chocolate(bl)	6% Brown(ch), 12% Brown(bl)(ch), 6% Blue(ch), 12% Red:Brown(ch), 25% Red:Brown(bl)(ch), 12% Cream:Blue(ch), 6% Brown Tortie(ch), 12% Brown Tortie(bl)(ch), 6% Blue Tortie(ch)
Cream:Lilac	12% Brown(bl)(ch), 12% Blue(ch), 25% Red:Brown(bl)(ch), 25% Cream:Blue(ch), 12% Brown Tortie(bl)(ch), 12% Blue Tortie(ch)

QUEEN - BROWN TORTIE(ch)

Brown	25% Brown, 25% Brown(ch), 12% Red:Brown, 12% Red:Brown(ch), 12% Brown Tortie, 12% Brown Tortie(ch)
Brown(bl)	12% Brown, 12% Brown(bl), 12% Brown(ch), 12% Brown(bl)(ch), 6% Red:Brown, 6% Red:Brown(bl), 6% Red:Brown(ch), 6% Red:Brown(bl)(ch), 6% Brown Tortie, 6% Brown Tortie(bl), 6% Brown Tortie(ch), 6% Brown Tortie(bl)(ch)
Brown(ch)	12% Brown, 25% Brown(ch), 12% Chocolate, 6% Red:Brown, 12% Red:Brown(ch), 6% Red:Chocolate, 6% Brown Tortie, 12% Brown Tortie(ch), 6% Chocolate Tortie
Brown(bl)(ch)	6% Brown, 6% Brown(bl), 12% Brown(ch), 12% Brown(bl)(ch), 6% Chocolate, 6% Chocolate(bl), 3% Red:Brown, 3% Red:Brown(bl), 6% Red:Brown(ch), 6% Red:Brown(bl)(ch), 3% Red:Chocolate, 3% Red:Chocolate(bl), 3% Brown Tortie, 3% Brown Tortie(bl), 6% Brown Tortie(ch), 6% Brown Tortie(bl)(ch), 3% Chocolate Tortie, 3% Chocolate Tortie(bl)
Blue	25% Brown(bl), 25% Brown(bl)(ch), 12% Red:Brown(bl), 12% Red:Brown(bl)(ch), 12% Brown Tortie(bl), 12% Brown Tortie(bl)(ch)

Appendix B

QUEEN – BROWN TORTIE(Ch) (Cont'd)

Blue(ch) 12% Brown(bl), 25% Brown(bl)(ch),
12% Chocolate(bl), 6% Red:Brown(bl),
12% Red:Brown(bl)(ch), 6% Red:Chocolate(bl),
6% Brown Tortie(bl), 12% Brown Tortie(bl)(ch),
6% Chocolate Tortie(bl)

Chocolate 25% Brown(ch), 25% Chocolate, 12% Red:Brown(ch),
12% Red:Chocolate, 12% Brown Tortie(ch),
12% Chocolate Tortie

Chocolate(bl) 12% Brown(ch), 12% Brown(bl)(ch), 12% Chocolate,
12% Chocolate(bl), 6% Red:Brown(ch),
6% Red:Brown(bl)(ch), 6% Red:Chocolate,
6% Red:Chocolate(bl), 6% Brown Tortie(ch),
6% Brown Tortie(bl)(ch), 6% Chocolate Tortie,
6% Chocolate Tortie(bl)

Lilac 25% Brown(bl)(ch), 25% Chocolate(bl),
12% Red:Brown(bl)(ch), 12% Red:Chocolate(bl),
12% Brown Tortie(bl)(ch), 12% Chocolate Tortie(bl)

Red:Brown 12% Brown, 12% Brown(ch), 25% Red:Brown,
25% Red:Brown(ch), 12% Brown Tortie,
12% Brown Tortie(ch)

Red:Brown(bl) 6% Brown, 6% Brown(bl), 6% Brown(ch),
6% Brown(bl)(ch), 12% Red:Brown,
12% Red:Brown(bl), 12% Red:Brown(ch),
12% Red:Brown(bl)(ch), 6% Brown Tortie,
6% Brown Tortie(bl), 6% Brown Tortie(ch),
6% Brown Tortie(bl)(ch)

Red:Brown(ch) 6% Brown, 12% Brown(ch), 6% Chocolate,
12% Red:Brown, 25% Red:Brown(ch),
12% Red:Chocolate, 6% Brown Tortie,
12% Brown Tortie(ch), 6% Chocolate Tortie

Red:Brown(bl)(ch) 3% Brown, 3% Brown(bl), 6% Brown(ch),
6% Brown(bl)(ch), 3% Chocolate, 3% Chocolate(bl),
6% Red:Brown, 6% Red:Brown(bl),
12% Red:Brown(ch), 12% Red:Brown(bl)(ch),
6% Red:Chocolate, 6% Red:Chocolate(bl),
3% Brown Tortie, 3% Brown Tortie(bl),
6% Brown Tortie(ch), 6% Brown Tortie(bl)(ch),
3% Chocolate Tortie, 3% Chocolate Tortie(bl)

Cream:Blue 12% Brown(bl), 12% Brown(bl)(ch),
25% Red:Brown(bl), 25% Red:Brown(bl)(ch),
12% Brown Tortie(bl), 12% Brown Tortie(bl)(ch)

Cream:Blue(ch) 6% Brown(bl), 12% Brown(bl)(ch), 6% Chocolate(bl),
12% Red:Brown(bl), 25% Red:Brown(bl)(ch),
12% Red:Chocolate(bl), 6% Brown Tortie(bl),
12% Brown Tortie(bl)(ch), 6% Chocolate Tortie(bl)

STUD	Possible colours shown as a % of the litter
Red:Chocolate	12% Brown(ch), 12% Chocolate, 25% Red:Brown(ch), 25% Red:Chocolate, 12% Brown Tortie(ch), 12% Chocolate Tortie
Red:Chocolate(bl)	6% Brown(ch), 6% Brown(bl)(ch), 6% Chocolate, 6% Chocolate(bl), 12% Red:Brown(ch), 12% Red:Brown(bl)(ch), 12% Red:Chocolate, 12% Red:Chocolate(bl), 6% Brown Tortie(ch), 6% Brown Tortie(bl)(ch), 6% Chocolate Tortie, 6% Chocolate Tortie(bl)
Cream:Lilac	12% Brown(bl)(ch), 12% Chocolate(bl), 25% Red:Brown(bl)(ch), 25% Red:Chocolate(bl), 12% Brown Tortie(bl)(ch), 12% Chocolate Tortie(bl)

QUEEN - BROWN TORTIE(bl)(ch)

Brown	12% Brown, 12% Brown(bl), 12% Brown(ch), 12% Brown(bl)(ch), 6% Red:Brown, 6% Red:Brown(bl), 6% Red:Brown(ch), 6% Red:Brown(bl)(ch), 6% Brown Tortie, 6% Brown Tortie(bl), 6% Brown Tortie(ch), 6% Brown Tortie(bl)(ch)
Brown(bl)	6% Brown, 12% Brown(bl), 6% Brown(ch), 12% Brown(bl)(ch), 6% Blue, 6% Blue(ch), 3% Red:Brown, 6% Red:Brown(bl), 3% Red:Brown(ch), 6% Red:Brown(bl)(ch), 3% Cream:Blue, 3% Cream:Blue(ch), 3% Brown Tortie, 6% Brown Tortie(bl), 3% Brown Tortie(ch), 6% Brown Tortie(bl)(ch), 3% Blue Tortie, 3% Blue Tortie(ch)
Brown(ch)	6% Brown, 6% Brown(bl), 12% Brown(ch), 12% Brown(bl)(ch), 6% Chocolate, 6% Chocolate(bl), 3% Red:Brown, 3% Red:Brown(bl), 6% Red:Brown(ch), 6% Red:Brown(bl)(ch), 3% Red:Chocolate, 3% Red:Chocolate(bl), 3% Brown Tortie, 3% Brown Tortie(bl), 6% Brown Tortie(ch), 6% Brown Tortie(bl)(ch), 3% Chocolate Tortie, 3% Chocolate Tortie(bl)
Brown(bl)(ch)	2% Brown, 6% Brown(bl), 6% Brown(ch), 12% Brown(bl)(ch), 2% Blue, 6% Blue(ch), 2% Chocolate, 6% Chocolate(bl), 2% Lilac, 1% Red:Brown, 3% Red:Brown(bl), 3% Red:Brown(ch), 6% Red:Brown(bl)(ch), 1% Cream:Blue, 3% Cream:Blue(ch), 1% Red:Chocolate, 3% Red:Chocolate(bl), 1% Cream:Lilac, 1% Brown Tortie, 3% Brown Tortie(bl), 3% Brown Tortie(ch), 6% Brown Tortie(bl)(ch), 1% Blue Tortie, 3% Blue Tortie(ch), 1% Chocolate Tortie, 3% Chocolate Tortie(bl), 1% Lilac Tortie

Appendix B

Blue	12% Brown(bl), 12% Brown(bl)(ch), 12% Blue, 12% Blue(ch), 6% Red:Brown(bl), 6% Red:Brown(bl)(ch), 6% Cream:Blue, 6% Cream:Blue(ch), 6% Brown Tortie(bl), 6% Brown Tortie(bl)(ch), 6% Blue Tortie, 6% Blue Tortie(ch)
Blue(ch)	6% Brown(bl), 12% Brown(bl)(ch), 6% Blue, 12% Blue(ch), 6% Chocolate(bl), 6% Lilac, 3% Red:Brown(bl), 6% Red:Brown(bl)(ch), 3% Cream:Blue, 6% Cream:Blue(ch), 3% Red:Chocolate(bl), 3% Cream:Lilac, 3% Brown Tortie(bl), 6% Brown Tortie(bl)(ch), 3% Blue Tortie, 6% Blue Tortie(ch), 3% Chocolate Tortie(bl), 3% Lilac Tortie
Chocolate	12% Brown(ch), 12% Brown(bl)(ch), 12% Chocolate, 12% Chocolate(bl), 6% Red:Brown(ch), 6% Red:Brown(bl)(ch), 6% Red:Chocolate, 6% Red:Chocolate(bl), 6% Brown Tortie(ch), 6% Brown Tortie(bl)(ch), 6% Chocolate Tortie, 6% Chocolate Tortie(bl)
Chocolate(bl)	6% Brown(ch), 12% Brown(bl)(ch), 6% Blue(ch), 6% Chocolate, 12% Chocolate(bl), 6% Lilac, 3% Red:Brown(ch), 6% Red:Brown(bl)(ch), 3% Cream:Blue(ch), 3% Red:Chocolate, 6% Red:Chocolate(bl), 3% Cream:Lilac, 3% Brown Tortie(ch), 6% Brown Tortie(bl)(ch), 3% Blue Tortie(ch), 3% Chocolate Tortie, 6% Chocolate Tortie(bl), 3% Lilac Tortie
Lilac	12% Brown(bl)(ch), 12% Blue(ch), 12% Chocolate(bl), 12% Lilac, 6% Red:Brown(bl)(ch), 6% Cream:Blue(ch), 6% Red:Chocolate(bl), 6% Cream:Lilac, 6% Brown Tortie(bl)(ch), 6% Blue Tortie(ch), 6% Chocolate Tortie(bl), 6% Lilac Tortie
Red:Brown	6% Brown, 6% Brown(bl), 6% Brown(ch), 6% Brown(bl)(ch), 12% Red:Brown, 12% Red:Brown(bl), 12% Red:Brown(ch), 12% Red:Brown(bl)(ch), 6% Brown Tortie, 6% Brown Tortie(bl), 6% Brown Tortie(ch), 6% Brown Tortie(bl)(ch)
Red:Brown(bl)	3% Brown, 6% Brown(bl), 3% Brown(ch), 6% Brown(bl)(ch), 3% Blue, 3% Blue(ch), 6% Red:Brown, 12% Red:Brown(bl), 6% Red:Brown(ch), 12% Red:Brown(bl)(ch), 6% Cream:Blue, 6% Cream:Blue(ch), 3% Brown Tortie, 6% Brown Tortie(bl), 3% Brown Tortie(ch), 6% Brown Tortie(bl)(ch), 3% Blue Tortie, 3% Blue Tortie(ch)

STUD	Possible colours shown as a % of the litter
Red:Brown(ch)	3% Brown, 3% Brown(bl), 6% Brown(ch), 6% Brown(bl)(ch), 3% Chocolate, 3% Chocolate(bl), 6% Red:Brown, 6% Red:Brown(bl), 12% Red:Brown(ch), 12% Red:Brown(bl)(ch), 6% Red:Chocolate, 6% Red:Chocolate(bl), 3% Brown Tortie, 3% Brown Tortie(bl), 6% Brown Tortie(ch), 6% Brown Tortie(bl)(ch), 3% Chocolate Tortie, 3% Chocolate Tortie(bl)
Red:Brown(bl)(ch)	1% Brown, 3% Brown(bl), 3% Brown(ch), 6% Brown(bl)(ch), 1% Blue,3% Blue(ch), 1% Chocolate, 3% Chocolate(bl), 1% Lilac, 2% Red:Brown, 6% Red:Brown(bl), 6% Red:Brown(ch), 12% Red:Brown(bl)(ch), 2% Cream:Blue, 6% Cream:Blue(ch), 2% Red:Chocolate, 6% Red:Chocolate(bl), 2% Cream:Lilac, 1% Brown Tortie, 3% Brown Tortie(bl), 3% Brown Tortie(ch), 6% Brown Tortie(bl)(ch), 1% Blue Tortie, 3% Blue Tortie(ch), 1% Chocolate Tortie, 3% Chocolate Tortie(bl), 1% Lilac Tortie
Cream:Blue	6% Brown(bl), 6% Brown(bl)(ch), 6% Blue, 6% Blue(ch), 12% Red:Brown(bl), 12% Red:Brown(bl)(ch), 12% Cream:Blue, 12% Cream:Blue(ch), 6% Brown Tortie(bl), 6% Brown Tortie(bl)(ch), 6% Blue Tortie, 6% Blue Tortie(ch)
Cream:Blue(ch)	3% Brown(bl), 6% Brown(bl)(ch), 3% Blue, 6% Blue(ch), 3% Chocolate(bl), 3% Lilac, 6% Red:Brown(bl), 12% Red:Brown(bl)(ch), 6% Cream:Blue, 12% Cream:Blue(ch), 6% Red:Chocolate(bl), 6% Cream:Lilac, 3% Brown Tortie(bl), 6% Brown Tortie(bl)(ch), 3% Blue Tortie, 6% Blue Tortie(ch), 3% Chocolate Tortie(bl), 3% Lilac Tortie
Red:Chocolate	6% Brown(ch), 6% Brown(bl)(ch), 6% Chocolate, 6% Chocolate(bl), 12% Red:Brown(ch), 12% Red:Brown(bl)(ch), 12% Red:Chocolate, 12% Red:Chocolate(bl), 6% Brown Tortie(ch), 6% Brown Tortie(bl)(ch), 6% Chocolate Tortie, 6% Chocolate Tortie(bl)
Red:Chocolate(bl)	3% Brown(ch), 6% Brown(bl)(ch), 3% Blue(ch), 3% Chocolate, 6% Chocolate(bl), 3% Lilac, 6% Red:Brown(ch), 12% Red:Brown(bl)(ch), 6% Cream:Blue(ch), 6% Red:Chocolate, 12% Red:Chocolate(bl), 6% Cream:Lilac, 3% Brown Tortie(ch), 6% Brown Tortie(bl)(ch), 3% Blue Tortie(ch), 3% Chocolate Tortie, 6% Chocolate Tortie(bl), 3% Lilac Tortie

Appendix B

Possible colours shown as a % of the litter
QUEEN – BROWN TORTIE (Cont'd)

Cream:Lilac

6% Brown(bl)(ch), 6% Blue(ch), 6% Chocolate(bl),
6% Lilac, 12% Red:Brown(bl)(ch), 12% Cream:Blue(ch),
12% Red:Chocolate(bl), 12% Cream:Lilac,
6% Brown Tortie(bl)(ch), 6% Blue Tortie(ch),
6% Chocolate Tortie(bl), 6% Lilac Tortie

QUEEN - BLUE TORTIE

Brown

50% Brown(bl), 25% Red:Brown(bl),
25% Brown Tortie(bl)

Brown(bl)

25% Brown(bl), 25% Blue, 12% Red:Brown(bl),
12% Cream:Blue, 12% Brown Tortie(bl), 12% Blue Tortie

Brown(ch)

25% Brown(bl), 25% Brown(bl)(ch),
12% Red:Brown(bl), 12% Red:Brown(bl)(ch),
12% Brown Tortie(bl), 12% Brown Tortie(bl)(ch)

Brown(bl)(ch)

12% Brown(bl), 12% Brown(bl)(ch), 12% Blue,
12% Blue(ch), 6% Red:Brown(bl),
6% Red:Brown(bl)(ch), 6% Cream:Blue,
6% Cream:Blue(ch), 6% Brown Tortie(bl),
6% Brown Tortie(bl)(ch), 6% Blue Tortie,
6% Blue Tortie(ch)

Blue

50% Blue, 25% Cream:Blue, 25% Blue Tortie

Blue(ch)

25% Blue, 25% Blue(ch), 12% Cream:Blue,
12% Cream:Blue(ch), 12% Blue Tortie,
12% Blue Tortie(ch)

Chocolate

50% Brown(bl)(ch), 25% Red:Brown(bl)(ch),
25% Brown Tortie(bl)(ch)

Chocolate(bl)

25% Brown(bl)(ch), 25% Blue(ch),
12% Red:Brown(bl)(ch), 12% Cream:Blue(ch),
12% Brown Tortie(bl)(ch), 12% Blue Tortie(ch)

Lilac

50% Blue(ch), 25% Cream:Blue(ch),
25% Blue Tortie(ch)

Red:Brown

25% Brown(bl), 50% Red:Brown(bl),
25% Brown Tortie(bl)

Red:Brown(bl)

12% Brown(bl), 12% Blue, 25% Red:Brown(bl),
25% Cream:Blue, 12% Brown Tortie(bl), 12% Blue Tortie

Red:Brown(ch)

12% Brown(bl), 12% Brown(bl)(ch),
25% Red:Brown(bl), 25% Red:Brown(bl)(ch),
12% Brown Tortie(bl), 12% Brown Tortie(bl)(ch)

Red:Brown(bl)(ch)

6% Brown(bl), 6% Brown(bl)(ch), 6% Blue,
6% Blue(ch), 12% Red:Brown(bl),
12% Red:Brown(bl)(ch), 12% Cream:Blue,
12% Cream:Blue(ch), 6% Brown Tortie(bl),
6% Brown Tortie(bl)(ch), 6% Blue Tortie,
6% Blue Tortie(ch)

STUD	Possible colours shown as a % of the litter
Cream:Blue	25% Blue, 50% Cream:Blue, 25% Blue Tortie
Cream:Blue(ch)	12% Blue, 12% Blue(ch), 25% Cream:Blue, 25% Cream:Blue(ch), 12% Blue Tortie, 12% Blue Tortie(ch)
Red:Chocolate	25% Brown(bl)(ch), 50% Red:Brown(bl)(ch), 25% Brown Tortie(bl)(ch)
Red:Chocolate(bl)	12% Brown(bl)(ch), 12% Blue(ch), 25% Red:Brown(bl)(ch), 25% Cream:Blue(ch), 12% Brown Tortie(bl)(ch), 12% Blue Tortie(ch)
Cream:Lilac	25% Blue(ch), 50% Cream:Blue(ch), 25% Blue Tortie(ch)

QUEEN - BLUE TORTIE(ch)

Brown	25% Brown(bl), 25% Brown(bl)(ch), 12% Red:Brown(bl), 12% Red:Brown(bl)(ch), 12% Brown Tortie(bl), 12% Brown Tortie(bl)(ch)
Brown(bl)	12% Brown(bl), 12% Brown(bl)(ch), 12% Blue, 12% Blue(ch), 6% Red:Brown(bl), 6% Red:Brown(bl)(ch), 6% Cream:Blue, 6% Cream:Blue(ch), 6% Brown Tortie(bl), 6% Brown Tortie(bl)(ch), 6% Blue Tortie, 6% Blue Tortie(ch)
Brown(ch)	12% Brown(bl), 25% Brown(bl)(ch), 12% Chocolate(bl), 6% Red:Brown(bl), 12% Red:Brown(bl)(ch), 6% Red:Chocolate(bl), 6% Brown Tortie(bl), 12% Brown Tortie(bl)(ch), 6% Chocolate Tortie(bl)
Brown(bl)(ch)	6% Brown(bl), 12% Brown(bl)(ch), 6% Blue, 12% Blue(ch), 6% Chocolate(bl), 6% Lilac, 3% Red:Brown(bl), 6% Red:Brown(bl)(ch), 3% Cream:Blue, 6% Cream:Blue(ch), 3% Red:Chocolate(bl), 3% Cream:Lilac, 3% Brown Tortie(bl), 6% Brown Tortie(bl)(ch), 3% Blue Tortie, 6% Blue Tortie(ch), 3% Chocolate Tortie(bl), 3% Lilac Tortie
Blue	25% Blue, 25% Blue(ch), 12% Cream:Blue, 12% Cream:Blue(ch), 12% Blue Tortie, 12% Blue Tortie(ch)
Blue(ch)	12% Blue, 25% Blue(ch), 12% Lilac, 6% Cream:Blue, 12% Cream:Blue(ch), 6% Cream:Lilac, 6% Blue Tortie, 12% Blue Tortie(ch), 6% Lilac Tortie

Appendix B

Chocolate	25% Brown(bl)(ch), 25% Chocolate(bl), 12% Red:Brown(bl)(ch), 12% Red:Chocolate(bl)(ch), 12% Brown Tortie(bl)(ch), 12% Chocolate Tortie(bl)(ch)
Chocolate(bl)	12% Brown(bl)(ch), 12% Blue(ch), 12% Chocolate(bl), 12% Lilac, 6% Red:Brown(bl)(ch), 6% Cream:Blue(ch), 6% Red:Chocolate(bl), 6% Cream:Lilac, 6% Brown Tortie(bl)(ch), 6% Blue Tortie(ch), 6% Chocolate Tortie(bl), 6% Lilac Tortie
Lilac	25% Blue(ch), 25% Lilac, 12% Cream:Blue(ch), 12% Cream:Lilac, 12% Blue Tortie(ch), 12% Lilac Tortie
Red:Brown	12% Brown(bl), 12% Brown(bl)(ch), 25% Red:Brown(bl), 25% Red:Brown(bl)(ch), 12% Brown Tortie(bl), 12% Brown Tortie(bl)(ch)
Red:Brown(bl)	6% Brown(bl), 6% Brown(bl)(ch), 6% Blue, 6% Blue(ch), 12% Red:Brown(bl), 12% Red:Brown(bl)(ch), 12% Cream:Blue, 12% Cream:Blue(ch), 6% Brown Tortie(bl), 6% Brown Tortie(bl)(ch), 6% Blue Tortie, 6% Blue Tortie(ch)
Red:Brown(ch)	6% Brown(bl), 12% Brown(bl)(ch), 6% Chocolate(bl), 12% Red:Brown(bl), 25% Red:Brown(bl)(ch), 12% Red:Chocolate(bl), 6% Brown Tortie(bl), 12% Brown Tortie(bl)(ch), 6% Chocolate Tortie(bl)
Red:Brown(bl)(ch)	3% Brown(bl), 6% Brown(bl)(ch), 3% Blue, 6% Blue(ch), 3% Chocolate(bl), 3% Lilac, 6% Red:Brown(bl), 12% Red:Brown(bl)(ch), 6% Cream:Blue, 12% Cream:Blue(ch), 6% Red:Chocolate(bl), 6% Cream:Lilac, 3% Brown Tortie(bl), 6% Brown Tortie(bl)(ch), 3% Blue Tortie, 6% Blue Tortie(ch), 3% Chocolate Tortie(bl), 3% Lilac Tortie
Cream:Blue	12% Blue, 12% Blue(ch), 25% Cream:Blue, 25% Cream:Blue(ch), 12% Blue Tortie, 12% Blue Tortie(ch)
Cream:Blue(ch)	6% Blue, 12% Blue(ch), 6% Lilac, 12% Cream:Blue, 25% Cream:Blue(ch), 12% Cream:Lilac, 6% Blue Tortie, 12% Blue Tortie(ch), 6% Lilac Tortie
Red:Chocolate	12% Brown(bl)(ch), 12% Chocolate(bl), 25% Red:Brown(bl)(ch), 25% Red:Chocolate(bl), 12% Brown Tortie(bl)(ch), 12% Chocolate Tortie(bl)
Red:Chocolate(bl)	6% Brown(bl)(ch), 6% Blue(ch), 6% Chocolate(bl), 6% Lilac, 12% Red:Brown(bl)(ch), 12% Cream:Blue(ch), 12% Red:Chocolate(bl), 12% Cream:Lilac, 6% Brown Tortie(bl)(ch), 6% Blue Tortie(ch), 6% Chocolate Tortie(bl), 6% Lilac Tortie
Cream:Lilac	12% Blue(ch), 12% Lilac, 25% Cream:Blue(ch), 25% Cream:Lilac, 12% Blue Tortie(ch), 12% Lilac Tortie

STUD	Possible colours shown as a % of the litter
	QUEEN - CHOCOLATE TORTIE
Brown	50% Brown(ch), 25% Red:Brown(ch), 25% Brown Tortie(ch)
Brown(bl)	25% Brown(ch), 25% Brown(bl)(ch), 12% Red:Brown(ch), 12% Red:Brown(bl)(ch), 12% Brown Tortie(ch), 12% Brown Tortie(bl)(ch)
Brown(ch)	25% Brown(ch), 25% Chocolate, 12% Red:Brown(ch), 12% Red:Chocolate, 12% Brown Tortie(ch), 12% Chocolate Tortie
Brown(bl)(ch)	12% Brown(ch), 12% Brown(bl)(ch), 12% Chocolate, 12% Chocolate(bl), 6% Red:Brown(ch), 6% Red:Brown(bl)(ch), 6% Red:Chocolate, 6% Red:Chocolate(bl), 6% Brown Tortie(ch), 6% Brown Tortie(bl)(ch), 6% Chocolate Tortie, 6% Chocolate Tortie(bl)
Blue	50% Brown(bl)(ch), 25% Red:Brown(bl)(ch), 25% Brown Tortie(bl)(ch)
Blue(ch)	25% Brown(bl)(ch), 25% Chocolate(bl), 12% Red:Brown(bl)(ch), 12% Red:Chocolate(bl),12% Brown Tortie(bl)(ch), 12% Chocolate Tortie(bl)
Chocolate	50% Chocolate, 25% Red:Chocolate, 25% Chocolate Tortie
Chocolate(bl)	25% Chocolate, 25% Chocolate(bl), 12% Red:Chocolate, 12% Red:Chocolate(bl), 12% Chocolate Tortie, 12% Chocolate Tortie(bl)
Lilac	50% Chocolate(bl), 25% Red:Chocolate(bl), 25% Chocolate Tortie(bl)
Red:Brown	25% Brown(ch), 50% Red:Brown(ch), 25% Brown Tortie(ch)
Red:Brown(bl)	12% Brown(ch), 12% Brown(bl)(ch), 25% Red:Brown(ch), 25% Red:Brown(bl)(ch), 12% Brown Tortie(ch), 12% Brown Tortie(bl)(ch)
Red:Brown(ch)	12% Brown(ch), 12% Chocolate, 25% Red:Brown(ch), 25% Red:Chocolate, 12% Brown Tortie(ch), 12% Chocolate Tortie
Red:Brown(bl)(ch)	6% Brown(ch), 6% Brown(bl)(ch), 6% Chocolate, 6% Chocolate(bl), 12% Red:Brown(ch), 12% Red:Brown(bl)(ch), 12% Red:Chocolate, 12% Red:Chocolate(bl), 6% Brown Tortie(ch), 6% Brown Tortie(bl)(ch), 6% Chocolate Tortie, 6% Chocolate Tortie(bl)
Cream:Blue	25% Brown(bl)(ch), 50% Red:Brown(bl)(ch), 25% Brown Tortie(bl)(ch)
Cream:Blue(ch)	12% Brown(bl)(ch), 12% Chocolate(bl), 25% Red:Brown(bl)(ch), 25% Red:Chocolate(bl), 12% Brown Tortie(bl)(ch), 12% Chocolate Tortie(bl)

Appendix B

QUEEN – CHOCOLATE TORTIE (Cont'd)

Red:Chocolate	25% Chocolate, 50% Red:Chocolate, 25% Chocolate Tortie
Red:Chocolate(bl)	12% Chocolate, 12% Chocolate(bl), 25% Red:Chocolate, 25% Red:Chocolate(bl), 12% Chocolate Tortie, 12% Chocolate Tortie(bl)
Cream:Lilac	25% Chocolate(bl), 50% Red:Chocolate(bl), 25% Chocolate Tortie(bl)

QUEEN - CHOCOLATE TORTIE(bl)

Brown	25% Brown(ch), 25% Brown(bl)(ch), 12% Red:Brown(ch), 12% Red:Brown(bl)(ch), 12% Brown Tortie(ch), 12% Brown Tortie(bl)(ch)
Brown(bl)	12% Brown(ch), 25% Brown(bl)(ch), 12% Blue(ch), 6% Red:Brown(ch), 12% Red:Brown(bl)(ch), 6% Cream:Blue(ch), 6% Brown Tortie(ch), 12% Brown Tortie(bl)(ch), 6% Blue Tortie(ch)
Brown(ch)	12% Brown(ch), 12% Brown(bl)(ch), 12% Chocolate, 12% Chocolate(bl), 6% Red:Brown(ch), 6% Red:Brown(bl)(ch), 6% Red:Chocolate, 6% Red:Chocolate(bl), 6% Brown Tortie(ch), 6% Brown Tortie(bl)(ch), 6% Chocolate Tortie, 6% Chocolate Tortie(bl)
Brown(bl)(ch)	6% Brown(ch), 12% Brown(bl)(ch), 6% Blue(ch), 6% Chocolate, 12% Chocolate(bl), 6% Lilac, 3% Red:Brown(ch), 6% Red:Brown(bl)(ch), 3% Cream:Blue(ch), 3% Red:Chocolate, 6% Red:Chocolate(bl), 3% Cream:Lilac, 3% Brown Tortie(ch), 6% Brown Tortie(bl)(ch), 3% Blue Tortie(ch), 3% Chocolate Tortie, 6% Chocolate Tortie(bl), 3% Lilac Tortie
Blue	25% Brown(bl)(ch), 25% Blue(ch), 12% Red:Brown(bl)(ch), 12% Cream:Blue(ch), 12% Brown Tortie(bl)(ch), 12% Blue Tortie(ch)
Blue(ch)	12% Brown(bl)(ch), 12% Blue(ch), 12% Chocolate(bl), 12% Lilac, 6% Red:Brown(bl)(ch), 6% Cream:Blue(ch), 6% Red:Chocolate(bl), 6% Cream:Lilac, 6% Brown Tortie(bl)(ch), 6% Blue Tortie(ch), 6% Chocolate Tortie(bl), 6% Lilac Tortie
Chocolate	25% Chocolate, 25% Chocolate(bl), 12% Red:Chocolate, 12% Red:Chocolate(bl), 12% Chocolate Tortie, 12% Chocolate Tortie(bl)
Chocolate(bl)	12% Chocolate, 25% Chocolate(bl), 12% Lilac, 6% Red:Chocolate, 12% Red:Chocolate(bl), 6% Cream:Lilac, 6% Chocolate Tortie, 12% Chocolate Tortie(bl), 6% Lilac Tortie

STUD	Possible colours shown as a % of the litter
Lilac	25% Chocolate(bl), 25% Lilac, 12% Red:Chocolate(bl), 12% Cream:Lilac, 12% Chocolate Tortie(bl), 12% Lilac Tortie
Red:Brown	12% Brown(ch), 12% Brown(bl)(ch), 25% Red:Brown(ch), 25% Red:Brown(bl)(ch), 12% Brown Tortie(ch), 12% Brown Tortie(bl)(ch)
Red:Brown(bl)	6% Brown(ch), 12% Brown(bl)(ch), 6% Blue(ch), 12% Red:Brown(ch), 25% Red:Brown(bl)(ch), 12% Cream:Blue(ch), 6% Brown Tortie(ch), 12% Brown Tortie(bl)(ch), 6% Blue Tortie(ch)
Red:Brown(ch)	6% Brown(ch), 6% Brown(bl)(ch), 6% Chocolate, 6% Chocolate(bl), 12% Red:Brown(ch), 12% Red:Brown(bl)(ch), 12% Red:Chocolate, 12% Red:Chocolate(bl), 6% Brown Tortie(ch), 6% Brown Tortie(bl)(ch), 6% Chocolate Tortie, 6% Chocolate Tortie(bl)
Red:Brown(bl)(ch)	3% Brown(ch), 6% Brown(bl)(ch), 3% Blue(ch), 3% Chocolate, 6% Chocolate(bl), 3% Lilac, 6% Red:Brown(ch), 12% Red:Brown(bl)(ch), 6% Cream:Blue(ch), 6% Red:Chocolate, 12% Red:Chocolate(bl), 6% Cream:Lilac, 3% Brown Tortie(ch), 6% Brown Tortie(bl)(ch), 3% Blue Tortie(ch), 3% Chocolate Tortie, 6% Chocolate Tortie(bl), 3% Lilac Tortie
Cream:Blue	12% Brown(bl)(ch), 12% Blue(ch), 25% Red:Brown(bl)(ch), 25% Cream:Blue(ch), 12% Brown Tortie(bl)(ch), 12% Blue Tortie(ch)
Cream:Blue(ch)	6% Brown(bl)(ch), 6% Blue(ch), 6% Chocolate(bl), 6% Lilac, 12% Red:Brown(bl)(ch), 12% Cream:Blue(ch), 12% Red:Chocolate(bl), 12% Cream:Lilac, 6% Brown Tortie(bl)(ch), 6% Blue Tortie(ch), 6% Chocolate Tortie(bl), 6% Lilac Tortie
Red:Chocolate	12% Chocolate, 12% Chocolate(bl), 25% Red:Chocolate, 25% Red:Chocolate(bl), 12% Chocolate Tortie, 12% Chocolate Tortie(bl)
Red:Chocolate(bl)	6% Chocolate, 12% Chocolate(bl), 6% Lilac, 12% Red:Chocolate, 25% Red:Chocolate(bl), 12% Cream:Lilac, 6% Chocolate Tortie, 12% Chocolate Tortie(bl), 6% Lilac Tortie
Cream:Lilac	12% Chocolate(bl), 12% Lilac, 25% Red:Chocolate(bl), 25% Cream:Lilac, 12% Chocolate Tortie(bl), 12% Lilac Tortie

Appendix B

STUD	Possible colours shown as a % of the litter QUEEN - LILAC TORTIE
Brown	50% Brown(bl)(ch), 25% Red:Brown(bl)(ch), 25% Brown Tortie(bl)(ch)
Brown(bl)	25% Brown(bl)(ch), 25% Blue(ch), 12% Red:Brown(bl)(ch), 12% Cream:Blue(ch), 12% Brown Tortie(bl)(ch), 12% Blue Tortie(ch)
Brown(ch)	25% Brown(bl)(ch), 25% Chocolate(bl), 12% Red:Brown(bl)(ch), 12% Red:Chocolate(bl), 12% Brown Tortie(bl)(ch), 12% Chocolate Tortie(bl)
Brown(bl)(ch)	12% Brown(bl)(ch), 12% Blue(ch), 12% Chocolate(bl), 12% Lilac, 6% Red:Brown(bl)(ch), 6% Cream:Blue(ch), 6% Red:Chocolate(bl), 6% Cream:Lilac, 6% Brown Tortie(bl)(ch), 6% Blue Tortie(ch), 6% Chocolate Tortie(bl), 6% Lilac Tortie
Blue	50% Blue(ch), 25% Cream:Blue(ch), 25% Blue Tortie(ch)
Blue(ch)	25% Blue(ch), 25% Lilac, 12% Cream:Blue(ch), 12% Cream:Lilac, 12% Blue Tortie(ch), 12% Lilac Tortie
Chocolate	50% Chocolate(bl), 25% Red:Chocolate(bl), 25% Chocolate Tortie(bl)
Chocolate(bl)	25% Chocolate(bl), 25% Lilac, 12% Red:Chocolate(bl), 12% Cream:Lilac, 12% Chocolate Tortie(bl), 12% Lilac Tortie
Lilac	50% Lilac, 25% Cream:Lilac, 25% Lilac Tortie
Red:Brown	25% Brown(bl)(ch), 50% Red:Brown(bl)(ch), 25% Brown Tortie(bl)(ch)
Red:Brown(bl)	12% Brown(bl)(ch), 12% Blue(ch), 25% Red:Brown(bl)(ch), 25% Cream:Blue(ch), 12% Brown Tortie(bl)(ch), 12% Blue Tortie(ch)
Red:Brown(ch)	12% Brown(bl)(ch), 12% Chocolate(bl), 25% Red:Brown(bl)(ch), 25% Red:Chocolate(bl), 12% Brown Tortie(bl)(ch), 12% Chocolate Tortie(bl)
Red:Brown(bl)(ch)	6% Brown(bl)(ch), 6% Blue(ch), 6% Chocolate(bl), 6% Lilac, 12% Red:Brown(bl)(ch), 12% Cream:Blue(ch), 12% Red:Chocolate(bl), 12% Cream:Lilac, 6% Brown Tortie(bl)(ch), 6% Blue Tortie(ch), 6% Chocolate Tortie(bl), 6% Lilac Tortie
Cream:Blue	25% Blue(ch), 50% Cream:Blue(ch), 25% Blue Tortie(ch)
Cream:Blue(ch)	12% Blue(ch), 12% Lilac, 25% Cream:Blue(ch), 25% Cream:Lilac, 12% Blue Tortie(ch), 12% Lilac Tortie
Red:Chocolate	25% Chocolate(bl), 50% Red:Chocolate(bl), 25% Chocolate Tortie(bl)
Red:Chocolate(bl)	12% Chocolate(bl), 12% Lilac, 25% Red:Chocolate(bl), 25% Cream:Lilac, 12% Chocolate Tortie(bl), 12% Lilac Tortie
Cream:Lilac	25% Lilac, 50% Cream:Lilac, 25% Lilac Tortie

STUD	Possible colours shown as a % of the litter
	QUEEN - RED:Brown
Brown	50% Red:Brown, 50% Brown Tortie
Brown(bl)	25% Red:Brown, 25% Red:Brown(bl),
	25% Brown Tortie, 25% Brown Tortie(bl)
Brown(ch)	25% Red:Brown, 25% Red:Brown(ch),
	25% Brown Tortie, 25% Brown Tortie(ch)
Brown(bl)(ch)	12% Red:Brown, 12% Red:Brown(bl),
	12% Red:Brown(ch), 12% Red:Brown(bl)(ch),
	12% Brown Tortie, 12% Brown Tortie(bl),
	12% Brown Tortie(ch), 12% Brown Tortie(bl)(ch)
Blue	50% Red:Brown(bl), 50% Brown Tortie(bl)
Blue(ch)	25% Red:Brown(bl), 25% Red:Brown(bl)(ch),
	25% Brown Tortie(bl), 25% Brown Tortie(bl)(ch)
Chocolate	50% Red:Brown(ch), 50% Brown Tortie(ch)
Chocolate(bl)	25% Red:Brown(ch), 25% Red:Brown(bl)(ch),
	25% Brown Tortie(ch), 25% Brown Tortie(bl)(ch)
Lilac	50% Red:Brown(bl)(ch), 50% Brown Tortie(bl)(ch)
Red:Brown	100% Red:Brown
Red:Brown(bl)	50% Red:Brown, 50% Red:Brown(bl)
Red:Brown(ch)	50% Red:Brown, 50% Red:Brown(ch)
Red:Brown(bl)(ch)	25% Red:Brown, 25% Red:Brown(bl),
	25% Red:Brown(ch), 25% Red:Brown(bl)(ch)
Cream:Blue	100% Red:Brown(bl)
Cream:Blue(ch)	50% Red:Brown(bl), 50% Red:Brown(bl)(ch)
Red:Chocolate	100% Red:Brown(ch)
Red:Chocolate(bl)	50% Red:Brown(ch), 50% Red:Brown(bl)(ch)
Cream:Lilac	100% Red:Brown(bl)(ch)
	QUEEN - RED:Brown(bl)
Brown	25% Red:Brown, 25% Red:Brown(bl),
	25% Brown Tortie, 25% Brown Tortie(bl)
Brown(bl)	12% Red:Brown, 25% Red:Brown(bl), 12% Cream:Blue,
	12% Brown Tortie, 25% Brown Tortie(bl),
	12% Blue Tortie
Brown(ch)	12% Red:Brown, 12% Red:Brown(bl),
	12% Red:Brown(ch), 12% Red:Brown(bl)(ch),
	12% Brown Tortie, 12% Brown Tortie(bl),
	12% Brown Tortie(ch), 12% Brown Tortie(bl)(ch)
Brown(bl)(ch)	6% Red:Brown, 12% Red:Brown(bl),
	6% Red:Brown(ch), 12% Red:Brown(bl)(ch),
	6% Cream:Blue, 6% Cream:Blue(ch), 6% Brown Tortie,
	12% Brown Tortie(bl), 6% Brown Tortie(ch),
	12% Brown Tortie(bl)(ch), 6% Blue Tortie,
	6% Blue Tortie(ch)
Blue	25% Red:Brown(bl), 25% Cream:Blue,
	25% Brown Tortie(bl), 25% Blue Tortie

Appendix B

STUD	Possible colours shown as a % of the litter
Blue(ch)	12% Red:Brown(bl), 12% Red:Brown(bl)(ch), 12% Cream:Blue, 12% Cream:Blue(ch), 12% Brown Tortie(bl), 12% Brown Tortie(bl)(ch), 12% Blue Tortie, 12% Blue Tortie(ch)
Chocolate	25% Red:Brown(ch), 25% Red:Brown(bl)(ch), 25% Brown Tortie(ch), 25% Brown Tortie(bl)(ch)
Chocolate(bl)	12% Red:Brown(ch), 25% Red:Brown(bl)(ch), 12% Cream:Blue(ch), 12% Brown Tortie(ch), 25% Brown Tortie(bl)(ch), 12% Blue Tortie(ch)
Lilac	25%Red:Brown(bl)(ch), 25% Cream:Blue(ch), 25% Brown Tortie(bl)(ch), 25% Blue Tortie(ch)
Red:Brown	50% Red:Brown, 50% Red:Brown(bl)
Red:Brown(bl)	25% Red:Brown, 50% Red:Brown(bl), 25% Cream:Blue
Red:Brown(ch)	25% Red:Brown, 25% Red:Brown(bl), 25% Red:Brown(ch), 25% Red:Brown(bl)(ch)
Red:Brown(bl)(ch)	12% Red:Brown, 25% Red:Brown(bl), 12% Red:Brown(ch), 25% Red:Brown(bl)(ch), 12% Cream:Blue, 12% Cream:Blue(ch)
Cream:Blue	50% Red:Brown(bl), 50% Cream:Blue
Cream:Blue(ch)	25% Red:Brown(bl), 25% Red:Brown(bl)(ch), 25% Cream:Blue, 25% Cream:Blue(ch)
Red:Chocolate	50% Red:Brown(ch), 50% Red:Brown(bl)(ch)
Red:Chocolate(bl)	25% Red:Brown(ch), 50% Red:Brown(bl)(ch), 25% Cream:Blue(ch)
Cream:Lilac	50% Red:Brown(bl)(ch), 50% Cream:Blue(ch)

QUEEN - RED:Brown(ch)

STUD	Possible colours shown as a % of the litter
Brown	25% Red:Brown, 25% Red:Brown(ch), 25% Brown Tortie, 25% Brown Tortie(ch)
Brown(bl)	12% Red:Brown, 12% Red:Brown(bl), 12% Red:Brown(ch), 12% Red:Brown(bl)(ch), 12% Brown Tortie, 12% Brown Tortie(bl), 12% Brown Tortie(ch), 12% Brown Tortie(bl)(ch)
Brown(ch)	12% Red:Brown, 25% Red:Brown(ch), 12% Red:Chocolate, 12% Brown Tortie, 25% Brown Tortie(ch), 12% Chocolate Tortie
Brown(bl)(ch)	6% Red:Brown, 6% Red:Brown(bl), 12% Red:Brown(ch), 12% Red:Brown(bl)(ch), 6% Red:Chocolate, 6% Red:Chocolate(bl), 6% Brown Tortie, 6% Brown Tortie(bl), 12% Brown Tortie(ch), 12% Brown Tortie(bl)(ch), 6% Chocolate Tortie, 6% Chocolate Tortie(bl)
Blue	25% Red:Brown(bl), 25% Red:Brown(bl)(ch), 25% Brown Tortie(bl), 25% Brown Tortie(bl)(ch)

STUD	Possible colours shown as a % of the litter
Blue(ch)	12% Red:Brown(bl), 25% Red:Brown(bl)(ch), 12% Red:Chocolate(bl), 12% Brown Tortie(bl), 25% Brown Tortie(bl)(ch), 25% Chocolate Tortie(bl)
Chocolate	25% Red:Brown(ch), 25% Red:Chocolate, 25% Brown Tortie(ch), 25% Chocolate Tortie
Chocolate(bl)	12% Red:Brown(ch), 12% Red:Brown(bl)(ch), 12% Red:Chocolate, 12% Red:Chocolate(bl), 12% Brown Tortie(ch), 12% Brown Tortie(bl)(ch), 12% Chocolate Tortie, 12% Chocolate Tortie(bl)
Lilac	25% Red:Brown(bl)(ch), 25% Red:Chocolate(bl), 25% Brown Tortie(bl)(ch), 25% Chocolate Tortie(bl)
Red:Brown	50% Red:Brown, 50% Red:Brown(ch)
Red:Brown(bl)	25% Red:Brown, 25% Red:Brown(bl), 25% Red:Brown(ch), 25% Red:Brown(bl)(ch)
Red:Brown(ch)	25% Red:Brown, 50% Red:Brown(ch), 25% Red:Chocolate
Red:Brown(bl)(ch)	12% Red:Brown, 12% Red:Brown(bl), 25% Red:Brown(ch), 25% Red:Brown(bl)(ch), 12% Red:Chocolate, 12% Red:Chocolate(bl)
Cream:Blue	50% Red:Brown(bl), 50% Red:Brown(bl)(ch)
Cream:Blue(ch)	25% Red:Brown(bl), 50% Red:Brown(bl)(ch), 25% Red:Chocolate(bl)
Red:Chocolate	50% Red:Brown(ch), 50% Red:Chocolate
Red:Chocolate(bl)	25% Red:Brown(ch), 25% Red:Brown(bl)(ch), 25% Red:Chocolate, 25% Red:Chocolate(bl)
Cream:Lilac	50% Red:Brown(bl)(ch), 50% Red:Chocolate(bl)

QUEEN - RED:Brown(bl)(ch)	
Brown	12% Red:Brown, 12% Red:Brown(bl), 12% Red:Brown(ch), 12% Red:Brown(bl)(ch), 12% Brown Tortie, 12% Brown Tortie(bl), 12% Brown Tortie(ch), 12% Brown Tortie(bl)(ch)
Brown(bl)	6% Red:Brown, 12% Red:Brown(bl), 6% Red:Brown(ch), 12% Red:Brown(bl)(ch), 6% Cream:Blue, 6% Cream:Blue(ch), 6% Brown Tortie, 12% Brown Tortie(bl), 6% Brown Tortie(ch), 12% Brown Tortie(bl)(ch), 6% Blue Tortie, 6% Blue Tortie(ch)
Brown(ch)	6% Red:Brown, 6% Red:Brown(bl), 12% Red:Brown(ch), 12% Red:Brown(bl)(ch), 6% Red:Chocolate, 6% Red:Chocolate(bl), 6% Brown Tortie, 6% Brown Tortie(bl), 12% Brown Tortie(ch), 12% Brown Tortie(bl)(ch), 6% Chocolate Tortie, 6% Chocolate Tortie(bl)

Appendix B

Brown(bl)(ch)	3% Red:Brown, 6% Red:Brown(bl), 6% Red:Brown(ch), 12% Red:Brown(bl)(ch), 3% Cream:Blue, 6% Cream:Blue(ch), 3% Red:Chocolate, 6% Red:Chocolate(bl), 3% Cream:Lilac, 3% Brown Tortie, 6% Brown Tortie(bl), 6% Brown Tortie(ch), 12% Brown Tortie(bl)(ch), 3% Blue Tortie, 6% Blue Tortie(ch), 3% Chocolate Tortie, 6% Chocolate Tortie(bl), 3% Lilac Tortie
Blue	12% Red:Brown(bl), 12% Red:Brown(bl)(ch), 12% Cream:Blue, 12% Cream:Blue(ch), 12% Brown Tortie(bl), 12% Brown Tortie(bl)(ch), 12% Blue Tortie, 12% Blue Tortie(ch)
Blue(ch)	6% Red:Brown(bl), 12% Red:Brown(bl)(ch), 6% Cream:Blue, 12% Cream:Blue(ch), 6% Red:Chocolate(bl), 6% Cream:Lilac, 6% Brown Tortie(bl), 12% Brown Tortie(bl)(ch), 6% Blue Tortie, 12% Blue Tortie(ch), 6% Chocolate Tortie(bl), 6% Lilac Tortie
Chocolate	12% Red:Brown(ch), 12% Red:Brown(bl)(ch), 12% Red:Chocolate, 12% Red:Chocolate(bl), 12% Brown Tortie(ch), 12% Brown Tortie(bl)(ch), 12% Chocolate Tortie, 12% Chocolate Tortie(bl)
Chocolate(bl)	6% Red:Brown(ch), 12% Red:Brown(bl)(ch), 6% Cream:Blue(ch), 6% Red:Chocolate, 12% Red:Chocolate(bl), 6% Cream:Lilac, 6% Brown Tortie(ch), 12% Brown Tortie(bl)(ch), 6% Blue Tortie(ch), 6% Chocolate Tortie, 12% Chocolate Tortie(bl), 6% Lilac Tortie
Lilac	12% Red:Brown(bl)(ch), 12% Cream:Blue(ch), 12% Red:Chocolate(bl), 12% Cream:Lilac, 12% Brown Tortie(bl)(ch), 12% Blue Tortie(ch), 12% Chocolate Tortie(bl), 12% Lilac Tortie
Red:Brown	25% Red:Brown, 25% Red:Brown(bl), 25% Red:Brown(ch), 25% Red:Brown(bl)(ch)
Red:Brown(bl)	12% Red:Brown, 25% Red:Brown(bl), 12% Red:Brown(ch), 25% Red:Brown(bl)(ch), 12% Cream:Blue, 12% Cream:Blue(ch)
Red:Brown(ch)	12% Red:Brown, 12% Red:Brown(bl), 25% Red:Brown(ch), 25% Red:Brown(bl)(ch), 12% Red:Chocolate, 12% Red:Chocolate(bl)
Red:Brown(bl)(ch)	6% Red:Brown, 12% Red:Brown(bl), 12% Red:Brown(ch), 25% Red:Brown(bl)(ch), 6% Cream:Blue, 12% Cream:Blue(ch), 6% Red:Chocolate, 12% Red:Chocolate(bl), 6% Cream:Lilac
Cream:Blue	25% Red:Brown(bl), 25% Red:Brown(bl)(ch), 25% Cream:Blue, 25% Cream:Blue(ch)

STUD	Possible colours shown as a % of the litter
Cream:Blue(ch)	12% Red:Brown(bl), 25% Red:Brown(bl)(ch), 12% Cream:Blue, 25% Cream:Blue(ch), 12% Red:Chocolate(bl), 12% Cream:Lilac
Red:Chocolate	25% Red:Brown(ch), 25% Red:Brown(bl)(ch), 25% Red:Chocolate, 25% Red:Chocolate(bl)
Red:Chocolate(bl)	12% Red:Brown(ch), 25% Red:Brown(bl)(ch), 12% Cream:Blue(ch), 12% Red:Chocolate, 25% Red:Chocolate(bl), 12% Cream:Lilac
Cream:Lilac	25% Red:Brown(bl)(ch), 25% Cream:Blue(ch), 25% Red:Chocolate(bl), 25% Cream:Lilac

QUEEN - CREAM:Blue

Brown	50% Red:Brown(bl), 50% Brown Tortie(bl)
Brown(bl)	25% Red:Brown(bl), 25% Cream:Blue, 25% Brown Tortie(bl), 25% Blue Tortie
Brown(ch)	25% Red:Brown(bl), 25% Red:Brown(bl)(ch), 25% Brown Tortie(bl), 25% Brown Tortie(bl)(ch)
Brown(bl)(ch)	12% Red:Brown(bl), 12% Red:Brown(bl)(ch), 12% Cream:Blue, 12% Cream:Blue(ch), 12% Brown Tortie(bl), 12% Brown Tortie(bl)(ch), 12% Blue Tortie, 12% Blue Tortie(ch)
Blue	50% Cream:Blue, 50% Blue Tortie
Blue(ch)	25% Cream:Blue, 25% Cream:Blue(ch), 25% Blue Tortie, 25% Blue Tortie(ch)
Chocolate	50% Red:Brown(bl)(ch), 50% Brown Tortie(bl)(ch)
Chocolate(bl)	25% Red:Brown(bl)(ch), 25% Cream:Blue(ch), 25% Brown Tortie(bl)(ch), 25% Blue Tortie(ch)
Lilac	50% Cream:Blue(ch), 50% Blue Tortie(ch)
Red:Brown	100% Red:Brown(bl)
Red:Brown(bl)	50% Red:Brown(bl), 50% Cream:Blue
Red:Brown(ch)	50% Red:Brown(bl), 50% Red:Brown(bl)(ch)
Red:Brown(bl)(ch)	25% Red:Brown(bl), 25% Red:Brown(bl)(ch), 25% Cream:Blue, 25% Cream:Blue(ch)
Cream:Blue	100% Cream:Blue
Cream:Blue(ch)	50% Cream:Blue, 50% Cream:Blue(ch)
Red:Chocolate	100% Red:Brown(bl)(ch)
Red:Chocolate(bl)	50% Red:Brown(bl)(ch), 50% Cream:Blue(ch)
Cream:Lilac	100% Cream:Blue(ch)

QUEEN - CREAM:Blue(ch)

Brown	25% Red:Brown(bl), 25% Red:Brown(bl)(ch), 25% Brown Tortie(bl), 25% Brown Tortie(bl)(ch)
Brown(bl)	12% Red:Brown(bl), 12% Red:Brown(bl)(ch), 12% Cream:Blue, 12% Cream:Blue(ch), 12% Brown Tortie(bl), 12% Brown Tortie(bl)(ch), 12% Blue Tortie, 12% Blue Tortie(ch)

Appendix B

STUD	Possible colours shown as a % of the litter
QUEEN:Blue(ch) (Cont'd)	
Brown(ch)	12% Red:Brown(bl), 25% Red:Brown(bl)(ch), 12% Red:Chocolate(bl), 12% Brown Tortie(bl), 25% Brown Tortie(bl)(ch), 12% Chocolate Tortie(bl)
Brown(bl)(ch)	6% Red:Brown(bl), 12% Red:Brown(bl)(ch), 6% Cream:Blue, 12% Cream:Blue(ch), 6% Red:Chocolate(bl), 6% Cream:Lilac, 6% Brown Tortie(bl), 12% Brown Tortie(bl)(ch), 6% Blue Tortie, 12% Blue Tortie(ch), 6% Chocolate Tortie(bl), 6% Lilac Tortie
Blue	25% Cream:Blue, 25% Cream:Blue(ch), 25% Blue Tortie, 25% Blue Tortie(ch)
Blue(ch)	12% Cream:Blue, 25% Cream:Blue(ch), 12% Cream:Lilac, 12% Blue Tortie, 25% Blue Tortie(ch), 12% Lilac Tortie
Chocolate	25% Red:Brown(bl)(ch), 25% Red:Chocolate(bl), 25% Brown Tortie(bl)(ch), 25% Chocolate Tortie(bl)
Chocolate(bl)	12% Red:Brown(bl)(ch), 12% Cream:Blue(ch), 12% Red:Chocolate(bl), 12% Cream:Lilac, 12% Brown Tortie(bl)(ch), 12% Blue Tortie(ch), 12% Chocolate Tortie(bl), 12% Lilac Tortie
Lilac	25% Cream:Blue(ch), 25% Cream:Lilac, 25% Blue Tortie(ch), 25% Lilac Tortie
Red:Brown	50% Red:Brown(bl), 50% Red:Brown(bl)(ch)
Red:Brown(bl)	25% Red:Brown(bl), 25% Red:Brown(bl)(ch), 25% Cream:Blue, 25% Cream:Blue(ch)
Red:Brown(ch)	25% Red:Brown(bl), 50% Red:Brown(bl)(ch), 25% Red:Chocolate(bl)
Red:Brown(bl)(ch)	12% Red:Brown(bl), 25% Red:Brown(bl)(ch), 12% Cream:Blue, 25% Cream:Blue(ch), 12% Red:Chocolate(bl), 12% Cream:Lilac
Cream:Blue	50% Cream:Blue, 50% Cream:Blue(ch)
Cream:Blue(ch)	25% Cream:Blue, 50% Cream:Blue(ch), 25% Cream:Lilac
Red:Chocolate	50% Red:Brown(bl)(ch), 50% Red:Chocolate(bl)
Red:Chocolate(bl)	25% Red:Brown(bl)(ch), 25% Cream:Blue(ch), 25% Red:Chocolate(bl), 25% Cream:Lilac
Cream:Lilac	50% Cream:Blue(ch), 50% Cream:Lilac
QUEEN – RED:Chocolate	
Brown	50% Red:Brown(ch), 50% Brown Tortie(ch)
Brown(bl)	25% Red:Brown(ch), 25% Cream:Blue(bl)(ch), 25% Brown Tortie(ch), 25% Brown Tortie(bl)(ch)
Brown(ch)	25% Red:Brown(ch), 25% Red:Chocolate, 25% Brown Tortie(ch), 25% Chocolate Tortie

STUD	Possible colours shown as a % of the litter
Brown(bl)(ch)	12% Red:Brown(ch), 12% Red:Brown(bl)(ch), 12% Red:Chocolate, 12% Red:Chocolate(bl), 12% Brown Tortie(ch), 12% Brown Tortie(bl)(ch), 12% Chocolate Tortie, 12% Chocolate Tortie(bl)
Blue	50% Red:Brown(bl)(ch), 50% Brown Tortie(bl)(ch)
Blue(ch)	25% Red:Brown(bl)(ch), 25% Red:Chocolate(bl), 25% Brown Tortie(bl)(ch), 25% Chocolate Tortie(bl)
Chocolate	50% Red:Chocolate, 50% Chocolate Tortie
Chocolate(bl)	25% Red:Chocolate, 25% Red:Chocolate(bl), 25% Chocolate Tortie, 25% Chocolate Tortie(bl)
Lilac	50% Red:Chocolate(bl), 50% Chocolate Tortie(bl)
Red:Brown	100% Red:Brown(ch)
Red:Brown(bl)	50% Red:Brown(ch), 50% Red:Brown(bl)(ch)
Red:Brown(ch)	50% Red:Brown(ch), 50% Red:Chocolate
Red:Brown(bl)(ch)	25% Red:Brown(ch), 25% Red:Brown(bl)(ch), 25% Red:Chocolate, 25% Red:Chocolate(bl)
Cream:Blue	100% Red:Brown(bl)(ch)
Cream:Blue(ch)	50% Red:Brown(bl)(ch), 50% Red:Chocolate(bl)
Red:Chocolate	100% Red:Chocolate
Red:Chocolate(bl)	50% Red:Chocolate, 50% Red:Chocolate(bl)
Cream:Lilac	100% Red:Chocolate(bl)

QUEEN - RED:Chocolate(bl)

Brown	25% Red:Brown(ch), 25% Red:Brown(bl)(ch), 25% Brown Tortie(ch), 25% Brown Tortie(bl)(ch)
Brown(bl)	12% Red:Brown(ch), 25% Red:Brown(bl)(ch), 12% Cream:Blue(ch), 12% Brown Tortie(ch), 25% Brown Tortie(bl)(ch), 12% Blue Tortie(ch)
Brown(ch)	12% Red:Brown(ch), 12% Red:Brown(bl)(ch), 12% Red:Chocolate, 12% Red:Chocolate(bl), 12% Brown Tortie(ch), 12% Brown Tortie(bl)(ch), 12% Chocolate Tortie, 12% Chocolate Tortie(bl)
Brown(bl)(ch)	6% Red:Brown(ch), 12% Red:Brown(bl)(ch), 6% Cream:Blue(ch), 6% Red:Chocolate, 12% Red:Chocolate(bl), 6% Cream:Lilac, 6% Brown Tortie(ch), 12% Brown Tortie(bl)(ch), 6% Blue Tortie(ch), 6% Chocolate Tortie, 12% Chocolate Tortie(bl), 6% Lilac Tortie
Blue	25% Red:Brown(bl)(ch), 25% Cream:Blue(ch), 25% Brown Tortie(bl)(ch), 25% Blue Tortie(ch)
Blue(ch)	12% Red:Brown(bl)(ch), 12% Cream:Blue(ch), 12% Red:Chocolate(bl), 12% Cream:Lilac, 12% Brown Tortie(bl)(ch), 12% Blue Tortie(ch), 12% Chocolate Tortie(bl), 12% Lilac Tortie
Chocolate	25% Red:Chocolate, 25% Red:Chocolate(bl), 25% Chocolate Tortie, 25% Chocolate Tortie(bl)

Appendix B

STUD   **Possible colours shown as a % of the litter**
QUEEN – RED:Chocolate(bl) (Cont'd)

Chocolate(bl)	12% Red:Chocolate, 25% Red:Chocolate(bl), 12% Cream:Lilac, 12% Chocolate Tortie, 25% Chocolate Tortie(bl), 12% Lilac Tortie
Lilac	25% Red:Chocolate(bl), 25% Cream:Lilac, 25% Chocolate Tortie(bl), 25% Lilac Tortie
Red:Brown	50% Red:Brown(ch), 50% Red:Brown(bl)(ch)
Red:Brown(bl)	25% Red:Brown(ch), 50% Red:Brown(bl)(ch), 25% Cream:Blue(ch)
Red:Brown(ch)	25% Red:Brown(ch), 25% Red:Brown(bl)(ch), 25% Red:Chocolate, 25% Red:Chocolate(bl)
Red:Brown(bl)(ch)	12% Red:Brown(ch), 25% Red:Brown(bl)(ch), 12% Cream:Blue(ch), 12% Red:Chocolate, 25% Red:Chocolate(bl), 12% Cream:Lilac
Cream:Blue	50% Red:Brown(bl)(ch), 50% Cream:Blue(ch)
Cream:Blue(ch)	25% Red:Brown(bl)(ch), 25% Cream:Blue(ch), 25% Red:Chocolate(bl), 25% Cream:Lilac
Red:Chocolate	50% Red:Chocolate, 50% Red:Chocolate(bl)
Red:Chocolate(bl)	25% Red:Chocolate, 50% Red:Chocolate(bl), 25% Cream:Lilac
Cream:Lilac	50% Red:Chocolate(bl), 50% Cream:Lilac

QUEEN - CREAM:Lilac

Brown	50% Red:Brown(bl)(ch), 50% Brown Tortie(bl)(ch)
Brown(bl)	25% Red:Brown(bl)(ch), 25% Cream:Blue(ch), 25% Brown Tortie(bl)(ch), 25% Blue Tortie(ch)
Brown(ch)	25% Red:Brown(bl)(ch), 25% Red:Chocolate(bl), 25% Brown Tortie(bl)(ch), 25% Chocolate Tortie(bl)
Brown(bl)(ch)	12% Red:Brown(bl)(ch), 12% Cream:Blue(ch), 12% Red:Chocolate(bl), 12% Cream:Lilac, 12% Brown Tortie(bl)(ch), 12% Blue Tortie(ch), 12% Chocolate Tortie(bl), 12% Lilac Tortie
Blue	50% Cream:Blue(ch), 50% Blue Tortie(ch)
Blue(ch)	25% Cream:Blue(ch), 25% Cream:Lilac, 25% Blue Tortie(ch), 25% Lilac Tortie
Chocolate	50% Red:Chocolate(bl), 50% Chocolate Tortie(bl)
Chocolate(bl)	25% Red:Chocolate(bl), 25% Cream:Lilac, 25% Chocolate Tortie(bl), 25% Lilac Tortie
Lilac	50% Cream:Lilac, 50% Lilac Tortie
Red:Brown	100% Red:Brown(bl)(ch)
Red:Brown(bl)	50% Red:Brown(bl)(ch), 50% Cream:Blue(ch)
Red:Brown(ch)	50% Red:Brown(bl)(ch), 50% Red:Chocolate(bl)
Red:Brown(bl)(ch)	25% Red:Brown(bl)(ch), 25% Cream:Blue(ch), 25% Red:Chocolate(bl), 25% Cream:Lilac
Cream:Blue	100% Cream:Blue(ch)
Cream:Blue(ch)	50% Cream:Blue(ch), 50% Cream:Lilac
Red:Chocolate	100% Red:Chocolate(bl)
Red:Chocolate(bl)	50% Red:Chocolate(bl), 50% Cream:Lilac
Cream:Lilac	100% Cream:Lilac

Appendix C
Glossary

(An italicised word in the explanation indicates an entry in the glossary.)

Active: A cat that may be bred from and is recorded as such by the breeder on the *GCCF's* active register; otherwise it's registered as non-active.

Agouti: The colour between a tabby's stripes: non-agouti cats lose this background colour, which results in solid coloured coats.

Albino: An individual with little or no pigmentation in the skin, coat and eyes; the eyes are so translucent that you can see the blood within.

Allele: A mutant form of the normal gene; for example, the allele for chocolate (b-) is a mutant form of the black gene (B-).

Anaesthesia: The loss of feeling, particularly sensations of pain and touch, produced by disease or deliberately induced by the use of drugs (anaesthetics).

Assessment class: The equivalent of a *GCCF* Open class for cats with Preliminary recognition, in which they are judged against their *Standard of Points*.

Back-cross: In the case of the Tonkinese, the mating of a Tonkinese with one of its parent breeds, Burmese or Siamese; however the term usually refers to the back-cross of an *F1 hybrid*.

Base colour: The coat colour of a cat, which may be masked by the effects of the sex-linked gene; for instance, the base colour of a red cat is brown, chocolate or cinnamon.

Bloodline: A line or family of cats related by ancestry or *pedigree*.

Breed true: To produce kittens exactly the same as the parents in *type, coat pattern* and eye colour.

Calling: Refers to the noise and general behaviour of a *queen* during *oestrus*.

Carrier: An individual that possesses a characteristic that is not apparent in the *phenotype* but can be passed on to the offspring; *heterozygous* for a recessive gene. Of diseases – shows no symptoms but is able to pass the disease on to other cats.

Challenge Certificate (CC): An award given to an adult winner of a breed class if the winner is sufficiently worthy.

Champion: Under GCCF rules an entire adult cat that has won three *Challenge Certificates (CCs)* at three different shows and under three different judges.

Coat pattern: The pattern in which the colour of the fur is distributed.

Co-dominance: Where two genes express themselves equally in the *phenotype* such as the *tonkinese coat pattern*. This should not be confused with *incomplete dominance*.

Colostrum: The first milk produced by the *queen*, particularly rich in nutrients and antibodies and containing less lactose than usual.

Conformation: see *Type*.

Congenital: A characteristic arising before birth, which may be inherited or result from a disorder occurring in the womb.

Contemporary gene: Name given to a *lethal gene* found in certain American Burmese lines. The gene has been traced back as far as 20 generations. The term 'contemporary' generally refers to the modern-type Burmese in the United States, with very short muzzle, protruding eyes and exaggerated, domed forehead.

Cross-breed: The result of mating two distinct breeds deliberately.

Appendix C

Cryptorchid: Male cat whose testicles have not descended.

Dilute: A paler (diluted) version of a basic colour, such as blue, lilac, fawn or cream.

Dominance: When the expression of a gene overrides the expression of another at the same locus, eg *agouti* over non-agouti. Not the same as *epistasis* (masking).

Double recessive: When an individual is *homozygous* for two pairs of *recessive genes.*

Entire: Refers to an unneutered male with both testicles descended.

Epistasis: Where the expression of a gene masks the effects of another gene. For instance, the sex-linked gene masks the base colour of a male cat to produce a red or cream coat colour. This is not to be confused with a *dominant* gene.

Expression: The manifestation, presentation or appearance of the effect of a gene.

F1 Hybrid: Strictly speaking, a first-generation offspring produced by crossing two different breeds (not two related breeds as is the case with the Tonkinese).

First-cross: see *Out-cross.*

Fistula: An abnormal opening or passage between two hollow organs or structures, or between an organ and the exterior. The condition may be congenital or acquired.

Fixing: Fixing a characteristic by selective breeding or *inbreeding.*

Folic acid: A vitamin of the B complex, found in leafy greens, liver and kidney, a deficiency of which causes pernicious anaemia.

Foreign: Certain varieties of short-haired cats, generally of medium length and elegant type, for instance Tonkinese, Burmese, Abyssinian, Russian Blue.

Gene pool: The collective number of genes in an interbreeding population.

Genetic drift: This might occur within a limited gene pool where selective breeding is relaxed, for instance if more Siamese type than Tonkinese type were used in the breeding of Tonkinese.

Genotype: The genetic composition of an individual; hereditary characteristics that may or may not be expressed.

Gestation: Pregnancy.

Ghost marking: Faint tabby markings seen in the coat of some solid colours, especially in kittens; usually recedes and may even disappear (hence 'ghost') with successive moults. Heavy markings are sometimes referred to as 'barring'.

Grand Champion: Under *GCCF* rules, a *Champion* who has been awarded a Grand Challenge Certificate by three different judges.

Grand Premier: Under *GCCF* rules, a *Premier* who has been awarded a Grand Premier Certificate by three different judges.

Haw: The nictitating membrane of the eye, also referred to as the 'third eyelid'.

Heat: See *Oestrus.*

Heterozygote: An individual with two dissimilar *alleles* at a locus, for instance (cbcs), but usually refers to one dominant and one recessive allele, (Aa).

Homozygote: An individual with two similar alleles at a locus: (cbcb), (AA).

Hot: The incorrect reddish tinge sometimes seen in cream, blue-tortie and lilac-tortie.

Hybrid vigour (Heterosis): The exceptional vigour often observed in the progeny of an out-cross mating.

Inbreeding: Mating of closely related individuals such as brother/sister or parent/offspring.

Inbreeding depression: A result of inbreeding that fixes the deleterious genes and causes a decline in vigour.

Incomplete dominance: A condition in which neither gene of the pair is *dominant* over the other. The *heterozygote* (Ll) is intermediate in expression to the two *homozygotes* (LL) and (ll). This is not the same as *co-dominance*.

Intermediate Certificate (IC): An award given to an adult winner of breed classes of breeds with Provisional recognition.

Inoculate: To stimulate the body's immunity to a disease by introducing a small quantity of the agent of the disease as serum or *vaccine*, usually by injection.

Jowls: Especially well-developed cheeks caused by heavy musculature in adult males.

Karyotype: A charted record of the chromosomes of an individual or breed.

Kink: A deformity of the tail or spine; more commonly a visible fixed deviation of the last vertebra of the tail.

Lethal gene: A gene that, in the *homozygous* state, causes the death of the recipient foetus or newborn kitten.

Latent infection: A passive or dormant infection. Latency is the presence of the virus genes within the cells without the production of the infectious virus itself. These may be *shed* (passed on) when the host is under stress.

Line breeding: Breeding to concentrate the genes of certain individuals, usually by repeated *back-crosses*; another term for *inbreeding* but usually accepted as a term for breeding from less closely related individuals.

Locus: The specific location of a gene on the chromosome; plural is 'loci'.

Lordosis: An exaggeration of the spinal curve in the lumbar region; the arched back position of a *queen* when ready to mate.

Luxating patella: Subluxation of the knee cap; may be corrected by surgery.

Major genes: Genes that have major effects on the *phenotype*, all genes referred to as *mutant alleles* are major genes.

Mask: The dark coloured area of the face covering the *muzzle*, eyes and forehead.

Melanin: The colouring pigment of the hairs (eumelanin = black, phaeomelanin = yellow), the effects of which are reduced or altered by specific genes.

Merit Certificate: Awarded to cats in Assessment classes (breeds with Preliminary recognition) if they correctly meet the standard of points set for the breed.

Minor genes: Genes that have minor effects on the *phenotype*; polygenes.

Modifying genes: *Major* or *minor genes* (but usually minor genes) that modify the expression of another gene.

Mongrel: The result of a chance mating between unrelated or unknown breeds; not to be confused with *cross-bred*.

Monorchid: Male cat with only one descended testicle.

Mutant allele: Gene resulting from the mutation of a normal gene, having no relation to the individual's ancestry.

Muzzle: The projecting jaw and nose of the cat, including the whisker pads and chin.

Neuter: A sterilised cat of either sex.

Nose-break: The point at which there is a change in direction of the nose profile.

Nose leather: The exposed, furless area of the nose.

Oestrus: The period in which a female will permit mating; also known as 'heat'.

Outbreeding: A breeding programme that specifically avoids *inbreeding*.

Out-cross: The crossing or mating of two breeds to produce a third breed; for instance, the crossing of a Burmese with Siamese to produce Tonkinese.

Appendix C

Parturition: The moment of birth.

Paw pads: The furless, fleshy cushions of a cat's feet.

Pedigree: A document showing the genealogy of an individual, usually up to four generations; a cat with documented ancestry of correct breeding.

Pencilling: Pencil-like marks on the faces of tabbies; also known as 'ribbons'.

Phenotype: The physical expression of *genotype* in the individual: the way in which we see the effects of the genes. The phenotype can be affected by environmental factors; for example temperature, diet and sunlight.

Pip: A slight bump on, or deviation at, the end of the tail; a fault that is not usually visible but can be felt.

Prefix: A unique name registered by a breeder and used before the name of all kittens bred by that breeder.

Premier: Under *GCCF* rules, a neutered adult cat who has won three Premier Certificates at three different shows and under three different judges.

Queen: Female cat used for breeding. (Referred to as the dam.)

Recessive gene: An *allele* whose expression is dominated (over-ridden) by another allele at the same *locus.*

Recognition: Acceptance and official acknowledgement by a cat association of a standard describing a new breed, or variety, of cat.

Registration: The official recording of a cat's birth and ancestry.

Self-coloured: A cat with uniform fur coloration.

Shedding: Seasonal moulting. Also used to described the manifestation and passing on of a previously *latent infection* from a cat under stress to other cats or kittens.

Spaying: The neutering of a female cat or kitten.

Spraying: The directed urination of a cat (usually male) to mark territory.

Standard Of Points (SOP): The written standard against which the cats are judged in shows.

Statement Of Difference: A statement that clearly indicates how a new breed differs from any other.

Sternum: The breastbone, at the end of which is the cartilaginous *Xiphoid sternum.*

Stud: Male cat used for breeding. (Referred to as the sire.)

Stud tail: A build up of greasy secretion around the base of the tail, called so because it's most frequently found on entire male cats.

tonkinese: The name for a unique coat pattern, named for the Tonkinese breed, which exhibits the perfect example of this coat pattern.

Tonkinese variant: A Tonkinese that exhibits either a solid coat pattern (as in the Burmese) or a clearly pointed coat pattern (as in the Siamese).

Type: The structural shape of a breed of cat, also referred to as its *conformation.*

Vaccine: An antigenic preparation used to stimulate the production of antibodies and effect immunity to a specific disease (see chapter 7).

Wedge: Head shape seen in some varieties of *Foreign* breeds.

Whippy: Refers to a slender tail that tapers to a point; a fault in the *Tonkinese.*

Whisker pinch: The indentation at the point where the *muzzle* is attached to the skull.

Xiphoid sternum: The small piece of cartilage attached to the lower end of the sternum. (Also known as hooked sternum.)

Bibliography

This list includes some of the sources I have consulted in the preparation of this book.

Allen, E, **Bonning**, L and **Rowan Blogg**, J *Everycat, A Complete Guide to Cat Care, Behaviour and Health.* Methuin Australia Pty.

Bary-Saunders, A de *Your Cat, Its Care and Treatment.* W Fulsham & Co, 1927.

Bessant, Claire and **Viner**, Bradley *The Ultrafit Older Cat.* Smith Gryphon.

Breton, R Roger and **Creek**, Nancy J *Feline Genetics.* USA.

Franklin, Sally *The Complete Siamese.* Ringpress Books.

Gebhardt, Richard H *Complete Cat Care Book.* W H Smith.

Greer, Milan *The Fabulous Feline.* USA: The Dial Press, 1961.

Hawthorne, Tim *Complete Book of Cat Care.* Ringpress Books.

Hodson, Anna *Essential Genetics.* Bloomsbury Publishing, 1994.

Lane, D R ed *Jones's Animal Nursing.* Pergamon Press for BSAVA.

Lauder, Phyllis *Siamese Cats.* B T Batsford, 1974.

Pond, Grace and **Dunhill**, Mary *Cat Shows and Successful Showing.* Blandford Press.

Readers Digest *Readers Digest Illustrated Book of Cats.*

Richards, D S, **Pocock**, R, **Swift**, M and **Watson**, W *The Burmese Cat.* B T Batsford.

Richards, Dorothy Silkstone *A Handbook of Pedigree Cat Breeding.* B T Batsford.

Robinson, Roy, FI Biol *Genetics for Cat Breeders.* Pergamon Press, 1977.

Searle, A G *Comparative Genetics of Coat Colour in Mammals.* 1968.

Simpson, Frances *Cats for Pleasure and Profit.* Sir Isaac Pitman & Sons, 1905.

Sproule, Anna and Sproule, Michael *The Complete Cat.* Prion.

Taylor, David, BVMS, FRCVS *The British Veterinary Association Guide to Cat Care.* Dorling Kindersley.

Turner, Trevor, BVetMed MRCVS, and **Turner**, Jean, VN, eds *Veterinary Notes for Cat Owners.* Stanley Paul & Co.

Vesey-Fitzgerald , Brian *The Domestic Cat.* Pelham Books, 1969.

Vesey-Fitzgerald, Brian *Cats.* Penguin Books, 1957

Viner, Bradley *The Cat Care Manual.* Stanley Paul & Co.

Williams, Kathleen R *Breeding and Management of the Siamese Cat.* F B Williams & Co, 1950.

Useful addresses

Tonkinese Clubs:

Tonkinese Breed Advisory Committee
Mrs C Poole
7 Langworthy End
Holyport
nr Maidenhead, Berkshire   SL6 2HJ

Tonkinese Breed Club
UK (GCCF & FAB affiliated)
Mrs L Vousden
Lansdale
12 Robin Hood Lane
Winnersh, Berkshire   RG41 5LX

Tonkinese Breed Club USA (CFF-affiliated)
Mrs Norma Roy
361 Fremont Street
Manchester, NH 03103

Tonkinese Cat Club
Mrs D Bishop
2 Rose Walk
Seaford, E Sussex   BN25 3DH

Cat Fancy Organisations:

American Cat Association (ACA)
The Secretary
8101 Katherine Avenue
Panorama City
CA 91402, USA

American Cat Fanciers Association (ACFA)
PO Box 203
Point Lookout
Missouri 65726, USA

Cat Association of Britain (CA)
Company Secretary
Mill House
Letcombe Regis, Oxon   OX12 9JD

Cat Fanciers Association Inc (CFA)
PO Box 1005, Manasquan
NJ 08738-1005, USA

Cat Fanciers Federation Inc (CFF)
9509 Montgomery Road
Cincinnati
Ohio 45242, USA   Tel: 001 513 984 1841

Fédération Internationale Féline (FIFe)
Boerhaavelaan 23
NL – 5644 BB
Eindhoven, The Netherlands

Governing Council of the Cat Fancy (GCCF)
Hon Secretary
4-6 Penel Orlieu
Bridgewater
Somerset   TA6 3PG,

The International Cat Association (TICA)
PO Box 2684, Harlingen, Texas 78551, USA

(For reasons of space, only British, American and international organisations have been included here. Addresses for other national feline organisations can be obtained from the GCCF.)

General:

Agriculture, Fisheries and Food (Ministry of)
Animal Health, International Trade Division B
Hook Rise South
Tolworth, Surbiton, Surrey   KT6 7NF
(For local offices see your telephone directory.)

Cats Protection League (CPL)
17 Kings Road
Horsham
W Sussex   RH13 5PP

Disabled Animals Club
5 Pepperscoombe Lane
Upper Beeding
Steyning, W Sussex   BN44 3HS

Feline Advisory Bureau (FAB)
Taeselbury, High Street
Tisbury, Wiltshire   SP3 6LD

Royal Society for the Prevention of Cruelty to Animals (RSPCA)
Causeway
Horsham, W Sussex   RH12 1HG
(For local offices see your telephone directory.)

Society for Companion Animal Studies
1A Hilton Road
Milngavie
Glasgow   G62 7DN

The Toxoplasmosis Trust
61 Collier Street
London   N1 9BE
Helpline (Mon-Fri): 0171 713 0599

World Animal Handicap Foundation (WAHF)
Presidente, WAHF, Square Marie-Louise
40/11, 1040 Bruxelles, Belgium

Index

Index